Fixed for Life

The True Saga of How Tom Became Sally

Fixed for Life

The True Story of How Tom Became Sally

Irene Preiss

PFLAG/Dallas
PO Box 586369   Dallas, TX 75258

toExcel
New York San Jose Lincoln Shanghai

Fixed for Life

The True Saga of How Tom Became Sally

All Rights Reserved. Copyright © Irene Preiss 1999

No part of this book may be reproduced or transmitted in any form or by any means, graphic, electronic, or mechanical, including photocopying, recording, taping, or by any information storage or retrieval system, without the permission in writing from the publisher.

This edition published by toExcel Press, an imprint of iUniverse.com, Inc.

For information address:
iUniverse.com, Inc.
620 North 48th Street
Suite 201
Lincoln, NE 68504-3467
www.iUniverse.com

ISBN: 1-58348-728-X

Printed in the United States of America

11. But he said unto them, All *men* cannot receive this saying, save *they* to whom it is given.

12. For there are some eunuchs, which were so born from *their* mother's womb: and there are some eunuchs, which were made eunuchs of men: and there be eunuchs, which have made themselves eunuchs for the kingdom of heaven's sake. He that is able to receive *it*, let him receive *it*.

St. Matthew, Chapter 19, (KJV)

This book is dedicated to those who have questions about their gender or sexuality;
to the family members of those who have questions about their gender or sexuality;
to the counsellors for those who have questions about their gender or sexuality; and,
to those who have no questions at all about their gender or sexuality, but who will eventually encounter those who do.

Preface

A lot of people know something about transsexuality, but not much. And a lot that is known is inaccurate.

There are males who want to become females, and females who want to become males. Each year hundreds accomplish the change to some extent.

One thing that will help in the exploration of this phenomenon is to set a few definitions to help communications. A transsexual is one who undergoes surgery and certain chemical changes to help become the sex of his or her choice. A transgendered person is one who has taken on all the social and wardrobe attributes of a transsexual, but not has not had the surgery to complete the process. A transvestite is one who dresses in the clothing of the opposite sex for short periods of time because it's fun for them.

We are different from the gay community in many ways. In fact, there is no community for transsexuals. We seldom associate with others like ourselves once the change has been made. We do not hold rallies. We do not ask others to accept us. We do not do anything to call attention to ourselves. Lordy, no.

There are groups that offer counselling, and there are some national organizations that will provide wonderful services for pre-op transsexuals. These are enormously helpful. For one thing, they can help a person determine if surgery is the right thing to do.

Each of us just wants to blend in as a member of the sex we believe we should be, and get on with life in the best way we can, just like anyone else. If we can't blend in and be productive members of society, we have failed. Failure brings dire consequences. I have achieved the goal of blending in, and I want to tell you all about it.

> A lot of my friends have asked me
> Why would anyone want to change their sex?
> How can you do that?
> What happens during the process?
> What happens after the process?

Those are certainly fair questions, and the very ones I intend to answer, along with some answers to other questions not yet posed. My focus is on the male changing to female, but much of what I say can be easily transposed for females who want to become males.

The definitions provided above are simplistic, but accurate enough for the purpose of this account. There is a growing culture of sex-change people who are writing magazine articles for print, for posting them on the Internet. They conduct meetings periodically and even have annual conferences. I think these activities are very helpful and necessary for those who pursue the business of change. One problem with all the internal communication is the temptation to tinker with the language and definitions relevant to the culture. My first official involvement happened in 1973. Since then much of the vocabulary has changed a bit here and there. By the turn of the century one can only guess what will be in vogue. Having declared my caveat, I will say a few more things that will be used here to bring insight and understanding for the general reader. Or the afflicted. Or friends and family of the afflicted.

These definitions might seem a bit too simple, but the general ideas are not very complicated. It is very important to keep in mind that sex and gender are two different phenomena.

The word sex has two meanings. One meaning is an action word, like having sex with... We use the term sexual orientation to indicate who we want to have for a sex partner. Most males are heterosexual and are oriented toward having sex with females; and, most females are also heterosexual and oriented towards having sex with males. A splendid arrangement, that. It enables us to perpetuate the population as well as to enhance a loving relationship.

The other meaning of sex is a label, and refers to the kind of body you have, i.e., male or female. It is the designation made on your birth certificate, your driver's license, and a few other places. It is purely a physiological term. This is what the transsexual desires to change.

The term bisexual has come to national attention as a result of the spread of AIDS. Prior to that time, the phenomenon was known, but seldom talked about. If you are a bisexual, you do not brag about that fact to the sexual partner you happen to be with at the moment. Bisexuals have sex with men and with women, usually at different times. A bisexual male may follow the standard pattern of being a married man with children, but occasionally likes to sack out with some young stud. For that kind of male, heterosexuality and homosexuality are matters of time or circumstance. I think it was Woody Allen who said, "A bisexual is one who doubles his chances for a date on Saturday night."

I have nothing to say about the kind of sexual activity where someone gets hurt. Rape, pederasty, incest, and such are too contemptible to write about. Such unwelcome sexual activity has no place in this book.

That is about all I have to say about sex. Pretty simple, actually. Anything else is commentary on frequency, or technique, or whatever. Books, magazines, and movies abound for those who want commentary.

But what kind of sexual activity does a transsexual have? There is no simple answer I can give. Our sexual appetites share the same spectrum as the general population. It all depends upon the individual. It could be any of the above, or something more creative, but I do not know. Some transsexuals become asexual. What I do know is that a transsexual is more interested in a gender change. Am I trying to tell you that a transsexual changes his or her sex for reasons other than the sex act? You betcha I am!

Gender is a much more elusive topic than sex. In its simplest sense, gender is a social role. Females are supposed to become women. Males are supposed to become men. This assumes that there is a clear-cut distinction between male and female social behavior. It also assumes that there is a specific list of attributes that are male, and another specific list that are female attributes. Such limiting lists do not exist, though we all seem able to identify behavior as either manly or womanly. What causes a lot of confusion in recent decades is that the definitions of manhood and womanhood have been undergoing some wrenching changes. Some of that is due to the need for women to abandon the traditional home-and-hearth role and get out there and earn money. Women also have been in need of a fair shake in society, such as equal status with the males, and the opportunity to pursue whatever goals they wish. So the women's movement caused some good stuff to happen for women, but it has left the men wondering about themselves. Men feel that their gender is being called into question when their wives drive off to work in the morning, and they tend the home fires and line up for unemployment insurance. Not fun.

It has been said that only Nature tells a girl she has become a woman. Nature's message includes a special mental, emotional, and spiritual package along with the physical gift.

Only society can tell a boy he has become a man. The young male develops the physical attributes of an adult male, but being a sexually-potent boy is not the same as being a man.

But Nature, with its endless manifestations of diversity, will occasionally switch consciousness packages with the physical packages. Nature is like that. Look around you for examples of Nature's diversity.

So much for the overall aspects of sex and gender. Essentially, gender is what gets exhibited when one is not engaged in sexual activity. For some folks, gender is all there is because there is no sex going on for them.

Gender, then, is a social role that includes—but is not limited to—what one wears, how one presents oneself to society, and the kinds of friendships one makes. To make a satisfactory gender change, one really needs to make a sex change. A feminine mind-set can exist inside a masculine body. For that mind-set to express itself properly, the body must be changed. Before a responsible surgeon will do the change to the body, one must prove to psychologists and a psychiatrist that one can function successfully as the opposite sex, and that the candidate for surgery is not crazy. But I am getting ahead of myself.

I think the phenomenon of immigration is a fair metaphor for transsexuals. Immigrants travel from their native lands for many reasons. In general, the reasons involve the expectation for a better life. In the process, one risks a lot. One can easily lose friends, wealth, social position, family ties, possibly suffer derision, and be taken advantage of. It is a perilous journey, but it can be worth it. The possibility of achieving the goal provides the motivation to take the risks. One gets to that point where life itself is no longer desirable without taking a shot at it. It requires a certain strength and perhaps desperation to migrate. Some fail, but the survivors achieve their goal and become stronger than before.

Preface

Yes, I wanted to be abroad, but not to leave this country. All I wanted to do was to move over to "the girls' side of the room." Spatially, it was a simple step, but mentally it was intergalactic travel.

My interest in wanting to migrate to womanhood began at an early age, about the time I became aware that women were different from men. It was an ill-defined desire; there were no sex-change role models to observe; there was no literature written to explain my desire; and, worst of all, I felt there was no one I could talk to about such a shameful topic. My strategy back then was to suppress the desire, concentrate on developing the social expectations for my sex, and with practice and prayer, I would eventually lose interest in wanting to become a woman. Well, I was able to do part of that. I did meet the expectations of society for a male, but I did not lose my desire to become female.

Goodness knows I tried to be a normal male. I'll tell you about all the things I did to achieve manhood, in anybody's generation. But being normal meant I had to suppress a desire that was basic to my nature. A kind of psychic resistance was set up that caused pressures of unreal force. Psychological ruptures and explosions did occur. I'll tell you about those, too. Some were funny, some were pathetic, all were instructive.

In my middle years, I began writing for myself as an attempt to find out who and what I was. The initial effort, prior to this manuscript, began over 20 years ago when I enrolled in a course to learn Ira Progoff's system of Jungian journal writing. My best friend and lover back then, Annie, (who you will soon meet) suggested we take the course. I bought a spiral notebook and a new pen, and we showed up for the evening class. I was more or less motivated. As the instructor promised, our initial writings would seem useless and stilted, but we were admonished and encouraged to keep at it. I forget exactly when or how it happened, but I found that such writing was becoming important to my daily mental health. The content and tone of my rambling evolved into some telling prose that eventually, among other things, showed me those areas of my life controlled by me and those which were controlled by others. Those revelations, which had nothing to do with selfishness or sacrifice but did have a lot to do with guilt and anger, love and compassion, and contradictions, soon enabled me to see which areas of my life were contented and which had the frustrations, and whether I could do anything about them.

All of that was followed by decades-long internal dialog about individual spirit, societal expectations, attempts to understand the nature of The Management of this planet, and the relationships of everything to everything else. While those internal searches continue to this day, I did produce some answers though they were tentative or provisional. I was able to make some sense of it all, and with understanding came action.

One action item was to dredge up a lot of my past, write it down as completely and as honestly as possible for the purpose of explaining to myself why I was confused about a number of things, and then look for ways to make repairs or adjustments for the future. Hurtful as it seemed at the time, I knew I had to be ruthless about being complete and honest if I expected to get any sensible direction. I believe that it helped in many ways. In 15 years I filled quite a few spiral notebooks before I was through with the exercise. Life became better, and then I thought maybe I could extract and abstract enough copy to make a book for others, especially for those whose gender or sexuality is in question. And for the people who live with those in their sphere of discontent.

I also tried to get rid of the desire for womanhood through psychotherapy. I was told that the only way to rid myself of the desire was not to want to fulfill the desire. (I think that is close to being a tautology, but what are therapists for?)I spoke with ministers about how to deal with a desire I could not seem to shake off. I was told by both of them that God speaks to us through our desires. Love, they said, was to be my guide.

Much of my life was a battle between what those closest to me had a right to expect versus what my inner desires were screaming for. I honored my commitments pretty well, better than most husbands and fathers. I was used to living between a rock and a hard place for all those decades, but as I neared my 60th birthday it looked like a load of gravel was coming down on top. I had to make a move or be destroyed.

Such a life caused me and those closest to me an unreal amount of mental anguish back then, and perhaps even today. I think I caused a world of hurt to descend upon a number of innocent family members who most certainly did not deserve it. It needn't have been that way, but when you don't understand the phenomenon of transsexualism, you and your loved ones can be in for misery beyond belief.

Preface

I hope, with all the passion I have, that those who are transsexuals, either potentially or for sure, that you will read my story, measure your feelings and life's experiences against mine, then make some very careful decisions that will not cause harm to befall those whom you love and who love you.

I refuse to give anyone advice, or try to talk anyone into or out of making a sex change. I will tell you what happened to me, and if you can get something from it to help you, then the telling will have been worth the effort.

The first chapter is an account that will capsulate the basic proposition of "my condition." That chapter is followed by a chronological telling of the mess that used to be my life. Consider it to be a journey from ignorance to understanding.

Chapter 1

August 1971

"Nobody, but nobody walks like that!" He hollered it once more in the good-humored voice of a drunk before his lady could shush him.

It was after 0100 (1:00 a.m.) The Officers' Club bar would close soon, and I wanted out before the indiscriminate, unattached, horny Marine officers began their final sweep for bed partners. In that milieu and at that time, even I was not exempt from invitations to someone's Bachelor Officer Quarters bedroom.

"Not man, nor woman, nor any beast of the field walks like that!"

I was almost to my car. I had to admit that all those gins over the rocks were affecting my walk. With my key in the ignition now and doors locked, I felt safe for the first time in hours. I had risked my hide and a whole lot more.

It had taken me hours to get ready. The day at sea serving with Fleet Training Group, San Diego, had been a long one, but not different from the others. Up at 0530, muster at 0615 with the Duty Officer, collect our clipboards, stopwatches, operation orders, and a cup of what had to be last week's coffee.

A motor launch from the ship in training (a destroyer) came alongside our pier at 0630. By 0700 we were climbing up the sea ladder and over the gunwale of our ship-for-the day. By 0800 we passed Pt. Loma Lighthouse and entered the Pacific Ocean. We had the customary meeting in the wardroom where the plans were reviewed, last minute changes made, and final drags on our cigarettes. As we stepped out on deck, General Quarters sounded. The unmistakable cadence of gongs was followed by the boatswain's pipe and the redundant verbal announcement. Naval tradition. We observers went to our assigned stations to evaluate the performance of the crew during their emergency drills.

My morning assignment was to observe a Damage Control Party-the people who deal with disasters such as fires, structural damage caused by bombs, torpedoes, or collisions. If they knew their jobs, my work would be easy. If not, I would have to lecture, demonstrate, or motivate to improve their performance. I played "what if" a lot. "What if you have a torpedo hit in this compartment and your shoring timbers are too long (or too short) for immediate use?" Etc.

The afternoon assignment consisted of evaluating the lowering and hoisting of a 24-foot boat using radial davits during light sea conditions. No one got maimed or killed. It was a miracle.

By 1830 our launch was back at the pier. We walked to our building, filed our reports, turned in our gear, said fare-thee-well to each other, and split for liberty.

I entered my room at the B.O.Q., grabbed a can of beer from the refrigerator, ripped off the tab and let it flow. Stripping to my shorts, I sat and asked myself if I really had the guts to go to the dance at the Marine Officers' Club as Sally.

I looked at the pile of sweat-stained khakis on the other chair and belched a loud one. My insignia were pinned on my collars: on one side the silver and blue of a warrant officer, grade 4; on the other the crossed gold anchors of a Boatswain.

I was proud of that uniform and proud of myself for having earned the privilege to wear it. A chief warrant boatswain is typically a big, heavy, banana-fingered ape with a gravel voice, hard steely eyes, beetle brows, and a generally menacing countenance. I did not fit the description. I was six feet tall, 180 pounds and looked a lot younger than my 43 years. On deck, however, I managed to compensate somehow. Compensating had become a way of life for me since the age of nine.

There really was no question about being Sally that night. As I showered away the salt and the sweat, I knew that in a few minutes I would turn into a facsimile of a woman-as feminine as I could be.

But did I really want to go to the O-Club at the Marine Corps Recruit Depot for God sakes? My answer was yes and my reason was clear.

You are a strong person, you live as a man among men. No one ever called you sissy or hinted in any way that you were less than a tough, centered guy with backbone.

My current Naval assignment created an attitude in me that gave me the guts to do anything I felt like doing. At that moment I felt like being Sally and trying my wings in the social context of hard drinking and wild dancing in a way that only Marines know how to do.

By 2130 I was as ready as I would be: a very close shave, makeup thick enough to cover even the imaginary defects, a black wig styled to compensate for the masculine topography of nose, chin, and forehead. Clean underpinnings, seven pairs of pantyhose to hide the hairs on my legs, a black A-line skirt, a white blouse with stand up collar to hide my Adam's apple, and long sleeves to hide the hair on my arms. Golden pendant earrings. Clip ons, of course.

I had another beer as I looked myself over. Yes, I admitted, you do not look anything like that son of a bitch who hollered and yelled throughout that damage control drill this morning, or that martinet on safety procedures witnessing that lethal boat move up and down this afternoon. Good. That's what I want. Let The Bosun look and act like a bosun, let Sally look and act like Sally. Further, I want Sally to be a lady: to look, act, and speak as a lady. Why?

A fair question, with no answer then. I had a drive, a compulsion of sorts that said, *Do it! Just shut up with the questions and the attempted logic and do it. Never mind reasons, just do it. You know how miserable you get when you can't find the time or the place to do it. You know that other people's compulsions are more socially acceptable than yours, that they can elevate their consciousness by mountain climbing, by scuba diving, or other risky recreations that lift themselves out of themselves. So your drive is to explore your femininity. Do it.*

Dozens of very good arguments said don't do it. But in any contest between one's subconscious and one's rational mind, the subconscious will win every time. The conscious, rational mind will find a way to justify the decision of the subconscious. By definition, that is the job of the rational mind-to rationalize.

Do it, dummy. You won't know exhilaration, joy, transcendence, conquest, or deep satisfaction until you do it.

Was there a devil trying to get in me or one trying to get out?

Never mind. Do it.

But if I'm caught I'd be in real trouble.

You will be in worse trouble later when you can't, if you don't do it tonight. You have been out before as Sally. You have been shopping, been to dinner, had drinks, and sat through films. You are all right. You need to create and develop the persona of Sally. There is so much more for you to know. You must let Sally grow. She is another dimension of you. More than a sister. You need to open your mind to the consequences of being a Gemini. Who did you think the other twin was, Dick Tracy?

But what if I get caught? And get into trouble?

You're not afraid to pit yourself against the Marines, are you? Do it. You don't know what is out there for Sally. So far you have learned how to get yourself reasonably presentable and not have people stare at you anymore. You have no social self, no personality, no life of your own as Sally. Yet.

But I should not give Sally a free reign.

Screw the shoulds! Who says should? You or someone else? All you have done is to work on a visual image, right?

Right.

Has it hurt or harmed you in any way?

No.

All right, then. Try for more. What you have done until now is only preparation for the real thing. There is more, a lot more for you after you develop a social self. Do it!

Okay.

The Lance Corporal at the gate waved me in-like a fox gesturing to a hen. I parked my car as close to the club as I could-for a quick retreat if I needed one. An exiting couple opened the door for me. I smiled a thank you and entered the foyer. I heard an animal sound come from the man. Before I could panic, his lady said, "Come on, Fred. We're going home."

I checked my coat as directed and cautiously penetrated further into the club. It was a Thursday, but if a bar is open, the Marines will make it New Year's Eve. Wild Caribbean music, maybe a hundred energetic dancers and drinkers. All of them wanting to be in a place other than where they had been during the day. Me too. I felt as though I belonged. I found an empty table and sank into a deep overstuffed chair. I felt some panic when the cocktail waitress came for my order.

"What'll it be, hon?"

"A gin over with a twist, please."

"And for you?"

Oops, not a lady's drink. I've got to remember that.

"That is for me."

"Oh, you're by yourself tonight?"

"Yes."

She came back in a few minutes with the drink and the report that single women were in short supply tonight. Everyone was home getting ready for tomorrow night.

"You won't be alone much longer, hon."

Two sips later I was asked to dance. A neat, keen-eyed gentleman wanted me to dance with him!

Can anyone imagine what that invitation did to me? Can anyone else understand what kind of fireworks went off in my head? Sweet Jesus! I wanted to be a woman that night, and here was a handsome young officer who regarded me as a woman that he wanted to dance with. In a psychic way, it could only be compared with my first pre-teen orgasm. For over three decades I'd had countless fantasies about being accepted and treated as a woman. Now it was happening. I sipped my gin for courage, for time, and to adjust the pitch of my voice.

"I'm sorry, but I've been on my feet all day…"

He asked if I was alone. Yes. He asked if he could sit with me. Yes. He asked lots of questions-the usual pick-up stuff I'd used in other times, other places. I took the attention away from me by asking him the kinds of questions I'd been asked in other times, in other places. It was remarkable how those "tapes" played in my head when I needed them. It was not the last time I would need those old soundtracks.

He said he was a jet pilot from the Naval Air Station in Lemoore. He said he came here a lot because this was the only place you could find a woman on a Thursday night. I cooled his jets with reticence and a Giaconda smile. He left after I'd finished the drink he bought me. The cocktail waitress brought me another drink.

"It's from the bartender, hon. He wants you to stick around."

Another officer came over and sat down. He started his pitch for a dance. I was beginning to feel more relaxed in my new role and pleased with my initial success. Mostly I think I enjoyed being the quarry. I had a twinge that maybe I was enjoying the role too much. His pitch was clever and it actually motivated me to accept. Cripes! What is happening to me? We lasted through the frenetic classic Proud Mary. It was so crowded no one could be identified as a bad dancer. The music ended and I asked if we could sit down. He squired me back to the table, ordered another drink for me, and thanked me for the dance. He said he couldn't sit still, and was off.

The jet pilot came back wanting to dance. I told him I had to get up early and "be on the floor all day tomorrow." I didn't know what that meant, but it sounded good.

Driving back to my room, I began the self-evaluation of my debut. Okay, so my walk needs work. All day I walk as a sailor walks-to compensate for the rolling of a ship at sea. Tonight I tried to walk like a lady. My handicaps were not knowing how, and the eight gins that precessed my gyroscope.

The critique continued in my room as I peeled off the seven pairs of pantyhose, all the other things, creamed my face, removed the nail polish, climbed in for my second shower, dried, and crashed in my chaste, single bed.

I was dead tired, yet exhilarated. I'd taken another step away from manhood. I was thrilled by my success and ecstatic with the new consciousness that was emerging. Was it legal to feel that good?

But I had transgressed. I had done something no real man would do regardless of how much courage it took to do it. I had a fuzzy remembrance of a story by Joseph Conrad about some castaways who had to resort to cannibalism until their rescue, and how they were never the same again. Don't mess with taboos.

I knew I was crude and had a lot of things to learn about to create a truly fine lady-like presentation. Yet, I had been accepted as a woman. Was there something about my manner, my presence that projected woman? How could that be if I was really a man among men?

You projected it because it is there. It has been dormant, but there since birth. Don't fiddle with the analysis, Tom. Relax and enjoy it. You've got lots more to learn aside from the physical presentation. That is only your ticket for admission into a world where you belong, where you have only the slightest glimmer of what is there. Remember how you felt when the jet pilot asked you to dance?

Yes.

Well, sport, that barely scratches the surface on the magnificence of the life ahead of you. It is not all roses and perfume and flowing skirts. There is an abundant supply of agony to go with the ecstasy, but it is for you and you are destined for it.

Okay. When can I go for it? I've got all these responsibilities and obligations and this big nose. How and when can I get there?

Quit with the stumbling blocks. They are only temporary. Even your nose. You will get your chance to be a woman when you are ready.

When will I be ready?

When you are ready to handle it, Tom. You haven't finished with your male agenda.

Chapter 2

Some of what we learn is not accurate. Sometimes we misunderstand what others say to us and end up with a wrong idea. One thing I learned, when maybe five or six years old, was that I should have been a girl. How did I learn that? Simple. In my presence, I heard my mother tell other adults that I should have been a girl. It was hard to misunderstand such a simple, direct message. What she meant, I learned some years later, was that the first child in the family was supposed to be a boy and the second child should be a girl. It was a family planning concept circa the 1920s. There was a line in the then popular song, Tea For Two, that said, "A boy for you and a girl for me." Neat.

What I abstracted from that comment, made so many times, was that I was a disappointment being a boy and somehow my fault. By extension then, everyone including myself would have been a lot happier if I had been a sister to my older brother. He came on cue, I did not.

I know now that the whole idea is silly, a misunderstanding of the most grievous order. But it did happen, and it is very easy for me to comprehend what she really meant and very easy to comprehend the way in which I misunderstood it. Someone once said that the greatest problem in communications is the illusion that it has been achieved.

The result of that misunderstanding *could* be the reason why I've always wanted to be female. Or, it could be a reason. I am neither a psychiatrist nor a psychologist, and therefore I am not qualified to diagnose myself or anyone else. Various philosophical systems offered alternative notions to explain *why* the *Tea-For-Two* concept triggered such feelings, but it would be some decades later before I encountered them. What I *do* know is what happened to me, and I know my reactions to the stimulus. I know those things better than anyone. The meanings and interpretations are for the experts.

Loaded with guilt for disappointing my parents, one can easily imagine what I thought each time I was scolded for being late, spilling or breaking something, et cetera. Right. *I am a disappointment. They don't like me. I'll bet they would like me if I were a girl. How can I get to be a girl?*

Of course I knew I could never be a girl. At least my rational mind told me that. But my rational mind does not control my fantasies. I mean, when you are a little kid and not in control of very much in your life, and you may not be too happy with what is going on, the fantasy is a wondrous thing. It is the opiate of childhood. In the fantasy, you are in charge. You will employ the fantasy to lift yourself out of where you are and go somewhere that is absolutely where you want to be. I fantasized a lot over the years to try to fix the mistake of being born male.

Why did I not just wise up one day after I comprehended what my mother really meant? My only answer-even now, in my eighth decade on this planet-is that I like what I'm doing. It makes no difference that I believe I know the reason why I went off in the "wrong direction." The fact is that I did take a wrong turn. I know I took a wrong turn, but I like it. Why do I like it? I don't know. I can furnish no conventional logic or rationale for wanting to live as a female any more than you can explain to me why you like chocolate ice cream, or anything else you like.

Aside from the foregoing, my childhood was pretty normal. I had the usual mix of dreams and nightmares. The dreams changed, of course, as I aged. My nightmares remained the same.

The dreams were mostly of adventure. Steam locomotives pulled their long trains of boxcars, missing my house by three short blocks. My friends and I would play in the creek bed next to the tracks. When there was water we built dams or tossed in boats to shoot the rapids. In summer all we could do was to start on next season's dams or put pennies on the tracks and see them flatten into ellipses. Poor Abe Lincoln. At night, the wail of the steam engines signalled adventure to distant places where there was no third grade teacher demanding a recitation of the times tables.

The dreams were enhanced by my father who had been a fireman in his youth, sometimes working on the same locomotive with his father who was an engineer. By the time my father left his home in Missouri to join a logging crew in Washington, he had traveled by rail to every state in the Union except Florida. Some stories he could tell.

I was nine when Amelia Earhart passed through our local airport, Mills Field. I did not get to see her, but I remember well the confusion I felt. This *woman* was the pilot of an airplane bound for strange sounding places in the Pacific. Until this fact manifested, I'd only known the fiction of people like Pat O'Brien, Errol Flynn, or John Wayne doing such derring-do. It was the first social anomaly I can remember.

No one knew what happened to Amelia, but Mills Field grew a lot five years later when America joined up in WWII. A lot of Army Air Corps planes were stationed there-mostly P-38s. After the war, the expanded air facility was renamed San Francisco International Airport, then grew some more. And more.

My father worked 12 to 14 hours per day, seven days a week as the founder, owner, builder and only worker of a gasoline station. In the early 1930s money was scarce. He had worked at menial jobs until he could make a down payment on a corner commercial lot. He dug the pits for the storage tanks by himself, aided only by pick and shovel. He erected the station house and lubrication rack by himself. How he did it I don't know, but I watched it happen. My mother and I carried his lunches and dinners from home, a mile and a half away.

Times were tough during the Depression. I knew my father mostly by reputation. Old family friends would come by our house. My mother was a warm, giving woman who had a knack for making people feel comfortable. There were lots of visitors. Usually they would say that they had just stopped by the gas station to see Art before coming to the house. Then I would hear their respectful commentaries about my father. Sometimes anecdotes from the old days in Washington. The visitors knew my father as a logger, an insurance salesman, a clerk in his uncle's law office, a naval officer, or until recently, the owner of a clay sewer pipe factory.

As the gasoline business improved, my father bought an automobile. He came home for his meals unless his new employee was sick. I did get to see him more frequently by the time I was ten or eleven. My brother (five years older) sometimes worked at the gas station. I was directed to stay home and help my mother. The stated reason was that I wasn't old enough to work there. The real reason remains moot.

What impressed me most about my father was his strength of character. He was tough, strong, intelligent as well as street-smart, fair, honest, and in all respects a gentleman by anyone's standards. He never played with me and seldom ever had a private conversation with me. He worked very hard, long hours-endlessly. No vacations.

His factory in Washington was buried as everyone's house of cards fell flat on that day in 1929. My uncle loaned him the money to get us moved to California, the land of opportunity. His first job in the Bay Area was at Swift's Meat Packing plant tying string around salami for an hourly rate of ten cents. Oh he was a tough man. He endured hardships and indignities for his family. A heroic figure. Whenever he spoke, I listened. He pounded away at the virtues he personified daily. He actually practiced what he preached.

One of the rules was that females were special, and they deserved respect, consideration, and protection. I was admonished to display courtesy and politeness whenever in the presence of a female of any age. Fine. I had no problem with any of those verities. I did have a problem believing that females could do no wrong, but that was not the point. My mother supported my father totally. His messages were reinforced when he was not present, which was most of the time. If I screwed up, and little boys have a way of doing that, I would be hollered at and sometimes punished, mildly. The real punishment was going on inside my head. Always, my first thought was that I had failed my father; then, I didn't mean to screw up; and invariably, *if I were a girl, they would like me better.* I must have had a desperate need to gain my parents' approval. That kind of experience happened a lot in my pre-teen years, then stopped. I don't know why it did. Maybe I just learned not to screw up.

In the fall of 1940, my brother joined the Naval Reserve. He was seventeen and still in high school. The war in Europe was reported daily in the newspapers and on the radio. A lot of us kids were building models of the airplanes and warships of the day. Strombecker had the simplest kits to build. I made their PT boats, destroyers, B-25 bombers, Hurricanes, Spitfires, submarines, and aircraft carriers. All that production of war vehicles took place on an old breadboard which rested on my lap while listening to the radio programs. Most people under 50 today find it impossible to imagine a world without television.

Listeners of radio drama had to use their imaginations as well as the development of listening skills. Conversation, not just talk, was a daily activity. And games; home-made games, sometimes invented on the spot. I think people talked more and felt a natural responsibility for one's own entertainment. Everyone had a library card and used it. Movies happened for kids on Saturdays-the ten-cent matinee. Flash Gordon, Zorro, Hopalong Cassidy, The Three Stooges and more. Usually one of those, then a cartoon, then the featured film.

I was reading the Sunday comics when the announcement came on December 7, 1941. The world was stunned as everyone knows, but the upheaval in my home was profound. In less than an hour, my brother was in his uniform and enroute to Yerba

Buena Island. The World's Fair next door on Treasure Island was closed but not really cleared away. The Navy became the owner and custodian then, and began the building of the Naval Station.

Our home was in Burlingame, about 20 miles south of San Francisco. By early 1942, the war was not fought in our backyard, but all of the logistics were there: shipyards, railroads, airfields, supply centers, docking facilities for ships, receiving stations and points of embarkation for troops. And the entertainment for those people. Sons and daughters of my parents' friends would telephone from the Presidio, or Alameda, or Treasure Island and ask if they could come visit. Our house was like a USO. After awhile there were regulars who visited: WAVES stationed on Treasure Island. One of them was "connected"-her mother and my mother went to high school together. She would ask if it was all right to bring a friend or two for a weekend. Of course. Many of them would keep their civilian clothes at our house for relaxing in when they came. Sometimes, when home alone, I explored their skirts and blouses. And sandals. After awhile there was quite a wardrobe of various sizes and styles.

By summer of '42 my father had pressed for reinstatement in the Naval Reserve and was ordered to active duty as a lieutenant commander. A very happy man. I was 14 that summer and my fondest, most passionate dream then was that the war would not end before I could join the Navy. My dreams centered around becoming just like my father-a Navy man; tough, strong, unyielding, respected for successes, and for being a gentleman in any circumstance. If I could be like that, I would be able to get rid of the girl fantasies. There was also the dream of being a man who could overcome any obstacle, under any handicap.

So that was me in the summer of 1942. That was when I discovered girls. I could see they had radically changed from irritants to something approaching adventure. Amazing what could happen to them in a year. There were parties on Friday nights. Cokes, chips, boogie woogie, lights turned down, and inevitably the recognition of the sex differences and the excitement of touching, holding, caressing, kissing, and more. It amazed me how Barbara could be so desirable, so exciting, so lovable, when last year she was a world-class pest.

Later, in high school the maturation continued which produced a cosmopolitan view of companionship: I became friendly with a girl who came from a different grammar school. I saw Carolyn and fell in love. Even now, this moment as I write, I can still feel the special love we shared for two years. We came from different socio-economic groups, as they say today. Back then, we just said her dad made a lot more money than mine. We really loved each other with whatever capacity existed for us at that age. We had fine physical times, but there was more. We tried to understand our parents-to sort out why they acted the way they did. She would show me her latest creations from her sewing class. I would give my best oohs and aahs, despite my inability to perceive the quality of design and execution. I invited her to watch me play in water polo games, which she would sit through, bored. That was my first experience at learning about loving someone else: you give to them what they want if you have it to give. Attention, humor, sympathy, excitement. You give of yourself.

My job that summer was delivering the U.S. Mail. Leather bag on the shoulder. My route, miraculously, included Carolyn's house in the hillside section of town. She would have cold lemonade waiting for me every day. And kisses. Oh lord, those kisses! And that lovely soft skin. But I had mail to deliver.

In 1945 I had my 17th birthday and expected to enlist in the Navy. I was about to enter my senior year and my mother said no. I couldn't join the Navy until after I finished high school. I begged, pleaded, argued. No. In desperation I wrote my father a letter, putting it to him. I told him how impassioned I was, how I wanted in before the war was over, etc. He wrote to my mother from whatever secret island base he was assigned to, telling her to sign my enlistment papers provided I swear that I would eventually get a high school diploma. In those days one had to have a high school diploma in order to be educated. I swore and she signed. The day of my physical was the day Nagasaki experienced the A-bomb. I was finally sworn in on August 18, but did not get to boot camp until October. I missed the war, dammit.

So much for the dreams of my childhood. I wanted adventure and I got it in ways congruent with my age. All things considered it was a good life. On the other side-the nightmares.

Fear is a powerful emotion. It can be motivating or debilitating, depending. In my case, fear was a motivating force. I suppose that it could be construed as a positive because of the positive results. I am reminded of T.S. Eliot's couplet from Murder in the Cathedral, "By far the greatest treason is to do the right thing for the wrong reason." That was me. I learned to be tough, a real male to avoid anyone discovering my true feelings.

Specifically, it was the feeling, the awareness that I should have been born female. My nightmares (sleeping and waking) centered around two poles, like the focal points of an ellipse: the fear of knowing I wanted to be a girl but could not let anyone know, fearing what they would say and/or do to me; and second, *why* is this happening to me and what am I supposed to do about it?

The specific indicators were trivial in the beginning. Maybe most boys experienced these portents that later dissolved, when growing up. There was the fun of walking around the house when I was five or six in my mother's high heeled shoes.

Not very high, but higher than anything I had. Then the stockings. Finally the rest of it (what the hell), any and all of the undergarments and dresses that I could find, put on, and eventually replace as though undisturbed, I thought. No one ever said anything to me. I think my mother didn't know what to make of it. I have no idea whether she ever told my father or not. The situation was ignored by all parties.

I remember one day when I was nine, seeing Bobby, who lived across the street, wearing his mother's clothes, complete with lipstick, nail polish, a bandanna on his head, and pushing his old baby buggy up and down the sidewalk. That looked like fun. I asked my mother if I could do that too. She said no, I wouldn't like it if the other kids called me a sissy. I asked what sissy meant. She told me to ask my brother or any other boy. I went back outside and there were several of my playmates giving poor Bobby the business: jeering and name calling until he ran home to his mother. She came out and told the kids to leave Bobby alone. She wheeled the baby buggy back inside. I don't remember if it had rubber bumpers or not.

I never claimed to be smart, but I'm perceptive as hell. My assessment of that drama told me that my inner feelings and desires, regardless of the subject, had damn well better be socially acceptable or I had to keep my mouth shut. Being able to keep one's mouth shut is an important social skill. I learned it through fear.

Over the years I would have an occasional twinge of some desire to either be a girl (because they were more highly regarded) or to at least wear some of their wrappings. Not dolls. No playing house.

I played with a lot of kids more or less my age. After school we would do stuff. Like the sod fights, possible only in the spring. Choose up sides, go to a vacant lot where the ground was still moist and the grass was about two feet tall. Form up into armies-"You guys are the Germans and we're the Americans." WWI was our last war, but we just called it The War. Then we would reach down, grab a handful of grass, pull straight up and presto! There was a missile. The soft, moist earth would become fashioned into a compact hemisphere. Whirl the thing around like a sling, aim at the enemy, and let go. Pow! I don't know who invented that diversion, but it was fun. We became good at it. Knowing when to let go, of course was the secret. We got so good at clobbering each other, that our mothers complained that our clothes were getting too dirty too quickly. Guess how many automatic washers and dryers there were back then? Right, zero. Washing was done in sinks or tubs with a washboard. We introduced a technological breakthrough in the form of the garbage can lid, used as a shield. It added more fun and kept our clothes cleaner. Sort of. We played street games: kick-the-can, tag, softball.

I learned by observation that there were role models for boys and for girls. To simplify, there were two archetypes: John Wayne and Shirley Temple. We watched them and their facsimiles on the screen on Saturdays. Every kid was supposed to pick the correct role model and pattern one's behavior accordingly. If not, and you acted like the one wrong for you, you were either a sissy or a tomboy. I used to wonder why tomboys were considered amusing, but sissies were social outcasts. Tomboy, eh. Only girls could be tomboys, girls who acted like boys. I believed I was a tomboy and took enormous pleasure in the thought. For awhile my pals called me Tom-Boy. They didn't know why I asked them to call me that. It was one of my early experiences in gaining pleasure in female consciousness without being detected. Farfetched? Not for me, it wasn't. I thought it was clever.

My twin nightmares continuing into my teens were occasionally wanting to be a girl, or interested in girl things, and *not knowing why it persisted*; and the fear that someone would catch me at it and *call me a sissy* like poor Bobby. I felt sure that if I joined the Navy I would certainly become a man and get rid of the fear and the confusion. A popular admonition was, "Grow up and be a man." That's what they said, and that's what I set out to do by joining the Navy.

Chapter 3

San Francisco has always been a place of adventure for me, regardless of my age. While still in short pants I had been taken to Playland-at-the-Beach, a year-round amusement park complete with roller coaster and other rides, a diving bell, bearded ladies, tattooed men, cotton candy and everything else an amusement park should have. My special interests included the shooting gallery, the electric autos one could actually drive, and any hamburger stand. Playland was about a hundred yards from the Pacific Ocean, separated from it only by a highway. Just before it was torn down to build condos, I watched Gene Krupa and Stan Kenton perform there.

When my pals and I were twelve or so, we'd buy bus tickets to ride to the Greyhound terminal on Seventh Street and then get on a local trolley. The trolley's destination didn't matter. We just rode it to the end of the line to see where it went. Getting there was the entertainment. Eventually we discovered Fisherman's Wharf via cable car; the Ferry Building, and watched the stevedores load and unload ships having flags that were white, with a big red disc in the center. We found Twin Peaks' Tunnel, Golden Gate Park, Stern's Grove, the zoo, industrial shops, printing plants, and of course, the Civic Center.

When you consider that San Francisco was populated and built by lusty, unsophisticated adventurers it should not be surprising that City Hall was only three blocks away from the President Follies, a burlesque theater featuring the finest acts of that art form. By age fifteen we were able to buy tickets and enter that temple of adult entertainment. A whole new universe of human behavior was revealed to us. (What we saw back then in the burlesque house was tame compared with what we see on television today.) Sometimes, after sitting through several matinee performances, we started looking at some of the other patrons and discovered there were women in the audience. "Probably wives doing their homework for tonight," snickered one of my pals.

It came as no surprise, two years later, that the entrance to the recruiting station for the United States Navy in San Francisco had moved next door to the President Follies.

I climbed the wooden staircase to the second floor and presented myself for duty. Aside from the attendance clerk at Burlingame High School, this was my first encounter with a true bureaucrat. It was a long time later that I learned that the bureaucracy could work *for* you.

The petty officer at the front desk gave me the recruiting forms that had to be completed and signed by either of my parents before I could ask anybody anything about the physical exam, how soon I could go to boot camp, and so forth. I was worried about my eyesight. I'd just learned a few months before that I was myopic. I knew I had trouble with distance vision, but I hadn't known the medical term. I asked if myopia would keep me out of the Navy. The recruiter looked at me menacingly and slowly said, "Watch your mouth, kid. By the time we get through checking you out we're gonna know *everything* about you. And if you're good enough we'll enlist you. In the meantime, take those papers home and don't come back until they're all filled out."

I was thunderstruck! He said that they would know everything about me. Did that mean they would find out that I liked to wear women's clothes now and then? How could they know that? I was a gullable kid and thought they might find out somehow.

My eyesight was not good enough for the standard at that time. I did my very first con job on the pharmacists' mate who checked my visual acuity. He said I had 20/70 vision in both eyes and that 20/40 was the worst they could accept. I did not cry, but I did give an impassioned plea that I somehow pass that test so I could join up like my father and my brother. He wasn't much older than me. He listened and I knew he understood. Finally he looked down at the clipboard with my test data on it and said, "Geez I make lousy fours. These look like sevens. I'll just put these little marks on top of these sevens and they will look more like fours. Move on." I don't remember much else about that physical except for a doctor asking me, confidentially, if I liked to have sex with men. No. I had passed the physical and was sworn in with a group of others a week or so later. I had specified that I wanted to join the Naval Reserve because that was what my father and brother had done. Three weeks later I received a letter from the Navy stating that no more Reservists would go on active duty because the war was over and Reservists weren't needed. Of course, regular Navy enlistees were always in demand. I reenlisted as U.S.N. until my twenty-first birthday. In September, as my senior year began, I received orders to report to boot camp in San Diego. Cloud nine.

The train ride was an education. I climbed aboard at the station in Burlingame. Several of my friends cut class to be there to wave me off. Even my sweetheart, Carolyn. As the train started moving, I looked for a place to sit. Some battle-weary Marines made room for me and the small overnight bag specified in my orders. "Are you going to boot camp, kid?" I said I was. "Oh boy, you'll really enjoy MCRD!" I asked what MCRD meant. They all looked at me and at each other and then one said, "It means the Marine Corps Recruit Depot. You are going to boot camp and you don't know that?" I said I was going to the Navy boot camp. I was invited to pick up my ditty bag, as they called it, and move out of their presence. As I started to get up, the grizzliest of the lot said I should stay put. After all, the Navy *did* have the decency to transport them back from Saipan. The least they could do in return was to be nice to one of their recruits. Besides, I found out later, they wanted to swap some of their clothes for mine. When we recruits stood in formation on the platform of the train station in San Diego waiting for the bus, we all looked half civilian, half Marine.

Boot camp is a place where you will enter as one person and exit as that person plus a whole lot more. The duration of my boot training was ten weeks. Everyone's individual identity was displaced by a uniform, group consciousness. A seemingly inhumane regimen was designed and implemented to rebuild our self-concepts as members of a team who would instantly respond to command. In any military organization instant obedience to orders is paramount. No questions, no discussion, no reflections, no voting. If you are given an order, you will obey without hesitation. It did not take ten weeks for us to comprehend the idea, but it took that long for us to internalize it. There is a big difference.

Another thing we learned was that our bodies were being rebuilt-by Navy mess halls, by the marching, and the calisthenics.

It was an invaluable experience. Not just the ability to respond to orders, but the training in the basics of shipboard living, i.e., how to stand a watch, how to fight various kinds of fires, how to handle yourself around moving lines, booms, and such. We were trained not to be a hazard to our future shipmates.

The biggest lesson I learned in boot camp was to do a job whether I felt like it or not.

I also learned that I had fooled the Navy into thinking I was as tough and manly as anyone else in Company 45-448.

After a short leave for Christmas, we were sent to the receiving station on Treasure Island to await transportation to our duty stations. In 1939 and 1940, I had spent many days walking around the World's Fair, seeing exhibits and being amazed at some of the futuristic artifacts. The arts and sciences were on display. I saw an outdoor opera. I saw a Ford Assembly line. I saw Sally Rand, the infamous fan dancer. Now, in December of 1945, T.I. was mostly barracks, chow halls, administration buildings, and Navy schools. It was somber in those drizzly days. No color, no adventure.

Within three days of arrival, we boarded the USS Effingham, a troop transport, and headed west through the Golden Gate. It was my last contact with North America for the next two years.

The Effingham had been making shuttle runs, bringing home all military scheduled for discharge, and shipping out those of us who would be replacements wherever replacements were needed. The Pentagon had a problem ending the war without emasculating the armed forces needed to maintain the peace.

In mid-January of 1946, our transport anchored in Nagasaki's harbor. It was during evening twilight. I went up on deck to see what the town looked like. All I could see was a dull red-orange sky and a low silhouette of stick-like things, looking like a forest fire had been there. Later I learned that it looked the same during the noonday sun, but a little brighter-not much brighter. The "city" was quarantined. We did not exchange personnel from land. Our anchorage, with favorable wind conditions, was a rendezvous with other ships. That was my first clue that Japan was sick of the war, and many thousands were sick from the war.

On the last day of January 1946, I was one of five who were taken from the transport at night via a noisy landing craft to the inner tidal basin of Inchon Harbor. We were assigned to the USS YO 118. It was a yard oiler, but it had only carried water. The mission was to load fresh water from the inner harbor, and carry it to large ships anchored in the outer harbor. We scrambled up the ladder and found that it was hard to stand up on an icy, slightly curved deck. We were warmly welcomed, given dinner, a bunk assignment and soon it was lights out.

The next morning we new seamen were assigned to the main deck with fire axes to break up the ice so the crew could get the ship underway.

After an hour or so the captain hollered down from the bridge, "Does anyone want to strike for Quartermaster?" I got my hand up first and was invited to the bridge to meet my new mentors-Frank from somewhere in Pennsylvania, and a nice guy named Mario Biaggi, from Paterson, New Jersey. I went to work learning the crafts of piloting, being a helmsman, and one of the hardest things to learn: Morse code, and communicating by flashing light.

It was the opinion of Frank that I was a deadbeat and incapable of being a signal watchstander. I did not want to concur, but it was hard to learn. No logic involved. Memorize and respond fast. I worked hard. As a result, I learned two things: first, a cup of hot coffee can keep your hands from freezing in the winter winds of Korea. Second, I learned that if you can read the flashing light from another ship, you can take the message below to the pilothouse where the cold wind does not cause the eyes to water and freeze. I was motivated by pain to learn flashing light. I can still read twelve words per minute.

A lot of the guys wanted to go ashore in Inchon and get laid. I did not want to. We'd go ashore, eat a local meal, drink, and while most of them went off to find sex, one or two others and I would continue drinking. We were the virgins. No one ever derided us. They just thought we were stupid not to get laid. My story was that I wanted to save myself for my future wife in the States. Sure.

By May of '46 our captain was informed that our 179' water tanker was needed in Tsingtao, China. We were to steam in the company of an LST. On May 18 we were told to get underway when the LST gave the signal to do so. Around noontime a sampan came alongside. Two Korean men were on deck and asked if any of us wanted "to push-push." International language, but you have to mime it, partly. Our captain, a Warrant Boatswain, hollered down, "How much?" The ladies crawled through the hatch and stood on their deck. Their pimp said, gesturing to his treasures, "Sugar." A deal was made. For a 50-pound bag of sugar one of the ladies would go to the crew, and the other would go to the captain's bunk. Done. I was glad to have the excuse of staying on the bridge waiting for the signal to get underway. The crew began their pleasuring with one lady on the mess hall table, using someone's mattress. The captain climbed into his bunk with his exclusive partner. I was *on duty*.

Twenty minutes later the captain came up in the pilothouse with a Cheshire smile, tossed a foil wrapped package on the chart table and said, "OK, Wheels, it's your turn." Wheels is the nickname for a quartermaster-the rating badge insignia is an 8-spoked ship's steering wheel. I looked at the red and white foil packet with black lettering that said Trojan. My heart sank. Oh shit. The captain wants me to get laid. I can't refuse, but I don't want to, even with a reliable condom. Yet I felt obligated. I said I was saving myself for my future wife at home. He said I was to take the bag (the Trojan), go below and have a piece of ass in his bunk. It came out as an order. *Do your job whether you feel like it or not.*

I went to the next deck below, opened the door to his cabin and there was a much prettier female than I had remembered on deck. Naked, except for a pair of jade earrings, and a beautiful smile enhanced by one gold tooth in front. I was nervous and scared and she knew it. She was going to get a cherry boy. She would have given *us* the bag of sugar to get laid by a cherry boy. She was nice, gentle, but insistent.

We were both naked in the bunk. I had no earrings, though. In no time at all I was penetrating that small body. All those stories about the Oriental women having their labia major in a horizontal configuration were wrong, but it wouldn't have mattered. I had found the Gates of Cathay. Paradise Lost was found. Half a dozen strokes and I could care less about anything. A few more strokes and I could have died with a smile on my lips. Then it came. I came. She came. Delirious. I nuzzled her left ear as the most incredible sensation I'd ever known began to subside in the sweetest way imaginable. My mouth found her clip-on jade earring. I removed it with my mouth, positioned it between my front teeth, gave her a rictus smile, and we kissed. I had found bliss. I wondered how long it would take to get it up again. I wondered about the gallons of semen I thought I pumped-how long would it take to replace the stock for one more push-push.

We were still playing with the jade earring when we were interrupted by the captain hooting down the voice tube. "OK, Wheels, we've got the signal to get underway!" I've still got the earring. Why did I keep it all these years?

As we steamed out of the harbor, the sampan now a tiny speck, my face with a Cheshire smile, I suddenly realized it was my mother's birthday. The significance for me was that in a warped way, I had given her a grand present: See, Mom, your young son is not a sissy, even though he used to try on your clothes. He has now performed a clearly male act with a bonafide female, and found the whole thing to be smashing.

Two days later we entered Tsingtao Harbor. My only question, unanswered by the nautical charts and the Sailing Directions for the North China Coast was, "Is the poon better in China than in Korea?" I could hardly wait to find out.

For the next seven months I had liberty every night. We all followed the same pattern: go ashore to Fatso's Frisco Cafe, have a couple of beers while listening to Roy Acuff sing *On the Wings of that Great Speckled Bird*, and other sodbuster songs. Next it was off to one of the three cathouses. The choices were enchantingly named Whorehouse #1, Whorehouse #3, and The House of a Thousand Assholes.

Afterwards, we would regroup at Fatso's for ham and eggs and a cherry brandy cut with vodka. Next, we'd go to the Enlisted Men's Club or to the Alaska Club. The E.M. Club had a bar and dining room. Slightly institutional, not the kind of place Fats had, which had creaky wooden floors, rickety tables and chairs that sometimes broke. The "class" was further enhanced by bottled goods that never had labels, in any language.

The Alaska Club was a magnificently detailed copy of the stereotypical nightclub seen in films made in the thirties-the kind associated with Bogart, Cagney, Robinson, etc. The last time I went there, one of the hostesses suggested I try a Singapore Sling. I just had my 18th birthday, been screwing so many times I'd lost count, I'd passed the exams and been advanced to Quartermaster, Third Class. I was a man. I could do anything, including 20 words a minute flashing light, Frank. So sure, I'd try a Singapore Sling. It tasted like fruit juice. My booze consumption to that time had been limited to cherry brandy and vodka, and beer. I had started on my sixth sling when I thought a little fresh air would feel good. Oh. My youthful vigor got me to the front door. I took one step down the dozen or so steps to the sidewalk. The rest of the way down was achieved by gravity. My shipmates found me, put me in a rickshaw, and back to the ship to begin my first hangover. I've never lost consciousness through drink since then.

A few days later a contrite me began the drill all over, but ended up at the E.M. Club afterwards. There was an entertainer there, a most unusual man who looked about 40 who played a little concertina and sang. He had a strong supple voice, not a great voice, but like Fred Astaire, he knew his way around a song. That night I heard *Symphony* for the first time. I was spellbound by the song and by the feeling this non-singer put into it. He did other songs of course, mostly pop show tunes and a lot of European folk stuff.

My horizons expanded that night. I learned that I could have a rewarding evening on liberty all by myself.

A few weeks later, I asked around town if there was an Italian restaurant within rickshaw reach. A place called Villa Viana, out near American Beach, I was told. I found the place in the European community. It was a Georgian-style, two-story residence with a small sign identifying itself. It was first a home, and a restaurant second.

Upon entering, I noticed the living room contained four small dining tables. That was it. The people were friendly and I ate spaghetti, the real, non-Navy kind, for the first time in over a year. I was a curiosity for them because I was the only shipboard sailor to eat there. They were accustomed to other military but not my kind. Their curiosity resulted in us getting to know each other, and soon I was invited to "join the family." The family consisted of Mamma (Russian), Papa (Italian), Viana (almost a teenager), Mamma's two sisters, and a few military; one Marine for each of the sisters, Eddie, a CB chief for the houseboy, and me and Viana. The chief became interested in me, and I became interested in Viana as a friend. She was a lot younger, but smarter and more knowledgeable.

Being part of the family meant sitting at the great table in the official dining room for a European style dinner, consuming ardent spirits, lots of conversation, and no rush. It was magnificent. The meal was the means to an end, a vehicle for warm, interpersonal contact. I never thought I could enjoy the company of Marines.

I learned a lot about living while there. I learned that I could not get into bed with another man. Eddie finessed me into sharing a room with him when I was invited to stay over. When I realized what his game was, I slept in a chair that night.

The big thrill was the impromptu operatic entertainment after the dinner and after the customers had left the commercial dining room. Piano, a violin, tenors, sopranos doing selections from European opera. I was ecstatic. I was amazed. Who are these people who can eat, talk and laugh at the dinner table and suddenly jump up and do Verdi, Puccini, and Russian folk stuff? It blew my mind. The incredible sweetness of the music and the voices. More polished than the man at the E.M. Club, but mostly they added new dimensions of music for me.

Orders came in a few months for my ship to go back to Korea. We said our goodbyes and promised to stay in touch. Viana and I stayed in touch, then she visited my mother when her family finally had to leave Tsingtao, then Shanghai, then to California to keep ahead of the Communists. They eventually lost touch due to Viana becoming a Navy wife and transferring a lot, and my parents moved. One day no one knew where anyone else was.

Upon arrival in Fusan, Korea, we transferred our ship to the Korean Navy. We were all assigned to the USS Elkhorn (AOG7) as permanent crew. The Elkhorn was a tanker, 310' long and could carry sixteen thousand barrels of aviation gas, motor gas, or diesel fuel, or combinations thereof. In postwar years it was used mostly for carrying fuel for the generators of Army weather stations in some of the most remote locations in the Pacific. We spent most of our time at sea, steaming independently. Sometimes two or three weeks without sighting land; then, find that little atoll, pump their needs, and underway again within hours.

I was not immediately accepted by the Quartermaster gang. It was T.J. somebody from St. Augustine, Florida, who disliked me intensely. Because he was in charge of the group, his attitude had to be sanctioned by the others. For a while anyway. I am not sure why he had it in for me. If I had to guess, I'd say he thought I didn't know my job. That was true to some extent. I knew my job quite well on the former ship, but the new ship had equipment I'd only studied about, but never seen operate. The ship also was heavily involved with celestial navigation which was new to me. So old T.J. had it in for me and worked hard at making my life miserable. There are people who are like that. I got on well with the rest of the crew. I did learn all the new stuff within a month or so, but the psychological hazing continued until he was transferred almost a year later.

Watchstanding at sea is mostly monotonous stuff. You could get to know your watchmates as well as you wanted to. Ultimately you end up with yourself, inside your own head. You can think about things, daydream, or whatever.

Occasionally, I found myself nursing some wounds from T.J. If he really came down hard, I found myself later (on watch) in a dealing-with-it process similar to my childhood days when I was scolded for doing something wrong. I didn't anesthetize my wounds by thinking he would like me better if I were a girl. Instead I would think about things I really wanted. At my sophistication level, there were limits. The most pleasurable things I knew consisted of putting on women's clothes, screwing, and those magnificent evenings at Villa Viana. I worked them pretty hard in my imagination.

Of course there was more diversity with women's clothes. After a long while of mentally trying on underwear and dresses and shoes, I dared to dream of being able to wear a wig. Wow! If I could wear a wig and all the rest of the stuff maybe I could feel like a girl. Woman. Whatever age group I was.

Then the childhood fantasies came back in full force, but they became much more mature. I'd had intimate relations with women and now I was aware of some of the key differences in body form. I began devising ways to offset narrow hips, hide my genitals, create a bosom. On watch I'd give myself those problems to solve. Then a new set of problems: I am in San Francisco as a male. How can I turn into a female and travel to Los Angeles? The logistics were staggering. Obtaining a wardrobe, the appearance, ID, money, travel reservations, what to do when I got there, how to get back, and all the time go undetected. Months of watches went by working on that one.

It was all elective. My head would let me think about anything I wanted. I could be in the middle of choosing a pair of heels that would go with the green silk dress when one of my watchmates wanted to talk about the changing weather conditions or some such. It didn't matter what the distraction was. I'd participate in sidetracking when needed, because I could always return to Macy's shoe department later and it would always be there, just as I had left it.

I'd think of lots of different things on watch and so did everyone else. I had that one category that no one else had: dressing up and going out as a woman. I was sure no one else thought about it because since my early days, no one ever talked about real guys doing that. No one ever wrote anything about it, except maybe a spy, like the Scarlet Pimpernel. But it was expedient for him, not for the joy of it—or so we are told. How could I reconcile my desire to look and act like a female yet be horny and screw women? I don't know. Where is it written that I am *obliged* to reconcile those two discrete events?

Mostly, in those days, I'd think about woman stuff when my pain or boredom level really got to be too damned much. A place of last resort so to speak. Why? Because I also thought it was wrong to think about that kind of stuff, like masturbation. When the physical or psychic pain got to a high level, I'd say the hell with it, and started thinking about female clothing and how to go about doing it one day if I ever got back to the States and away from Navy folk.

I remember one night while anchored just off Truk Island. I was the only one on topside watch. I committed the unforgivable sin of not waking up the radioman at 0400 so he could copy messages. I was to be punished. Of course, I could have been summarily shot if that had happened during wartime. Evidently, my record of performance was pretty good, because at Captain's Mast, I was actually given my choice of punishment: either lose my rating as a Quartermaster, Third Class, or "volunteer" for 100 hours of extra duty. Without hesitation I chose the extra duty.

Later, anchored in Kwajalein Harbor, I was a few hours short of my hundred-hour sentence to clean the Diesel cargo bilges when two radio messages came to the ship. The first message was to the captain telling him to get the ship underway for Midway Island to pump off some aviation gasoline, and then proceed to Apra Harbor, Guam, to effect ship repairs. The second message was directed to our navigator, telling him that his father was dying and that he should proceed to the airfield and fly home on emergency leave. The captain informed me that since I had been the assistant to the navigator, I was now to function as navigator, in the lieutenant's absence.

I did it. I got us from Kwajalien to Midway, and then to Guam. We had no LORAN equipment. Nobody had invented satellites yet. I did it by shooting stars with a sextant and working out the sights to produce lines of position to provide the fixes. Morning sights and evening sights for stars, sun lines during the day. Yes, the captain checked my work for a few days and was satisfied. I had learned a lot working for the navigator. He told me more about celestial navigation than I wanted to hear. But now I used that knowledge to get us there, directly. I was a high school dropout, nineteen years old, and navigated a U.S. Navy ship for two weeks.

To this day I'm not sure which made me the proudest: doing my 100 hours of scut work without complaint, being promoted to second class, or navigating the ship to two destinations. I'm not sure it matters which made feel the best. What I learned was that even though I thought I was some kind of pansy for thinking so much about someday wearing women's clothes, I had shown one and all that I was skilled in my craft and that I could do some pretty shitty jobs without complaint. I actually had those silly bastards believing that I was as much a man as any of them.

In Guam we drank beer. The smallest unit you could buy in the exchange was a case. It never occurred to us to buy one and share it. So, when in Rome,... One of the results of drinking that much beer in a few hours is the need to urinate. One of the anatomical capabilities of the male is the ability to urinate efficiently in a standing position. One consequence of drinking that quantity is the capacity for novel thinking. The result: we practiced writing our names in urine on the hillside roads above Apra Harbor while walking backwards.

Something began to happen as a result of that trio of events in 1947. In my mind I discovered that I had capacities not previously known to me. It was like discovering a whole new wing to a house I'd lived in for a long time. It occurred to me that for all practical purposes I could be a man among men *and* still have space for developing some kind of feminine consciousness too. My life did not have to be an *either or* situation. But what kind of feminine consciousness? I didn't even have that vocabulary back then, let alone the concept. It was a crude, clumsy thought, but I was beginning to see some kind of possibilities.

Oh hell! Where is there a book on this? I must be the only guy in the whole world who appreciates his manhood, yet wants to develop a womanhood of some sort. Well, there were to be endless watches in my future, and I would try to sort this thing out somehow. At that moment, the important thing was that I'd finished some kind of rite-of-passage and was no longer a confused boy. I was a man. A confused man.

In the fall of 1948, I was qualified to take the fleet competitive examinations for petty officer, first class. I knew I was going to leave the Navy at the end of my enlistment next May, but my ego demanded I compete. I did, and in January of 1949 I became a Quartermaster, First Class. Three years and three months earlier I was in boot camp, now I had a prestige that made it hard for me to stand firm on my decision to leave the Navy in May.

At the Separation Center, the same facility on Treasure Island I'd shipped out from in January of 1946, I went through the discharge process. It took a month for the administrative folk to process the paperwork. To keep us busy between interviews, some of us senior petty officers were assigned to the Shore Patrol headquarters on Clay Street near Montgomery Street in San Francisco. The tough, cop types running the station house were confounded by my status: I was supposed to check the drinking establishments in the North Beach area to ensure there were no intoxicated military personnel in them causing trouble. The problem was that I was not legally allowed inside those places because I had not yet had my 21st birthday. We all agreed to overlook that technicality.

The boon was this: We were each given a territory to patrol, and a list of the places that were off limits to the military because of the unsavory environments therein. In today's parlance-the gay bars. We salty old dogs snickered as we walked into each off-limits place to check on uniforms. On our off nights and in civilian clothes we could go back to some of the better places for kicks. I was jealous over the fact that the gay population had places to go for mutual support and good times.

Independently, I cruised every place in that spring of '49 only to learn from the gay men's bars, the lesbian bars, and even Finnochio's, that I was really weird by any of their standards. The most notorious places were The Black Cat Cafe on Montgomery Street and Mona's Candlelight Club on Broadway. I could not find a society of people like me. Not even in the city that offers everything. Almost everything.

On our last day in the Navy, a recruiter came by to give the pitch for signing up in the Reserves. I thought that made sense, so I enlisted in the Navy Reserve, kept my rating, and subsequently joined a training unit in San Jose, where I'd enrolled in college on the G.I. Bill. I got paid to attend those meetings every Thursday night.

From May until September I lived at home in Burlingame and took a job selling Fuller Brushes, door-to-door. It was fun and it was frustrating. I learned a new kind of discipline, but it was based on an old one. I rang those doorbells whether I felt like it or not.

One evening, after making 67 cold calls, I stopped at the Picadilly for a few beers and met two of my old high school pals who had gotten out of the Army a year earlier. They were students at San Jose State and suggested I enroll too, and take a room in their boarding house.

My first year was a disaster, scholastically. I had a blast, socially. By June of '50, I'd been placed on second probation and told to shape up or go play somewhere else.

The highlight of that year was the Halloween Costume Dance. Right. Carte blanche. All of the logistics were worked out in my head in about five minutes, but took a week to execute. Step one, line up the costume; two, find a date with a sense of humor. The costume had to be feminine, of course, but a costume. Goldstien's Theatrical Costumes in San Francisco had everything but a wig. I chose a flapper outfit, a chiffon shift with slip, shoes, and headband with plume. The wig came from a small wig shop in San Jose. No one had invented the inexpensive synthetics we know today. It cost serious money to rent a human-hair wig. Hand tied. I bought the under garments and cosmetics. I tested everything of course with great attention to detail. My debut, you see.

When I asked Joan, one of my classmates, if she would like to go to the dance with me she said, "Sure, what are you going to wear?" I told her about the flapper outfit. She was silent a moment and then said she would call me back. An hour later she said okay, she would go as a clown.

I picked her up and we drove to the dance out in Saratoga. She said she felt she was out with another girl. I was thrilled. I asked if that was all right. She said it was weird.

At the dance I received mixed reactions. Some thought I must be a fairy to wear such a pretty dress and take such care with the details. Others thought it was clever. No one mistook me for a girl. I was ecstatic because I was doing what I'd dreamed of doing, but disappointed that I didn't pass worth a damn. It *was* worth the investment. No one said anything about it to me afterwards.

No more opportunities for dressing that year. I did have a few things I picked up from the Goodwill and the cheaper shoe stores, but I never went out in them. I'd put them on, lock the door to my room, and wonder what the hell was going on.

One thing that went on was the police action in Korea. I was disappointed with myself and my lack of self-discipline, my lack of scholastic success, and my lack of ability to begin the fulfillment of my fantasies. I actually thought I might be happier in the Navy. Maybe I was not cut out to be a civilian. I had lots of success in the fleet, not much in school. I decided to volunteer to go on active duty to fight the Commies. When I contacted the Navy, they said I should not bother to volunteer because my orders were on their way. That is what the Reserve is for. Sure enough, in a week I had orders to report to the USS Agerholm (DD 826) in San Diego, six weeks hence.

Chapter 4

The train ride to San Diego in September of 1950 was quite different from the troop train atmosphere I experienced in 1945.

First, there was a club car and I was old enough to transact business in it. Heineken's was a new beer for us Californians. I felt it incumbent upon me to make sure it was good enough to recommend to my friends.

Second, I had my seabag of clean, well-fitting uniforms stowed in the baggage compartment. I wore slacks and sportcoat, starched shirt open at the neck, and highly polished penny loafers. Hot stuff in 1950. No Marine would hustle me out of those duds.

Third, I had a very good idea of the action coming up and knew how to behave in an efficient, seamanlike manner. Upon arrival in San Diego, I would go to one of the uniform/lockerroom places on lower Broadway Street, rent a locker, get my blues pressed out, a shoeshine, store my civilian clothes, grab a cab and proceed to the 32nd Street Pier and report aboard my new home.

By the time the train left the Salinas stop, I was well-situated on a bar stool. The bartender knew my beverage and looked my way for a nod often enough. I had my operational plan worked out so that I could move on automatic until the time I would cross the side of the USS Agerholm and report for duty. It would be a new experience for me to serve on a combat ship. No sense in trying to speculate on the future. I had enough to sort out from the past.

What in the hell was going on with me? I'd had a year of civilian life as a non-studious student. I'd made a lot of friends, had my night out last Halloween, and met a lovely young lady on the last day of finals. One of my fraternity brothers introduced me to his date. Helen was beautiful. Fantastic cheekbones guaranteed to keep her beauty through old age. She was graduating and getting ready to return to her home on Oahu. I persuaded her not to be too hasty. Let's get to know each other. We dated several times by the time my orders came. A few days before train time I suggested we become engaged. Okay.

So why didn't I feel good about the engagement? I certainly picked a choice woman. She was good looking, had a degree in Home Economics, a reasonable sense of humor, and was healthy. All the good things. Bad things? None observed. Then why wasn't I more excited about the future as a married man? For one thing, getting married was the proper thing to do. Everyone said so. Privately, I believed that getting married and being physically and emotionally close to a woman would eliminate my desires to dress as a woman, or try to present myself as such in public or private. And should there be any residual desires along those lines, she would support me as a loving wife who would have compassion while I worked through this. A reasonable assumption.

A look from the bartender. A nod from me. Another beer.

Too bad about Carolyn. We were so tuned to each other just a few years ago in high school. Now we were strangers and each too proud or too stupid to reconcile. The disruption happened in the fall of 1948, several months before my discharge.

It was my first liberty in the U.S. after my ship moored in Oakland. I telephoned her at her dorm in Berkeley. A friendly but not too enthusiastic Carolyn agreed to a date that night. She'll warm up once we get together. I rented a car and drove to her dorm near Dwight and Hillside and waited in the lobby for her. The student receptionist eyed me curiously. I wondered why. I wore my best blues, clean white hat, and my shiny inspection shoes. New campaign ribbons, too. When my high school sweetheart entered the reception area, she stopped, mouth open, and stared. Why isn't she running into my arms? She walked to me, held out her hand and said mechanically that she was pleased to see me.

It took awhile for her to select a suitable coffee shop where no one would know her. It seemed I was an embarrassment for her in my uniform. After all, she was a junior at U.C. Berkeley and a political science major. The contemporary attitude was that the military were the bad guys. She was politically and philosophically opposed to me and my kind. Oh yes, she was still fond of me, but ...

We tried a second date a few weeks later. I wore all new clothes complete with white shirt and conservative tie. Contemporary Berkeley and Carolyn rejected this square as though I'd worn my uniform. In fact, it was the uniform of the class despised more than the military. The date lasted longer because we went to San Francisco for guaranteed anonymity. Over dinner I learned I did not know a damned thing about the important issues of the day. The U.N. for example and the heroic figures who were fighting for what seemed to me to be communist causes. I was very tired of being considered a loser and a know-nothing when, in *my* world, just the opposite was true. We parted that night without kisses. Oh how I remembered those kisses from earlier years!

Another look. Another nod. Another beer.

The six weeks in San Francisco required some reflection, too. After receiving my orders to active duty, I thought I'd better find a way to experience woman things somehow. I got a job with the Railway Express Co. in their warehouse near Pier 2 on the waterfront. I was a lumper: strong back, weak mind they said. I rented a room out near the Panhandle of Golden Gate Park. My plan was to work during the day and turn into a woman at night. Neat plan. In actuality it was far from successful. Not a total loss, but nearly so. My first lesson was that it was expensive to purchase a dockworker's wardrobe *and* women's clothes.

I was too embarrassed to ask to try on a dress, or to even suggest the dress was for me. Women's sizes do not correlate very well with men's sizes nor are they consistent. A man's 42 long suit or a 16 collar are universally standard. A woman's size 16 is almost meaningless. The manufacturer will play games with sizes and so will the stores. In Sears I might buy an 18 skirt, in Saks I'd need a 14.

I had just enough money to buy the clothes needed for the job, my rent, bus fare, food, some really cheap women's things, and on some days I could even buy more than one beer after work. I could not buy enough good stuff to walk around the block, let alone go into town to a restaurant. I supposed I was naive, all right. I looked younger than my years, with a sophistication level to match.

Another look. Another nod. Another beer.

What did I want for the rest of my life? Sure, I wanted to satisfy my urging to dress as a woman, but I still had no inkling of what that meant. Did it mean I should try to *become* a woman or just *pretend* once in awhile? How *does* a man become a woman? I couldn't see how. Why are there no books or movies about a man who wants to be a woman? Of course I did not know whether I wanted to be a woman or not. I wanted to know if it was possible, and what would it be like to be the other sex. There were no sources of information I could find that could help me. No one talked about it. I must be the only more-or-less typical male with these feelings, these urges, the pulling toward... toward what? No answer. That was maddening! A theme was becoming manifest and no way to find out what it meant.

Sure there is, Tom. Do it. Get yourself dressed the way you want, and you will begin to find out. You learn best through experience anyway. Until you actually get fully decked out, head to toe, skin out, appropriate paint, until then you will never know what it is all about.

Yeah, but how am I going to do that? I'm on my way to San Diego to join a crew on a combat ship. The logistics are impossible! And I've asked a girl to marry me!

For now it looks impossible. You have learned to wait. You know how to control your mind. As for the young lady, that is another matter. You hardly know her. You expect that marriage to her will solve your need to investigate femininity. Maybe you will tell her about this before you tie the knot.

If I do that, I'd be risking my chances for a happy marriage. I really think a good marriage will make this feeling go away.

Yes, I know you think that.

Another look. Another nod. Another beer.

Why did I begin to answer my question about the rest of my life by thinking of the female stuff? Sally. We will use Sally as the label. Why didn't I think first about career choices? I more or less learned some things about advertising and public relations. Why not that as a career choice? Why didn't I think about where my future family would live? Or how many kids. Why did I think about Sally first?

No more beers.

We were entering Union Station in Los Angeles. There would be a short wait before the Atcheson, Topeka and Santa Fe would let us board for the final hour and fifteen minutes of train ride to San Diego. I idly wondered how many Lincoln ellipses were made underneath me that day.

The A. T & SF had a different club car configuration. More tables and booths, less bar. There were only a few empty seats at tables when I got there. I asked a pleasant-looking guy if I could join him. Sure, sit right down. He was about ten years older than me and dressed about the same. We started talking the usual drivel: about the crowded train, weekend travel, rarely go to San Diego anymore, etc. He asked me what I did for a living. I said that I'd been a student of advertising at San Jose State. He said that he was a partner in an ad agency in West L.A. I said that my schooling was being interrupted by the Korean Police Action, that I was a Navy Reservist being recalled to active duty. He said that he was being recalled also. He hadn't been on active duty since early '46. I said that was when I got my first duty station. The exchange went on for a few more minutes. He asked what my orders said. I told him. Me too he said. Son of a bitch, we're going to be shipmates!

The bartender did not understand my nod system but the waitress did. We started our second round. I asked what his rate was. He smiled and said that he was a Lieutenant Commander. He would be the new executive officer of the USS Agerholm. Cripes! Here I am sitting and drinking with my new X.O. I could see the amused look on his face as all of this registered on mine. I told him I was a Quartermaster, First Class. It was his turn to be surprised. You are too young to be first class. I'm glad that we'll be shipmates, he said. The rest of the trip was spent in casual conversation with lots of beer. He bought, mostly.

The next day, Monday, we met on deck. After exchanging salutes and good mornings we smiled and went on about our separate duties.

Life on the Agerholm was profoundly different from my prior service. The ship spent a lot of time at sea, which was fine with me, but we never went anywhere or did any task. Drill, drill, drill. Spit and polish and drill. I'd been away for over a year, and my prior service was more like the *Mr. Roberts* Navy.

By the time we got underway for Korea, we had new weapons installed, gone through the mill at Fleet Training Group (the bastards), and I became a husband.

Our wedding in mid-November was well attended: her family and friends, my family, the fraternity house, old pals from Burlingame, and all the off duty crew from the ship. The reception was in the ballroom of the Sainte Claire Hotel in San Jose. The ship was in Mare Island. I was granted two weeks leave for the honeymoon. My parents had friends who let us use their weekend cabin in the Santa Cruz mountains. An idyllic fortnight. Eat, drink, make love, sleep,... . At one point I did wonder if her nightgown would fit me, but decided to postpone finding out.

In the third week of the marriage, we were back in San Jose. Helen, it turned out, had one more class to complete before receiving her diploma. The Agerholm was still in Mare Island. I commuted daily by public transportation.

Sometime in that third week I said that I wanted to wear her nightgown. She asked, bewildered, *why*? I said that I liked to wear women's clothes although I'd hardly had the chance to do so. She was upset. I mean really. She cried. She called me a homosexual. I don't know whether I was more hurt or more confused by such a stupid remark from someone who minored in psychology.

She could not find anything in print regarding my special form of "homosexuality." It took awhile to get her to stop saying that.

In December the Agerholm got underway for San Diego where we endured the derision of Fleet Training Group. Like boot camp all over again. Helen joined me a week later when she finished the quarter and got that degree. I thought sure she was going to serve me with divorce papers. "No," she said, "we'll work this out when you come back." The marriage was not going to crumble so quickly.

In August of 1951 we were steaming with the USS Iowa off the East Coast of Korea. The Navy announced a need for certain rates to apply for submarine school. Hot damn! I'd always wanted to serve on subs, but "the needs of the service" did not permit-until now.

In two weeks I had orders to proceed to the sub base in New London. I wondered about my eyesight but no one else seemed to care. In New London they cared. Very much. They tested every part of my body and my mind. Submariners must be healthy and stable under pressure. No pun intended. The tests did not reveal that I wanted to wear women's clothing. The only fault they could find after three weeks of inside/outside inspection was my myopia. Because of my rate, it was critical that my eyesight be perfect. "In fact," they said, "if you tried to join the Navy today, you would be rejected." No kidding? I flashed back to the magic sevens and fours next door to the President Follies. I also had a phantasmagoric view of all the flashing light and flag hoist signals I read in over four years at sea.

But Admiral Rickover had not produced an atomic sub just yet. Submarines, the diesel boats, still spent most of their time on the surface where weather-deck personnel such as myself had to have 20/20 eyesight. I was assigned to Gilmore Hall for about six weeks as Master-at-Arms. Then they gave me a pair of glasses and orders to the USS Newport News (CA 148).

I hated to leave New London. I'd never before seen the end of summer turn to fall and then winter. From wearing whites in September to peacoats and flat hats in November. I remember the beauty of the trees and their colors-changing almost daily. California does not have four distinct seasons.

The other thing I liked about New London was its position on the coast. I would alternately spend my weekends in New York or in Boston. Despite my best efforts, I could not find anyone like me in either city. Boy! I must really be weird. Even the sophisticated gay bars in Greenwich Village did not know of any place that catered to oddballs like me. Oh, there were places that had female impersonators. That was not what I meant.

The USS Newport News was moored in Portsmouth, Virginia. It would be there for two more months then deploy to the Mediterranean for a year.

Two months. Then what? I'd better make some plans. How much longer would the Navy need me? Want me? If I'd been accepted in sub school I would have reenlisted for four years (without my wife's consent). Would I go to the Med? What if the Navy releases me next month? Would I want to re-enlist? What if I have to suddenly become a civilian again? Maybe I should speak with my spouse about these matters.

After a short phone call to Helen, I started the search for an apartment. It was tough but I found a room. A bath, down the hall, was shared by only one other couple. I took it. Helen would be there in about a week or less. I had a private place and some spare time. What a deal.

Right, Tom, what are you waiting for? The stage is set. Get busy.
But I'm short of cash.
Buy something. Anything.

I went to the local department store to ask for a nightgown for my wife who would be here next week. I was counseled into a new line of nylon pajamas. When asked what size, I found myself responding with the brilliant line, "I don't know the number, but if they will fit me, they'll fit her." I bought slippers too. Later, in the room I put the stuff on. Wow. I spent the night. How many more days before Helen comes? What will I do with these things when she gets here? I can't throw the stuff away. I had done that too many times in the past. I'll hide the things.

Helen came a few days later. We were happy to see each other. Later, she found the stash. We had a heavy discussion which lead to nowhere. Then we mellowed out and that conversation lead us to bed.

A month later I was transferred to the USS Missouri (BB 63). The Mo was going to sea for a fleet exercise, LANTFLEX52. I was assigned to Admiral Stump's staff. Helen went back to Palo Alto to await my return. In February she reported the death of a rabbit. I was to be a father.

In March I was released from active duty in time for Spring Quarter at San Jose State. We rented a two bedroom unit of student housing for veterans: $27.50 per month.

My grades shaped up, never getting less than a B for the rest of my undergraduate years.

I struggled with the problem of reconciling fatherhood and Sally. So did Helen.

Our first son was born in late September of '52. During her few days in the hospital I was a bachelor again. Once more, the stage was set. I scrounged around the Goodwill store and found what I needed. I finally had the walk around the block I wanted two years earlier in San Francisco. It was in the early morning hours, and I wore, skin out, head to toe except a scarf on the head, the you-know-what. There is no way to adequately describe the physical and psychological sensations I felt on that warm, early morning walk. The sensory part included the thrill of all the nylon underthings moving on my skin as nothing else could, the air moving around my legs in nylon stockings. And the newness of balance wearing 3" heels, the movement of the cotton skirt as I moved.

The psychic awareness was twofold: I'd done it—I'd gotten a whole outfit together and made it outdoors alone. True, no one saw me, nor should they. I didn't want to be discovered. The other awareness was the sheer joy in my heart. I felt as though I had to have this, be this, only this, someday, somehow. In the meantime, well, tough it out.

Helen guessed that I had done what I did. We chatted about that until her milk almost turned sour. There was always an undercurrent of rejection in our marriage. I love you except for *that*. But *that* is a central part of me. No. It is an unnecessary thing for you to do. After all, you're a father now. Grow up!

We had our pleasant times, comfortable times until the need came, triggered by nothing special I could discern.

Helen heard about a psychologist on the college faculty who counseled students for a dollar an hour, once a week. I stumbled and fumbled on the couch, finally getting the trip blurted out. The poor man thought I was a homosexual. I managed to convince him I cared not for the male body. His comeback was that I must be a latent homosexual. I said that if I could be a homosexual, my life would get a lot simpler, but I *could not* be a homosexual. Besides, what has that, if possibly true in the future, got to do with me now? How am I going to deal with this problem now? His answer was classic: Only you can help yourself. Oh, thank you, Doctor. Why do I come here if you can't help me? I don't want to get rid of the woman development within me. I want to foster it. I have this conflict with my wife, you see. I'm sorry, our time is up. Great. I leave the couch more agitated than before.

I knew what I wanted to do, but I couldn't just walk out on a wife and infant son. You do your job whether you feel like it or not. I worked at it. I absorbed myself in study. Things went well for weeks or even months until I'd see a particularly well-turned-out woman wearing something that I'd want to wear. I could almost feel the sensation of her clothes on my body. Spooky. Then the pain of doing nothing about it.

In 1953 someone named Christine Jorgensen made international news. A man became a woman. Words could not describe the hope that came. I was not so sure I wanted to really become a woman like that. I just wanted to find out what it was like—I needed more than just a walk around the block. I read as much as I could about George becoming Christine. That was not my story, but to know such medical art existed gave me an unexplained hope. Why should I care? I didn't know.

In April of '55 son #2 arrived. In August I was graduated with a B.A. degree in education, a teaching credential, and a contract to teach school for $4,000 a year. We bought a three-bedroom, two-bath tract house. Everything was falling into place: the family, the career, the mortgage.

There was also the struggle with Sally. She wanted a turn. I didn't even know what that meant. All I did know was that there was this tremendous urge building within me. I was keeping the lid on my id, but sometimes there would be a leak and cause a mess and I would end up feeling like a loser because I was not a normal man as I should have been. The psychologists called it "a one-down position." She was a normal woman. I was not a normal man. Did I ever get sympathy, comfort, or compassion from her? No. Only the admonition to get my act cleaned up. Did she ever threaten to leave me? No.

It was almost thirty years later that I realized she was living in terror, but I interpreted her behavior as domineering. A lot of dumb things can happen when married couples don't talk with each other about sensitive issues. Son #3 came in '57.

I think the only thing that saved my sanity was the friendships I made with the teachers at the junior high school. Most of us guys were veterans so the universal comradeship manifested in daily support and Friday night poker once a month.

The next international blockbuster book to hit the media was *The Story of Bridey Murphy*. Here was the story of a woman who was under hypnosis. The hypnotist began an age-regression series of questions. He was so successful and his subject so cooperative, that he began to ask her about events before she was born. To his surprise, she gave answers as Bridey Murphy, an Irish woman of a previous century. The significance, of course, was that maybe reincarnation was not hokum after all. Within a week all of us on the faculty had read the book, were discussing it, and seeking out books on related topics.

The Edgar Cayce books soon appeared. Cayce was called "The Seer of Virginia Beach." He became famous in the 1930s because he could go into a trance state and travel in time, and a lot more. His books—still in print—were fascinating. But were they true or just b.s.? In our heated debates, it was pointed out that we could ask the same question about the Bible. Who was to verify the accuracy of the Holy Writ? A conversation stopper.

Reincarnation made sense because it was the only philosophical concept that explained why good things could happen to bad guys and bad things could happen to good guys. I have not yet been able to find a flaw or inconsistency in the system. Rather, it has helped me to reconcile the enormous parade of pain, sorrow, disappointment, and garden variety bullshit that I have encountered. Furthermore, more people in this world believe it than those who don't.

We had several years of serious discussions at school and after school on that and related topics as psychocybernetics and Eastern religions. Such a construct has enabled me to keep my sanity and save me from the shrinks who had no knowledge of my problem and didn't seem to care. Two therapists even asked me to find help elsewhere. They said they did not want to talk with me.

Anyone who goes to a psychiatrist ought to have his head examined.

Chapter 5

The decade from early 1960s to early 1970s was the worst decade of my life. There is no other period that is so marked by selective forgetting. A few events were significant and good.

I spent a lot of time trying to find a way to dress up in women's clothing, but I was not able to. That pain was compounded by the gaffs and jibes from my never-loving wife who knew when I was thinking of it. Sometimes we would fight about my *thinking* about it. I could never win, of course, if I played by her rules. "You are not a normal man. Grow up! You disgust me!" I felt she was right. Her anger was based on fear, but I did not know that then.

Neither one of us knew how to deal with the problem. We scraped enough money together for an appointment with a psychiatrist. He didn't know what the desire of mine was all about. The literature was still not available, even then, so that the therapists could educate themselves. Our intentions were to find a solution to my problem, but enlightenment that would have suggested a solution was not there. All we knew was that I was not a normal man, and by then I knew I would never be normal by the conventional definition of normal. I am still wondering what normal really is.

Was my brother-in-law normal? He used to climb granite mountains, using ropes, picks, and pinions until he changed his recreation to driving formula one racing cars, going round and round a racetrack. I could have done a ten-minute diatribe on the stupidity of risking one's life and the incredible expense involved just to court death. But Helen would never listen to me when I "got like that."

I was alone. No one to talk with about my disgusting, sick fantasies as she called them. My self-concept was about one notch above the motivation level for suicide. I would not kill myself, really, but the idea visited me a lot of times. One thing I'd learned from reading about reincarnation: You really chose your life's agenda and had yourself born into the appropriate time and place to work through your lessons. If you "dropped out" you would have to come back and do it again until you finished the agenda. I sure as hell didn't want to repeat *this* life. Or maybe I *was* repeating it now.

What was I to do? How was I going to gain equilibrium, achieve parity in my own house, and accommodate the aching need to put on *anything* feminine?

One of my Sunday school teachers used to say, "God never gives you a problem that you can't solve." Well, okay, that sounded good, but where is my solution to this dilly of a problem? The teachings of the Eastern philosophies contained the same concept. And the high school teacher who said, "Every problem carries the seeds of its own solution." Well? With all the homilies and cracker barrel philosophy for support, something good should come along and I would be watching for it. I told myself, in quiet moments, that a way out of this confusion was coming my way. I would be alert for it and would recognize it and know what to do.

Most of us from the faculty of Dartmouth School were on a Friday night field trip to the Falstaff Brewery to see how lager is made. On the guided tour, I noticed Diane noticing me and positioning herself near enough to make comments so that only I could hear. A nice technique for singling one from the herd. I was nearly overcome because no woman had ever done that to me until that evening in the spring of 1966. What an ego stroke!

More than an ego stroke. It was like a lifeboat loaded with shelter and provisions. I had spent years in the one-down position at home where I was supposed to get support, and had to fake a happy posture outside the home. I never asked the woman to like it or to participate. Just leave me alone for awhile and don't bitch about it. No.

So the attention I got from Diane was incredibly sweet. I knew right away I was about to add infidelity to my list of evil deeds, but it felt good; so good to look into those intelligent, loving eyes that were looking into mine. The fact that she was a tutor for me in the school of life did not occur to me for some time to come.

The affair lasted for four months, then ended as abruptly as it began. We had gotten too serious about each other. We had agreed from the outset that it was a physical attraction that brought us together, and there would be no divorce or talk of divorce. I was the one who wanted to break the rule.

She signed up for art classes at night at San Jose State. I signed up for education courses at night at Stanford. I needed distraction from a wound I believed would never heal. It healed, but I still have the scar. Soon after entering graduate school I began to notice some of the women on campus and what they wore. Nice clothes. Looked like fun to wear. But I was busy teaching math all day, sitting in night classes two nights per week, and lots of papers to write in between times. No time to spend thinking about how good it would feel to wear that dress with the wide belt above the full circle skirt. Border print.

Graduate school was everything it was supposed to be: interesting, relevant, exciting, and it actually stimulated thought. In 1968 I was awarded the master's degree. My ego was pumped up, I got a thousand dollars a year increase in salary at school, and I'd actually learned some things I could put into practice right away. Not bad for a guy who was a high school dropout. But I was still in love with that woman who felt more strongly about my marriage to Helen than I did.

One of the guys in our school had to earn one unit of upper division credit to qualify for something. We searched the fliers and found an ideal course: San Francisco State was going to teach a weekend class on suicide prevention and it would be held in a ballroom of the St. Francis Hotel. A bachelor weekend in San Francisco? Four of us signed up for the class.

The speaker who arrested my attention was a lovely, vivacious young woman named Sheri Cravan. She had just earned her doctorate degree in sociology. Her dissertation had been snapped up by a publishing house and it became a successful college bookstore item. The theme was bar hopping in San Francisco and the societies one can find in various kinds of cocktail lounges. My thought was that if there is anyone who can help me find out about men who dress like women, it would be Dr. Sheri. Before the weekend was over, I found out how I could phone her the following week.

During my telephone pitch, I haltingly explained my desire to find a way to dress as a woman and be in some area of town that would tolerate such nonsense. She was reluctant to talk about it at first and suggested I get psychiatric help. I eventually convinced her to meet with me, dressed as Sally, in the small bar on the street level of the Embassy Hotel. Cheap, clean, but no class. (Diane and I stayed there one night.)

No need to signal her. She spotted me right away as did everyone else in the bar. We had a couple of drinks, talked some, then she split.

What I got from the conversation was that I looked and acted like a man dressed up in women's clothing, wearing a cheap wig. A football player, she said. She was nice, she was kind, above all she was honest.

Her opinions were as follows: In her visits to the 3,600 known bars in San Francisco at that time, she had not found one that catered to men like me. She thought I had a lot of courage to do what I was doing. She urged me to get out of the bar and walk around-see what it was like. Go have coffee somewhere. On Polk Street I couldn't lose. She mentioned a couple of places that were weird enough to let me feel comfortable.

Finally, she said I should stay out of the gay bars. Why? I had always thought gay men were sissies, like any male who wanted to dress as a female. No. She said I was all mixed up on the terms sissy, weak, and gay. They were not synonyms at all. She said that either sex could be strong or weak, either sex could be gay or straight. Gay men, for example, celebrate their manhood by celebrating with each other's manhood. They may or may not be sissy. You, on the other hand, deny your manhood by wanting to project a female persona and to explore womanhood on whatever terms you can. Going to a gay bar is not a good idea for you. Yes, you are really different. And certainly I can't see any sissy or weakness in you. After she left I had one more gin over with a twist and then took a very deep breath as I set my high heels in motion on the sidewalks of San Francisco.

Only four months earlier, I had the opportunity to transfer from a one-night-per-week Navy Reserve training group in San Jose to a unit on Treasure Island. The T.I. group met one weekend a month, Friday evening through Sunday afternoon. We would meet for organizational purposes on Friday evening, then proceed to the O-club for beverages, liars' dice, and macho bonding. Saturday mornings at 0800 we would get underway on a minesweeper or a destroyer and conduct drills like the people down in Fleet Training Group, San Diego. At the end of a hard day we would go back to our rooms at the B.O.Q. to clean up and put on our business suits, and go to San Francisco for dinner and drinks. We had a lot of places to check out. Maybe four or five of us would spend the evening and a lot of money playing bachelor on that one night per month. Sundays were unpredictable. Sometimes we would get underway, or we would stay in port to conduct school on deck gear, or weapons, or on the bridge.

Of course, I knew even before my first meeting that this was a way to eventually get Sally put together and *out there*. Sure enough. After two such Saturday nights of tomcatting around, I declared to my fellow officers on the third Saturday that I had a date and would not be joining them.

I checked in at the Embassy on Polk and Turk Streets with a couple of grocery bags of clothing, shoes, etc. I had no wig but I wasn't going anywhere. I just wanted the satisfaction and relief of getting into the clothes and experimenting with makeup. It was a thirteen-year interval since that pre-dawn walk around the block in 1955. Thirteen years of psychic pain, frustration, anger, confusion were now coming to an end.

I had some shopping to do before the next T.I. weekend. I had to find a wig and some better-coordinated clothes. A big mystery was pantyhose, as were a lot of other things. A typical man does not understand what a woman has to think about when she shops for clothes. A partial checklist built into every feminine psyche includes size, color, and style. Simple, until one realizes that each woman has her own style and shopping to find what you want can be exhausting. Other items on the checklist: price range, what you are looking for, and what else it will go with. If you buy that suit, you will need a new blouse for it, and which blouse will go with your new suit and at least one other skirt/jacket you already have? Will the new colors work with what is home in your closet? Fabrics and textures are an issue too. Some skirt/jacket combinations call for a silk blouse or maybe a cotton blend. Ruffles? Tailored? Jewel neck? Covered buttons? Will it work with the new scarf? And more. Much more.

The purchase of the wig was the biggest challenge. This object had to be for the person who was going to wear it. Certain items of female clothing can logically be purchased as gifts: nightgowns, slips, but not bras. Maybe panties. Shoes are not gifts and they had better fit or the wearer is in trouble. A whole new classification of pain awaits if you have to walk a distance in women's shoes that don't fit.

The wig is a very special thing. It is there to serve as the lady's crowning glory. It has to be right in color, length and styling. The one who will wear it must try it on, and let the salesperson comb it to fit the face.

By this time I was a public school administrator as well as a family man. I had to have absolute anonymity in all of these transactions. So where can I go for my first plastic hair? I'll need a place where nobody knows me, where I can try them on until I find something that works, where I can get it cleaned and pressed in between times.

I let my fingers do the walking through the Yellow Pages to locate wig places at least fifteen miles away from home. I found three and jotted down their locations. Then I drove to them to see what they looked like from the street. I eliminated those in shopping centers, and that left just one.

It was on a well traveled boulevard less than a mile from the University of Santa Clara. There was a row of old, rundown shops. Jean West's Wig Shop was in between an insurance office and a vacuum repair place. I parked and went in. Jean West, herself, turned from her customer, looked at me with the most bright and powerful blue eyes I ever saw. She told me to sit for a few minutes and relax. Relax? Me? In a clearly feminine domain, with only one possible reason for me being there, and I'm supposed to relax? In a few minutes the elderly customer vacated the chair. A nice looking woman. Class, like the president of a garden club. She and Jean looked at me briefly and the customer nodded at her, then left.

Jean asked if she could help me. I said I wanted a wig for a play. I was to be a woman. Did she have something not too expensive? Of course. As we tried a few lengths and styles, we talked small talk until she said that it was her guess that I was not really going to wear the wig in a play. I was stunned. She quickly added that I should relax. I said, "Okay. I want the wig for myself so that I can go to a masquerade next month in San Francisco." "And after that?" she asked. "Whenever I can. I would like to dress up as a woman whenever I get the chance."

A barrier had been breached. That was the first time I had talked of "my problem" to another person-aside from head specialists and my doting, compassionate wife. It felt scary. It felt good. There it was, out in the open. She said that my saying it to a stranger must have taken some courage. I said that desperation was more like it. She smiled and told me to relax. Where had I heard that before? She assured me of the confidentiality I could expect, and she said that she could better serve my needs now. She asked a few questions while combing and teasing the wig that I liked best. No, I was not interested in men. Yes, I'd really like to look like a woman if possible. No, I don't think I want to be like Christine Jorgensen. Too soon to tell. It was exciting to be able to talk with a "friendly" about all this.

Eventually the black wig I had chosen was shaped as good as it needed to be to balance my nose and chin. I began to see that women really live in a different world of concerns. If you have a problem with your body, there is a way to fix it. Or to compensate for it. You had better do something. Misshapen men are all right, misshapen women are not. Men can't resort to cosmetic fixes. Women can.

As I was paying out the $39.50 for the wig, Jean asked if I had any friends who were like me. I said no, that I felt sure there were not any other straight guys like me who wanted to dress up once in awhile. It was a very lonely place to be. She said I did not have to be lonely ever again if I didn't want to be. She has three other customers like me. "One of them is a dentist, one is a high school teacher, and another is a retired Cadillac dealer. In fact, the woman who was in the chair when you came in used to be the owner of the local GM agency. She lives by herself as herself all the time. She has been a customer of mine for twelve years. When *he* came in back in the 50s, he was almost a basket case. I got him to relax and helped him with his first wig-human hair.

That turned the trick. I've only seen *her* since he retired five years ago. Maude is a lovely woman who has gone through everything you have. She spotted you the minute you came in, and knew. She said that I could give you her telephone number if you want to talk about anything." If I want to talk about anything? I called Maude and she gave me her address, and said to stop by after three o'clock the next day. I had trouble paying attention to anything and could hardly sleep that night. Here was a chance to find out about *everything*.

Consider the probability: Since age ten I've wanted to talk with someone who knew what it was like to be male and wanted to be female, maybe. I looked for thirty years. I looked for books in the library. None. I looked in bars in special sections of several major cities. No one. I interviewed a knowledgeable professor. Nothing. I paid for shrink time. No way. I selected a wig shop at random, and BINGO!

Maude was a wonderful woman. She looked like someone's grandmother. Dignified, yet warm, content, and able to put me at ease right away. "I won't tell you to relax as Jean West said to you." We had coffee and cigarettes at the dining table in her kitchen. She told me that she knew I had a thousand questions and, not to worry, she would answer them all as best she could. She said she knew I had deep psychological pain, but we won't talk about that because it wouldn't get us anywhere. She said that she would help me do what I wanted to do by giving me the best information she had. She was not interested in doing anything such as helping me shop or giving me lessons in makeup. She had no interest in pushing me in any direction, like into or away from the path she chose. Fair enough.

Maude retired at age fifty-five. She had saved money and made investments. After her divorce from a wife like mine, she moved to an apartment and became Maude. She never told me her male name. Who cares anyway? She gave me some highlights of her life, her one-night visits to a hotel or motel to dress up, keeping it secret from everyone.

I'd certainly found a kindred soul. She encouraged me to ask questions. I had some. In a few minutes, two hours had passed and I had to get home for dinner. Damn! I was just getting warmed up. She said I could come back two days later. I did, of course.

It is impossible to remember all of what Maude explained to me twenty years ago because so much of what I know came from her and others. Who taught me certain things is unanswerable now. What I do remember was that two people, anatomically males, were engaged in what would otherwise have been a mother/daughter relationship. "Don't ever wear anything that is dirty or has any kind of spot on it. And, you will need a cover story-who you are, where you come from and so forth. Keep it simple and stick as close to the truth as you can." She told me a whole lot more, and all of that advice was very good at the time.

She introduced me to her friend, the high school teacher. Fred had been a bomber pilot in WWII and in Korea. I never saw him "dressed." He was almost Maude's boyfriend.

Maude gave me Bob somebody's phone number in East Bay. I called and made a date for the next Saturday when I was scheduled for the next Reserve week end. He told me to bring my stuff and we would have a fine evening, the three of us. "Three?" "Yes. Valerie is my roommate. You will like her." O.K.

Bob and Valerie lived in a two-bedroom apartment in Alameda, just south of Oakland. I rang the bell. Bob answered, greeted me warmly and relieved me of some of my load. He led me upstairs to his bedroom and his walk-in closet. Cripes! At least ninety percent of the hangar goods were women's clothes. And dozens of pairs of high heels. "All yours?" I asked. "All mine," he said. "Come on down stairs and meet Valerie. We'll have a drink and get acquainted. Change later."

Valerie was wearing a sleeveless black sheath. Pearls. Pendant earrings. Long, almost black hair. Bangs. Long red nails. A smile that was causing a stirring within me. "Hi, Sally." Sally? Oh, yes, me. "Hi," I managed.

Bob said that Valerie made the best fried chicken dinner ever. Then I noticed she was wearing an apron. We drank and made small talk. Finally, it was time to cook the dinner and for Sally and Alice to manifest.

Dinner was nice. We were three women at a candlelit table. The whole evening was a class act. Later, we stacked the dishes and drove to a local upscale bar, sat in low, soft swivel chairs and sipped after dinner drinks. I wondered about Valerie: How could such a lovely young woman be so friendly with Bob who liked to dress up as a woman? Are there women out there that will go along with such madness? Or just this one. We began sharing personal stuff and that was when I found out that Valerie was one of us. She had not been hiding anything. She was just Valerie. If others thought she was a woman, then fine, she thought she was, too. We were immediately friends that night because we three had endured the pain, the loneliness, the confusion *alone* in the past. We were able to be together and form a friendship on that basis, celebrating the fact that we didn't have to be alone anymore.

As we shared the personal stuff, I thought how strange it was that we three had the same kind of homelife, the same kind of teen years, middle class homes, a church-going family, we loved our parents, all enlisted in the military. Bob had gone to college and became a mechanical engineer. Valerie went to work at the local GM plant.

Her job, as a male, was to put tires on the wheels in the truck division. I could not see this lovely young woman doing that kind of work and I said so. She smiled that beautiful smile and said that it was easy if you knew how to make the tools work for you. "It's all in the wrist." I asked why she didn't work as a woman. She said that she didn't want the reduced wages that women received. She was saving up for the surgery, you see.

Alice (Bob) was tall and thin with a triangular face. When she wore a wig she looked just fine without makeup. She was bright, funny, and curious about a lot of things. Her present job was chief engineer for a coffee company somewhere in the Bay Area. Her responsibilities included the design and installation of all the automated equipment that would transform green coffee beans into the packaged products that one sees in the grocery store. Quite a job for someone who society considers a weirdo.

It was Alice's idea that we leave those sophisticated surroundings and shoot some pool.

On the other side of town there was a small beer bar with one pool table. The neighborhood was scary, the place inside was disreputable, but the well-lighted pool table stood in pristine presence, like a shrine.

There were others like us there. Whether they were rough, ugly, pretty, young, or old, all of us understood that we came from the same place: a quagmire of confusion, loneliness, fear, uncertainty. By the same kind of chance event that I had found Maude, each of these people had found their friend, who had a friend, and so on. There are lots of places nowadays where "our kind" are tolerated if not openly welcomed. The managers of bars and restaurants are nice to us because they know we have money to spend, because they know we will not wreck the place, and because the owner might like to dress up once in a while, too.

The thing most people don't know is that there are an awful lot of us on this earth. Because most societies take a dim view of us expressing ourselves we have to hide our condition and never let anyone know or we will lose friends, lose our jobs, and alienate relatives.

Many of us are fortunate to find friends to be with and places to go to. We feel, to some extent, that we have a "bum rap"; that we did not ask for these feelings, we did not suddenly one day say that we thought it would be a good thing to develop an interest in an activity that society doesn't want. Dealing with transvestism or transsexualism is a mental or psychological equivalent of dealing with Downs Syndrome, cystic fibrosis, or diabetes. You've got it, you didn't catch it, it just came with the package delivered to the maternity ward. The how, what, why, who of what goes on in that packaging center is a mystery to all of us.

A few games of snooker and eight-ball were played while the rest of us drank beer and got acquainted. It was my first encounter with so many like me. There was a blend of male and female postures, voices, appearances. Some were like truck drivers, others like secretaries. Some were sedate and cool in a most feminine way until it was time to try for the three-ball in the corner pocket. The sudden transformation to male stance and display of authority as the cue sent the cue ball to do its job was astonishing. Then, three-ball dispatched, the player would return to the oh-dear-me-did-I-do-that? countenance.

In an hour or so we left for some time with each other again. We drove to one of the posh Westside restaurants for the nightcap. A lovely place on the edge of the bay. Huge windows and dim lighting so that one could view the lights of the Bay Bridge, San Francisco, and vessels at anchor. We talked about the evening, especially sharing what we talked about with "the girls" at the pool table.

It was a result of that conversation that I perceived the difference between a transvestite and a transsexual, according to me. Good and knowledgeable people such as Drs. John Money and Harry Benjamin know a lot more about the phenomena than I will ever know. Anyone truly interested in the conditions should read their stuff. I have read some, and they are good writers. But where were they when I needed them? My interest here is to tell my story and to give my reactions and my feelings in my life. Neither of those learned men can do that as well as I can.

Alice, I thought, was a transvestite-wanting to dress up and present herself in society for a limited period of time on an occasional basis. Have fun. Valerie was a transsexual. She really wanted to become a woman, full-time, forevermore. She was taking estrogen pills, getting electrology treatment, letting her hair grow long, had her ears pierced, and was saving the money for that special operation.

I sat there nursing my favorite bedtime drink of coffee, brandy, lemon twist, in a stemmed glass (no sugar), and wondering which pile I belonged in-the TV or the TS. What I was aware of was my feeling of exhilaration in being accepted and treated as a woman that night. Whether the service personnel I encountered knew what was going on with me, they gave me the woman treatment. I felt wonderful. There was some kind of awakening going on. Difficult to describe but a lot like opening a door to a room not visited before-and wondering whether this is a good and comfortable place to be. Interesting, but is it my cup of tea? No answer then, except I knew I had a lot to assimilate and ponder as a result of that night's whirl.

The three of us, or sometimes just Alice and I, would connect on those Saturday nights, once a month. The entertainment and adventure were pretty much the same each time. We became more comfortable and trusting as the months went by. Valerie said she would be going to New York soon for the *big one*. She wanted to drop me a note. I gave her my school district address and the proper name to put on it. A month later I was handed a postcard by my secretary-a very nosey woman-who said, "My, my. You have girlfriends all over."

The card was from Valerie with the message, "Everything came off all right!"

Chapter 6

I closed the door to my office-a rare event-and requested phone calls to be held for awhile. I needed a few minutes alone. The news from Valerie hit me sideways. I was holding a picture postcard with Rockefeller Center on one side and an unsettling message on the other. Why was I so unsettled? I felt like sharing the good news with someone, but who? Certainly not my gossipy secretary, or anyone else I could think of. I was very happy for Valerie. I felt proud, in a sense, to have been a close friend of someone who crossed the finish line. Christine Jorgensen was a national figure and therefore slightly unreal to me. Valerie was my friend. Undefined feelings were present too. Later, much later, I was able to admit that envy was one of those feelings.

Well, good for Valerie. I hoped her life would be to her satisfaction. I knew I would never hear from her again. That was her rule. Once the operation is complete, one is ready for total immersion in society as an "I was born this way woman."

By the time one gets that far, medical science can do no more. One has been socialized partly in the real world, partly by one's sisters. The sisters can do no more. Now is the time to leave the nest and fly away, so to speak. The Lot's Wife story is an appropriate parable here.

I stared at the huge 3' x 4' color photograph on the wall across from my desk. It was a scene of the Mendocino coast-small islets with pine trees; large rocks surrounded by the froth of the Pacific Ocean: a narrow strip of sandy beach that I would mentally walk on when I needed a break from things like the b.s. one encounters as a public school administrator. Today, Valerie's card put me on the beach.

I had known her for three years. We had spent a lot of Saturday nights together. Once, Alice and Sally went to a nice cocktail lounge where Valerie was moonlighting as a waitress. She was magnificent. Graceful.

I thought of how far she had progressed and how little I had. There was no doubt that I wanted to follow her path more so than Bob's path. Bob would be Alice as a lark, a recreation, something cute to do. An operation for him? Total living as a woman? Oh no. Not only no, but hell no.

So what about Sally? Sally was the transportation to a new consciousness. Dressing as Sally was a vehicle, a passport to another country. Did I want citizenship in that country? I didn't know. My assessment was that I was presently obliged to live the lifestyle or schedule of a transvestite (one Saturday night per month), but I had a disturbing notion that I was really a transsexual.

I had trouble accepting the label of a TS. The implications of that were staggering. It meant ending a life I had built and inhabited for over forty years. Ending that life would not be a problem for me, but it would have been devastating to those around me.

One concern was the ability to begin a new life as a woman without benefit of having any experience as a woman. Consider this: On Tuesday night, a forty-year-old-man goes to bed. On Wednesday she wakes up, gets dressed and… what? Does she go to work? Where? Does she have any identification? What does she say to those in her house? Does she kiss her wife good morning? While these questions sound stupid, they are real. And they are a simplistic representation of the enormity of it all. A change of sex involves more than a snip snip "down there." To create a whole new life at any age would be totally upsetting and mind-boggling for me, yet it would be overwhelming for others in my life.

It was a titillating thought, though. Books and movies had been in our literature since H. Allen Smith's *Turnabout*. Why were these literary efforts always written as farces? I saw nothing funny in the possibility for me.

Face it, Tom. You know your true direction.

Sure, but what about all my family, the marriage, my job? And building a whole new life?

Tom, we have been through this before. You listen, but you resist.

But I can't just bug out and live as a woman. Yes, I admit I think I want to, but I don't know for sure. I'd need a trial. When could I have an unbroken time of say forty-eight hours as Sally? I haven't even had *that* much continuous time.

True. You will find a way. You found a way for more frequent time by connecting up with Treasure Island, and the two-week trips to San Diego each year. Not a whole lot, but a real improvement. Right?

Yes.

There will be more. It will come.

When, dammit?

As I've said before: when you are ready to handle it.

I thought about my successes in life. I had acquired so much-everything *they* thought I should: a B.A. degree, an M.A. degree, credentials to teach in California schools from kindergarten through community college, I had been selected to become a district office administrator, I had a commission in the Naval Reserve, I had a mortgage on a two-story house on a Los Gatos hillside and populated with three fine sons and a wife who was a loving mother. According to *them out there*, I had it all.

I felt like a prisoner. Sentenced to a male life I didn't want. I didn't want it because I always felt that I maybe wanted to be a female, but overwhelmed by the irrationality of it, by the logistics, the expense, even the feasibility that this large person could be a believable woman. The hope that I could someday find out never left me.

I was also aware that I had been acting all my life. Somewhere between childhood and boyhood I learned which role I was expected to perform. I'd worked at it and had been successful. I had been assured that by achieving the status I had, that I would feel fulfilled. Yes, there were good times, profound moments, and a pride in being good at it. There was, however, the persistent feeling from time to time that said, "Don't forget about me." Where did that come from? Who was "*me*"?

I've told you already, Tom. Your other half. You have two lives to lead this time around. You are not to forget your sister, but it is still your turn. You haven't finished your male agenda.

But what is there left for me to do? Haven't I done enough? And why doesn't she get her own body? Why mine?

Karma, Tom. You have accomplished much and accumulated many things. You have more to learn.

What?

You will know when the lessons are complete.

"I hate to interrupt boss," said my secretary, "but the superintendent wants to see you." The tide was coming in anyway. I cleaned the Mendocino sand off my shoes and went to see the big boss.

The title of my job was Director of Specially Funded Projects. I was in charge of thirteen women who actually worked with the school population selected for the special programs. My job was to write the proposals for the grants, get the State and Federal monies, set up the budget, monitor the programs, and act like a leader. A good leader is one who finds out what the people need to do their jobs, then gets those things for them. Sometimes they need direction, sometimes a pat on the back, sometimes a few new books, sometimes a day off. Whatever. The professional group I led consisted of a psychologist, a reading specialist, a math specialist, a nurse, and nine teacher aides. There was also my secretary, but no one could lead her. She was as disciplined as a cat.

I had been a leader of men, but never women. By the end of the second week on the job, I invited them all to lunch at the Los Gatos Lodge. A private room. Specially printed menus-no prices. I was paying and wanted them to order by choice, not by price. We had a drink or two, then I made The Speech. I cannot recall the complete text. The two main points were these: 1) I've never been a leader of women before, and 2) Whatever they needed to do their jobs, I'd get for them. I finished by giving my old Navy benediction: A group that *drinks* together *thinks* together. I returned home from that lunch at 7 p.m. There had been a lot to think about.

Two days later Kaye, my secretary, asked if I would have a minute to talk with Annie. Who was Annie? Kay said she was one of the teacher aides. I vaguely remembered her from lunch but we'd had no conversation. Now she was standing there in a cotton shift, hair pulled back into a bun, no makeup. A face no magazine would put on its cover, yet I thought she was an extremely attractive woman. There was a beauty in that face and that posture. I was captivated. A minute of awkward silence before I could ask how I could help. We sat down in my office, then she smiled for the first time. "You said you would get us what we needed. I need a parachute." "I'll get you one, Annie. What do you plan to do with it?" She said it was an important part of her remedial reading program. Oh?

Within a few days after I got the parachute from a surplus store, Annie and I went for coffee away from anyone we knew. It had been five empty years since Diane and I spent private time together. I recognized the symptoms, the cues, the whole drill. Annie and I had seen each other and that was it for me: We belonged together. We were slow and casual. We were both living in glass houses, and no way in a not-quite-rural community could we "carry on." That realization kept the lid on our behavior, but we both knew we were enchanted. Eventually, we found coffee shops and bars far enough away.

Don't blow it this time, Tom. Stick by the rules. This is an important lady. The most important woman you will ever know.

You've got it. But what are the rules?

You two will make them. Remember what I said.

Right.

One smart move I made was to encourage all of the group to attend the annual three-day conference of the California Mathematics Council held in Asilomar, on the Monterey Peninsula. The school district paid the registration and other expenses. I was going to buy us dinner. I made reservations for fourteen on Saturday night at the Naval Postgraduate School in Monterey. The O-Club was in the old Del Monte Golf and Country Club. Elegance unsurpassed. It had the ambience of old money. There was a five-piece orchestra. I danced at least twice with each member of the group. All the other dances were with Annie. I had gone to a lot of trouble just to hold the woman in my arms.

It was during the last dance that I nervously asked if she would like to join me on a Saturday night on Treasure Island. "I thought you'd never ask," whispered Annie.

I had to be captivated by her to surrender a coveted eight hours of being Sally. My routine for those three years of weekend drills was to go to a motel or hotel in San Francisco, become Sally, walk around different parts of downtown, have drinks (doubles at first to calm my nerves), eat in a restaurant, have after dinner drinks at a place with entertainment, then back to the rented room. Alone. It always hurt to turn from butterfly back to a caterpillar. An unnatural act, you might say.

There were other times (maybe two) when I did not do Sally. One time I wanted to go to a fund raiser for the Hungarian Freedom Fighters. It was held in California Hall- the social center for the Germanic community. They always had the best events. I was biting into my bratwurst when a familiar face crossed my field of vision. Viana! No mistake. Not even twenty-one years could change her. She was thrilled to see me. Her husband had retired from the Navy and they had settled in San Francisco. She hurriedly gave me her telephone number. She was part of a set of folk dancers that had to go on. What a lucky break! It had to be more than luck. And it had to be something else that caused me to misplace her unlisted phone number for almost five years.

It was a magic evening Annie and I had on Treasure Island that Saturday night in mid-December of 1971. We had a nice dinner at the elegant Nimitz Club, walked across the street to the B.O.Q. and my room on the third deck. All beds were singles. This room had one single.

We kicked off our shoes and stretched out on the floor to relax and talk some more. I nervously worked up to telling her about Sally, or what I knew about Sally.

We were carefully skirting around the word love. We both knew we were meant for each other.

After a few halting attempts I said, "I have a very special feeling for you, Annie. I hope we can spend a lot of time together. Before we go too far in our relationship, there is something I must tell you. The unsatisfactory marriage I have is due to not telling her before we were married. The simple fact is that I like to wear women's clothes and do my best to present myself as a woman in public. I do not know why. I am not a homosexual. It is just something I do because I have a need to. If that revelation is too unpalatable for you, it is better you know up front."

She asked if I expected her to participate. No. "Okay.", she said, "Let's see what we can do in a single bed."

I got in first and lay on my back. She wanted it that way. She climbed in and gradually lowered herself to the ready-and-waiting me.

We repeated the exercise in January.

She said that Treasure Island was a magic place for her. For me it was littered with milestones in my life: the World's Fair, embarkation point to two years in the Orient, processing for discharge and joining the Naval Reserve, damage control school, firefighting school, and now my one weekend a month duty station.

February of '72 brought special orders for another two weeks active duty at Fleet Training Group, San Diego. We T.I. Reservists were considered first class talent. Whenever FTG got overloaded on their schedule to put ships through their paces, we would be invited to do another two weeks to help them out. They were fine men, and it gave me pride to be considered good enough to be one of them. Enormous pride.

As I had done for nearly five years, I drove from the Bay Area to San Diego. I checked into the B.O.Q. on Sunday. The new facility seemed like a motel rather than a hotel. I got my gear hung up and everything in its place, including the Sally stuff. Out of sight, but handy. The next step was to drive out to one of the shopping centers near San Diego State. There was a beauty salon, open seven days, that would do wigs. I negotiated a two-day service and slowly strolled the mall for something in a size 16 I couldn't resist. I resisted everything but a pair of white patent heels that would be perfect with the navy blue dress I brought with me.

The days of the first week were uneventful, meaning all went as before. No problems. Everything was like clockwork. Ride the ships, do the drills, hold the critiques, return with the filled-out forms, go on liberty.

I was no longer interested in having Sally appear at the O-clubs. Instead I found the joys of Hotel Circle, a fairly closely grouped set of hotels/motels on both sides of Interstate 8. Each had their bars, coffee shops, nice dining rooms, and entertainment. In fact, I had spent the weekend in one as Sally-my first Friday night to Sunday afternoon totally as I wanted to be.

On the Saturday night of that weekend, I went to dinner at the Appleblossom Inn, and then to their lounge for the after dinner drink. Someone was playing the organ. Good upbeat stuff. The place was almost empty. I chose the cocktail table closest to the musician. She saw me and gave me a large smile. She finished her set and came to my table. "Hi, I'm Lisa. May I sit at your table during my break?" She was my height while she stood next to me where I was sitting. "Hi, I'm Sally. Please do sit. I'll buy you a drink. You play so well."

She sat and we talked small talk until it was time for her to resume playing. She asked if I had any requests. I named a few old favorites. She said she didn't know some of them. They were before her time. Thanks, Lisa.

On the next break she came straight to the table. "Are you a librarian?" "No," I said. "Why do you ask?" She said it was the way I looked and moved. And the harlequin-shaped glasses I wore. I told her I was a schoolteacher. We made more small talk. Before she went back to the organ, she asked if I would stay until her shift was over-another hour. Oh yes, Lisa.

What a thrill. Here was this tiny person, a very happy person who liked me as a woman. This was my first budding woman-to-woman friendship as Sally. Until now I had only talked to waiters, store clerks, and other service people. Now I was actually making a friendship with another person. I was glad the person was a female. I felt so pleased that she regarded me as a woman. But why did she want me to stick around?

It turned out, she said, that there was a guy at the bar who had made passes at her and she did not want to be seen leaving alone. She wanted me to leave with her and follow her home-in Poway, near Escondido. If the guy saw her leave with another woman, especially a big one, he might think she was a lesbian and leave her alone.

We arrived at her house around 1:30 a.m. She invited me in for coffee. She said her mother and brother would be asleep and we could talk. Soon after we sat together on a low couch, I became aware that my girdle was killing me. I guess I squirmed a little. She asked if I would like to take anything off. I said no. We rambled on, drinking coffee and smoking her cigarettes as mine were gone. Finally she asked if I lived as a woman all the time. Zowie! I stumbled and mumbled and finally asked her how she knew I was a guy. She said she knew the minute I walked into the lounge. I asked why she was so friendly to me. Her answer was that I seemed like a nice person, wearing an expensive dress and she was curious. She also wanted to protect me.

Protect *me*? Yes. She said that the manager spoke to her about the drag queen in the restaurant and that he would throw me out if I went into the lounge and caused trouble. Thinking fast, she told him I was an old friend and a house guest and please leave her alone.

Drag queen. What an insult! A drag queen is a person, usually a gay, who creates a grotesque caricature of a female. She said I should calm down as he was not accurate with his vocabulary.

In the next two hours Lisa had as much of my life story as she wanted. She told me a lot about herself and where she wanted to go with her career as a musician. I felt very comfortable with her, especially after I removed the girdle. She told me I could be a believable woman if I practiced more, removed an inch of makeup, and got rid of the harlequin glasses. We kissed goodnight at 5 a.m., chastely, and promised to stay in touch.

On my way back to my hotel room I noticed a bright red light in my rear view mirror. Oh shit. The CHP officer was a courteous, dispassionate bureaucrat. When he asked for my license I told him I did not have it with me. Then he asked for the registration. I handed it to him, explaining that I had borrowed my brother's car. He asked for my name and I said Sally. And that is how Sally's summons arrived at my home three weeks later, handed to me by my wife.

On Monday I did not ride a ship. I made a phone call to my office to see how things were going without me. Kaye said the superintendent wanted to speak with me. He made his point in his usual Teutonic manner: Cool it with these reserve activities or go back to being a classroom teacher.

By Thursday of that week I decided to request a transfer to the retired list. I had a total of 26 years and some months and certainly qualified for retired pay at age 60. The retirement orders came in early March, and that was the end of my monthly weekends away from home.

Annie and I became creative in finding ways to spend time together. We also double-dated occasionally with another pair like us.

Bill and Holly were also teachers in our district. Bill and I had taught together for years before I went into administration. As a foursome we had fine times at mythical education conferences in many distant cities.

By October of '72, I knew I had to leave home. I had the taste of freedom and now I was restricted to an occasional weekend. Sally was nowhere. Annie displaced her in fact, but not from my wish list. In November I had my plan. I would rent an apartment in January—after the holidays and then sort things out. Did I really want to live with Annie? Did I really want to live as Sally? Could I live as Sally?

Chapter 7

On December 30, 1972, I told Helen I was leaving. Moving out. I had rented an apartment in Mountain View. Telling her of my intention was just barely harder than not telling her. Desperation was my strength.

She was not happy. I was not happy, although I did feel an immense relief because I finally stopped the game—the twenty-two year marriage in which I was not normal, in which I was continually reminded of my abnormality, in which I could never win, in which she could never win. I had exhausted all of my physical and mental resources. I blamed no one except myself for my cupidity at age twenty-two for thinking that a good marriage would cure me, and for the stupidity of prolonging a bad situation for over two decades thinking that it was better than divorce.

Helen was a good woman. She was unable to change her feelings about me. I was unable to eliminate the drive to explore womanhood. I could not be in love with her because I did not feel good enough about myself to have any love to give. Her feeling for me was anger because I could not deliver on my marriage vows. I cannot presume to know exactly what was going on inside her, but I think it was fear and pain.

I said goodbye to my two younger sons. Their brother was away at college. They were not happy that I was moving out, but I think they knew at some intuitive level that they were living with two very unhappy parents. They did not know exactly why

I was leaving. I could not tell them the real reason. Besides, I was emotionally incapable of a long discussion with them. I was hurting from my own internal pain, hurting from the pain I had just caused their mother, worn out from the ordeal of garnering the courage to tell her I was leaving, and it was late at night. I knew I would be seeing them, and I promised I would telephone them in a day or so when I would have a phone installed. I would give them my number so that they could call me anytime.

That whole episode was so unbearable for me-the loss of being a member of that family, and the sense of failure I had as a husband and a father-that it would be almost twenty years later before I could begin to try to examine the feelings in that situation.

It was nearly midnight when I loaded two suitcases and a garment bag into my Pinto, and started my drive to Mountain View.

Was I supposed to be a woman or not? I was approaching my mid-forties and was desperate to have an answer. My mind was a battleground. Even my body was beginning to spoil: skin rash, gastrointestinal problems, and a great deal of muscle spasm. Standard medical treatment could not eliminate any of those symptoms. I was irritable and restless: a wreck inside and out.

I unlocked the door of my unfurnished apartment, opened a bottle of screwcap wine, found a plastic coffee cup, an ashtray, and sat on the floor of my new apartment. I needed furniture as well as answers.

My rational mind was still controlled by the inner custodian-the script written by my parents and the social norms of the 1930s. While those norms were very clear in my mind, I had a second system of thought that could displace the original system at any time. It was an eclectic system of notions and ideas abstracted from my readings and discussions of Eastern thought, from contemporary writings, and from my talks with my former paramour, Diane, and lately with Annie. My alternative system seemed more powerful, could explain more, and generally accommodated reality as I perceived it to be.

In conventional terms I was a rotten bastard. I broke my word given at the altar twenty-two years ago. I was causing pain and sorrow for those I left. Never mind what was happening to me. I was supposed to be totally selfless.

In the new system, I was pursuing growth. I was trying to get on with a life that had meaning and significance. I needed a chance to develop into something new. I did not know what was ahead. There was something deeper in me, more basic than my programming from the 1930s. I was tired of being a square peg in a round hole.

Yes, I was escaping. Escaping from feelings of inferiority, from acquiring trophies and recognition for things that meant little to me, from a slowly disintegrating body.

from the early stages of ennui. I had witnessed my father seek refuge from a bottle. I wanted my refuge to be another chance at life-as fully aware and as alert as I could be. I wanted to feel normal for me; not try to be normal according to someone else's standards. Who was in charge of my life? Them or me? Who was qualified to run my life? I had tried their way. Now it was my turn.

It took only three cigarettes and a half bottle of wine to arrive at that point of summation. I had taken the first step on a new path.

Congratulations, Tom. It has been a long time coming.

All those years of wanting to please others and never making it.

You are not finished with the need to please other people. What you are finished with is the need to please other people on their terms. Part of being female is the desire to please. You will soon discover that you will be selective regarding whom you choose to please.

Can I do that? Pick and choose like that?

Sure. Try it. Why should you continue the psychological masochism?

If I wanted to continue the masochism, I would not be sitting on this floor, leaning against this wall, drinking screwcap wine in this unfurnished studio apartment. I have made the strongest statement I can to end the masochism. I do not intend to be selfish, however.

I know that. I also know you are not capable of being selfish. Remember Ayn Rand's The Art of Selfishness you read a couple of years ago? It was an attempt to clarify that very point: You cannot give to others that which you do not have. Sound familiar?

Yes, I remember.

Well, then? What is your problem?

It just seems selfish to me to live a life my way. I want it, but I'm supposed to give, not get.

Do you remember the sermon of Rev. Scott last summer when he developed the point that giving and getting are really the same thing?

Yes, I remember that, too. He said that the only real getting comes from the feeling of giving.

Right!

But I have been trying to give all of my life-to please other people to feel good about myself. It hasn't worked very well.

True. The point, Tom, is this: There are an awful lot of other people in this world. They are all different from each other. What pleases one person will disappoint another.

I'm getting confused.

All right. Here's a metaphor that may help. You are a carnation, a very lovely red carnation with a marvelous scent, dewy petals, and on a long, straight stem. Your whole purpose is to be a beautiful carnation so that those who like carnations will be pleased with you because your beauty and your scent enrich their lives. Get it?

Not really.

Sometimes you have a head like concrete. The message is this: If you are a carnation, do not try to pass yourself off as a rose in order to please rose lovers. You will only disappoint them.

Oh. Now I get it.

I hope so. No matter how good you are, no matter how loving and sincere you are, no matter how many people love you, there will always be people who do not love you, and will never love you simply because who and what you are frosts their cojones.

I suppose only really great people are loved by everyone.

No one has ever been so great. You may recall that Jesus did not die of old age.

You mean that if I am true to myself and give to those who want what I've got to give, that my life will count for something and I will feel rewarded while I am giving to others?

You are on the right track, Tom.

Yes. Right track. A whole new world view was coming into focus. Some current topics needed resolution. I had responsibilities to my family. I needed to plan my next moves so that everything would make sense and lead toward a pattern of giving and getting in the best way.

I got up off the floor, dumped my ashtray, rinsed my plastic cup, unrolled my sleeping bag. I got into my one and only nightgown and went to sleep with the belief I was finally on my way.

Chapter 8

Annie came to visit on the first Saturday of 1973. She had her camper loaded with furniture and furnishings for my use. We shopped for food and all the little things an apartment needs when one first moves in. Dinner that night was idyllic. We had our favorite foods, beverages, music, and a conversation that continued all the way to testing the new bed. We lavished love upon each other. She was my support. I was... I'm not sure what I was for her. Maybe I'll understand someday.

At breakfast we began talking about what I planned to do next. I was exhilarated with the awareness of being free to decide. I was developing a love for Annie and told her so. I was also with the need to explore the possibility of being a woman, and reminded her of that, too. Obviously the two events were mutually exclusive. The only reasonable course of action was to designate alternate weekends for the alternate pursuits.

And so it was.

The routine was simple: Monday through Friday I, the male, would drive to my job at the school district office. Upon returning to my apartment, I changed clothes, did the makeup, cooked dinner, and either went to a grocery store or maybe a walk through a shopping mall. Sometimes a neighbor would stop by for a glass of wine or coffee. Their visits were unpredictable. Sometimes they would visit the old me, sometimes the new me. I thought I had them fooled into thinking that Sally was my sister. They went along with it anyway.

Every other weekend I was Sally from Friday night until Monday morning. I spent a lot of time trying to do the typical stuff a single woman does on a weekend, but I wasn't sure what that was. Mostly, I fidgeted with my facial paint job or my meager wardrobe. I was very sensitive about my appearance. Was I convincing? There was no one I could ask for help or commentary. I had to rely on the public to let me know how I was doing. No one ever said anything to me, but I could tell by the way some looked at me, like I was a walking version of a What's-Wrong-With-This-Picture puzzle.

I was still timid about buying female things for myself. The male would have to buy the clothes from the racks hoping they would fit. Once in a while they would, otherwise they would have to be returned. What a hassle that was. Frustration was mixed with the joy of knowing that I was at last getting started.

My new confidants were the ladies at the wig shop in Cupertino. It was a backwater, bedroom community and apricot orchard back then. That was before Apple Computers moved in and set up their headquarters. I had complete anonymity there, telling them only selected things about my real life, but dwelling mostly on what I wanted to do. (Jean West had closed her wig shop some months before.) They were as sympathetic as they were helpful. They gave me advice on wig styles, of course, and the kind of clothes I should wear and certain stores where I could buy them from friendly salespeople who would be understanding of my situation.

In March I gathered the courage to make an approach on Miss Lorraine's Modelling Studio in Los Altos. Miss Lorraine had been a fashion model for years. Her husband, Robin, had been an industrial psychologist. Their twin daughters were beautiful. As Sally, I stopped in on a Saturday morning and said that I wanted to enroll in their school. Robin and Lorraine interviewed me for a half hour before deciding to let me take classes. Evidentially they knew I was a man dressed as a woman as I walked in from the parking lot. It was their business to know such things. They let me think I was fooling them. They wanted to see what I would do and how I behaved. "Yes", they agreed, "you are not a whacko, nor would you be disruptive to our professional atmosphere."

They proceeded to tell me what I needed to be able to do if I wanted to present myself to the public and be convincing. They said I would have to learn to walk, talk, sit down, stand up, turn around, how to carry a purse, to put on and take off a coat, and a whole lot more. I was to learn about cosmetics, my colors, my style of dress, and how to choose hosiery colors for a particular outfit. And jewelry. I began to see that there were a million things to learn if I was going to be convincing and comfortable, too. I also saw that it was going to be fun. And expensive.

At first I had private lessons, sometimes with Lorraine, sometimes with the daughters. After several special Saturday lessons, I was integrated into classes with the 16 to 20 year-olds who wanted to become actresses, airlines hostesses, television personalities or the like. They were primed for my presence in their midst. They were very kind and accepted me without a negative word or gesture. Elbow to elbow in the dressing room we learned how to start with a freshly scrubbed face, apply cosmetics, and be ready for the camera in just ten minutes. I was always a few minutes late. I had more nose to cover than they. Nothing can compare with the feeling of being one of the girls. I don't know why.

Annie and I spent the other weekends together in my apartment. We enjoyed each other's minds and bodies. We made love, we made conversation. We played tourist in San Francisco. Visiting Chinatown on the Sunday morning after the New Year celebration and dragon parade became an annual pilgrimage, most years, for the next decade. We would stroll Grant Avenue from Clay to Columbus, carefully avoiding the serpent teams that were blessing the businesses. Loud drums, cymbals, and lots of firecrackers. A wok on the wild side, we called it. We were right for each other. If I had to remain as male for the rest of my life, then I wanted to live it with Annie.

Robin, Lorraine, and I became friends. We would often sit with wine and cigarettes after class and talk of this and that. Lorraine would insist that I hold my stemmed wine glass in a certain way, and if I had to smoke cigarettes, they should be handled thus and so.

It was during one of those after-hours sessions in May that Lorraine told us about her day at Stanford Hospital. She had been invited to speak to a group of transsexuals at the Gender Dysphoria Clinic. Naturally I asked what that was all about. She told me and we all agreed that I should investigate the program.

Was I a transsexual? A transvestite? What? Maybe it was time to find out from those professionals. What I did know for sure was that the more I explored the world of the female and experienced a few minor womanly events, the more I knew I was moving in the right direction. But did I want that sex change operation? Hey, that is an irreversible step! It is one thing to apply cosmetics that wash off, and to wear women's clothes that come off faster than they go on. But to have an operation to rearrange one's plumbing system...

I decided to call Maude to ask her about the program. She said it was a good place, good staff, and that she was getting ready for the surgery herself. She said that their screening program would tell me what I was.

I didn't know if I was serious about a sex change operation or not. How was I supposed to know? All I knew at the time was that I need to explore, to find out if I could function socially as a woman. If so, would I enjoy living the life of a woman? I had no interest in men. None. All I wanted to do was to scratch the itch of four decades of wanting to try to be a woman, but blocked from any real trials. I was scared about being on the streets as a woman. Oh, I went out all right, but I was afraid that someone might catch me and I would die of embarrassment, and my innocent family would be humiliated when the media informed the entire planet of my transgressions. That pathetic scenario is laughable now, but I have to point out that I had lived my entire life being directed by others. All the scripts and inner custodians were there to tell me I was wrong, a sinner, a pervert, a very bad and despicable person. I had felt so much negativism from those few old friends who knew of my plans that to survive I began to internalize my new credo: They are wrong. By definition, they are different from me. How dare they presume to know what is right for me? I think they were more concerned about themselves, and that my desires were unimportant. In particular, my former wife wanted me to give her love. I could not. I did not have it to give her. If you don't have it, you can't give it. I knew that I needed, above all else, the ability to create and give love. To do that, I had to feel centered; feel good about myself so that I would have that feeling of goodness to share with others. The few steps I had taken so far had resulted in clearing up my skin rashes, normalized my gastrointestinal intestinal track, and mellowed my disposition. I had the feeling that I was on target.

Wearing my new navy blue turtleneck sweater and pleated skirt set I went to the office of the Gender Dysphoria clinic in Stanford Hospital. Marty was the receptionist and personal assistant to Dr. Laub, head of Reconstructive Surgery. Marty was lovely. She listened to me stumble around for a moment, then smiled and gave me some forms to fill out. I completed them, handed them back, and was told to watch my mailbox for an appointment notice. In less than a week I was back for psychological tests and interviews. Not since the screening at submarine school in New London had I been put through such a wringer. The next step was a physical examination. The final phase was an interview with the staff psychiatrist. He had my file with all the test results. His evaluation was that I was borderline.

Borderline? My reaction to that was borderline anger and outrage. I protested. I cast some aspersions on the validity of their tests. I was warming up to a tirade, without intending to do so, when the good doctor smiled and said that I had just passed the final phase of the evaluation. He apologized for the game he played, but he said he had to have an emotional measure. All the other tests were either physical or cerebral. Now that my emotions were tested and a suitable response was observed, I could be welcomed into the program if I wanted to be. Oh, yes! I was given a list of internists to choose from. The internist would write the prescriptions for estrogens and would monitor my progress.

I chose a doctor in San Francisco. He interviewed me for nearly an hour. He wanted to make damn sure I knew what I was doing. I could only assure him that I was damned sure I needed to find out. He gave me prescriptions for Estinyl 0.5 mg and Provera 10 mg. Estinyl in that strength is uncommon. It took a few hours for the druggist to find them for me. I left the drug store with those two prescriptions. The Provera was white, the Estinyl was peach colored. Innocent little pills that would change my life. The *magic wand* came in two small apothecary bottles.

I started on a daily basis right away. At first I thought I was on tranquilizers. I felt different. In less than a week I noticed that I was not overreacting to ordinary irritations. It was an odd feeling. I was in some small way distanced from annoyances. Instead of being sucked into an angry posture, I found that I could actually choose my response to any external stimulus. I felt a new power in having that kind of control. I marvelled at the effect of the estrogen and wondered what else was in store for me. Plenty, it turned out.

In less than a month my chest became sensitive around the nipples, and the two mounds began to form. The growth was slow, but growth nevertheless.

The week after my admittance to the Gender Dysphoria Clinic, I received The Letter. I now had written permission from the doctor, the exalted, to go do it. Even now, over twenty years later, I get a tingly feeling whenever I read it. It was no literary masterpiece. It had misspellings and unconventional punctuation, but it was my ticket for admission to a new world. I was now legitimate. Now that I had permission and something to show if I got stopped by someone, I learned that I didn't need it. Aside from its inestimable psychological value, I've only used it where official records had to be changed, such as my driver's license, social security card, transcripts, certain charge cards, and ultimately a court ordered name change. It took me awhile to realize that I was still needing other people to give me approval for what I was beginning to pursue. Would I ever outgrow that need?

By early June of 1973 I was nearly overcome with happiness. I had started to rebuild my world. I had a growing number of friends who were supportive of my exploration. I had counsel on body motion, clothing, and cosmetics. The wig ladies continued to try new styles on me. And now I had a clinic in the Stanford Hospital offering me the chance to explore my femininity with a medical technology and a legal legitimacy I never would have dreamed of six months earlier.

There were two other key elements to the clinic's program: Find a licensed therapist for at least monthly visits, and attend the monthly group sessions at the clinic.

I attended my first meeting with others enrolled in the Gender Dysphoria program in July. It was a Thursday afternoon schedule. Attendance was required. That meant I had to take a day off work to be there. There were about twenty of us in the large meeting room, chairs in a circle. What a collection of humanity! I was reminded of that first meeting when I saw the barroom scene in the movie Star Wars some years later. Some of us looked like Halloween, some looked very nice, and everything in between. We were all quite serious about wanting to be women. We introduced ourselves, had short conversations, but mostly we assessed one another. Some of us were there for the first time, others were on the brink of surgery.

I met Tanya. She latched onto me as though I needed her guidance. She wanted to be my big sister. This was my first experience in a formal support group.

One of the staff chaired the meeting. After welcoming us he asked if anyone had anything to share with the group. Some of the most incredible things came out. "My mother thinks of me as her daughter now. She took me to her hairdresser last week for a perm. We can wear the same size skirts and blouses, but not the shoes. I'm learning to cook, too. My father is disgusted with us both, but especially me. He calls me a faggot and tries to ignore me." Another said simply, "My boss commented on my pierced ears." Most did not say much.

The chairman introduced our guest speaker. She was a staff nurse. She taught us how to inspect our partners for venereal warts. I supposed that it was a relevant topic for some in the group, or maybe the staff thought it would be relevant for all of us. I was amused, thinking of my early days in boot camp when they taught us how to "skin it back and milk it down" as part of the physical exam. I wondered what I was getting into here. I mean, I just wanted be a woman in a psychological and social sense, not to be a sex kitten. Or was I fooling myself? The question lingered for years.

After the meeting some of us approached each other for more getting-to-know-you conversation. That was how I met Stephanie. We were about the same age and had similar backgrounds. She had been a VA hospital administrator in the mid-West and had chucked it to come to California and become a woman. She had a license to be an X-ray technician and was trying to get the license reissued in her new name. We exchanged phone numbers and vowed to stay in touch. She said she was working on "a deal" and would let me know.

One evening Tanya called to ask if I would have time to meet Brenda. Sure. Brenda was to arrive that Saturday around noon. Okay. Brenda needs help in finding an apartment in your end of the peninsula. All right. She's one of us, you know. Fine.

I drove to San Jose, had coffee with Tanya and Jason, and waited for Brenda to drive in from San Diego. We discussed their recent newspaper article. Jason and Tanya wanted to get married. No problem except Tanya was born male and had been altered to become female. Jason had been born female and had gone through the horribly complex process to become a male. Both were generally regarded as the gender of their choice, but some fine print in California law blocked Jason from attaining full legal status as a male. Tanya, the extrovert, had arranged for reporters to interview and photograph them. A full page of the San Jose Mercury was devoted to their travail.

Brenda arrived shortly before noon. She was cute, had her own long blond hair, was 5' 4", and flashed an engaging smile. And I hated her right away. Well, not really hated her. It was my first experience with female jealousy. She was curious about Jason's operation.

The bearded Jason began to tell all. We learned that he never had boobs. After her hysterectomy, he had acquired a devilishly clever penis. It was fashioned by a long series of skin grafts from various parts of the stomach, abdomen, and hip areas. The phallus was fashioned first as a rectangle, then folded and sewn on the long axis to provide a hole, like a gun barrel. With a wink, Jason said that he could insert a plastic rod to create an instant erection should any of us girls be interested. He said there was sensitivity for him, but not like one's original organs. Tanya added that it was the same with her. A nice feeling, but mostly psychological.

Brenda and I left. We unloaded her stuff at my place. She was back in two hours with the keys to her new home. She too had found a studio, but hers was large enough for two. She was going to scout the clinic for a roommate. At the next monthly meeting, Brenda found Lorna. We kept in touch, but I often thought that we would never have any friendship were it not for this particular common bond.

Annie and I continued the alternate weekends together. I still marvel at my psychological agility... able to shift from male to female presentations in minutes. Technique was one thing. My ability to handle it was uncommon, I think. The male persona had over forty years to practice. The female persona had wanting expression for those same years. The two personae were mutually exclusive. I was either a *male* male, or I was doing my best at being a *female*.

An unexpected benefit of the estrogen therapy was a marked improvement in my sex life. Specifically, two things were happening. First, I was a lot slower in achieving orgasm. I'm sure an endocrinologist or urologist could explain the mechanics. In practice, it meant I could devote more time to foreplay and not have a premature ejaculation. The second benefit was in having a more sensitive nature. I was more observant of my partner, more concerned about what she was doing and feeling. I was better able to get in touch with her in bed or out. Needless to say, the first benefit lasted less than a year. The second continued development. Annie and I capitalized on this good fortune, albeit transitory.

The summer of 1973 was to be my last shot at being in charge of summer school. By that time I was seeing the end of the road for me in the public school system. My last hurrah as Superintendent of Summer School was to fashion a program that offered novel programs and experimental practices. Of all the aspects of that experience, the one that I remember with fondness was my ability to enable five women teachers to gain administrative experience. Four of them subsequently became permanent administrators. I had given them a chance to show their stuff... something no other administrator was willing to do.

Billy Joe and I were working on a pitcher of beer one afternoon after summer school. He, Holly, Annie, and I were now veterans in weekend travel. The four of us went to a lot of weekend seminars in distant cities. Billy had a quick mind, a keen wit, a sharp tongue, and a ready laugh. He was also the most sexist bastard I ever knew. He asked me what my plans were. Was I going to set up housekeeping with Annie or what?

I felt that I had three options open to me. Option One: I could return to my family and forget the idea of ever being Sally. Option Two: I could drop out of the male space to pursue womanhood. Option Three: I could set up housekeeping with Annie and her three daughters.

My response to Billy was that I had three options open to me. Option One: I could return to Helen. Option two: I could pursue a wild idea I've had for a long time. Option Three: I could set up housekeeping with Annie.

Naturally, he was curious about Option Two. I felt he would not understand or approve. I vagued out, saying that I didn't want to talk about it right then.

In early August, Annie asked what my plans were. She had been my main support during the time I was in that studio apartment. She knew I was going through some tough times, and she was always there (physically or on the telephone) whenever I needed to talk. She was well aware of my efforts to explore my feminine side, but she just did not want to talk about that. She was supportive of me for whatever I was doing, but did not want to hear the details of Sally's experiences.

I told her of my conversation with Billy Joe. My feeling, I explained, was that I loved her. I also was feeling a great pull toward being Sally. Yes, she allowed, but what do you *really* want to do? I said that I had to focus on being Sally, but if I did that, I would be on a one-way street with no coming back. And if I did that, I would always wonder what life would have been like with her. I ended by saying that I knew

I was being selfish, but how about this: We live together for a year in a house to see how that works out. At the end of the year, we will see how we are doing. I ended by saying that I would guarantee my presence for twelve months. I may need to be Sally from time to time, but I'll do that somewhere else.

Annie appreciated my honesty. She thought that maybe it was time for me to be a little selfish, if that was how I wanted to think about it. Her opinion was that we give it a try for a year. We could take a house in a nice neighborhood. She would lease her house for a year. If at the end of the year, we needed to split, then she would go back to her place and I could go to… wherever. Agreed.

It took us less than a week to find a good place. We were to take possession on September 15, 1973.

I was pleased with the arrangement and so was Annie. Her three teenage daughters seemed pleased, but a little unsure of me on an everyday basis.

As I was closing out of the studio, I realized how much had gone on during that nine-month gestation period. I had attended modelling school, attended classes at two different community colleges, became affiliated with the Gender Dysphoria Clinic, made some new friends, and acquired a second wardrobe. I had a collection of prescription pills that would lie dormant for the immediate future. They would retain their potency for another two years. I had to demonstrate my potency for the next twelve months.

Chapter 9

Life in the new menage in Los Gatos was good. We all went through our adjustment period in a reasonably civilized style. I had the responsibility of learning how to be a father figure for three girls. I had always wondered what girls were like in their natural habitat. Now I was able to observe them while they were not on stage. I had no sisters, no female cousins, no daughters. My conclusion was that they were no different from their male counterparts, except perhaps the amount of space and time each required in the water closet. While I never saw their bedrooms, my understanding was that I didn't want to. A mutual respect did develop in a short time.

My #3 son had expressed an interest in maintaining contact. Soon, he was like an adopted brother for the three young ladies. He was a frequent visitor. He had no idea about Sally.

Within a week, mail from our previous residences began to show up. The first time one of the girls brought in the letters came the question, "Who is this Sally person?" Annie said that we were accepting mail for that person. Period.

In October a mimeographed announcement came for Sally from the Jewish Community Center in Belmont. The only contact I had there was to attend a lecture they sponsored that May. I had been searching for social activities, saw the advertisement for a lecture entitled, How to Choose a Psychiatrist, and went. I remembered being asked for two dollars and to sign in on the clipboard. It was an entertaining and informative lecture.

I opened the forwarded letter and found it to be an invitation to attend the first organizational meeting to establish a women's center in San Mateo County. The meeting was scheduled for early November at the Jewish Community Center. Wow and golly!

A series of thoughts went through my head: An invitation for Sally to be a member of a group of women; but I had just made a commitment to be a husband/father figure; but I really want to check this out; but do I have the *cojones* to do it… to try to pass as a woman among women?

I knew that I had the freedom to be absent from the house whenever I wanted, but I could see logistical problems. Where is my "telephone booth" for making quick costume changes? How can I become one of them without giving them my phone number and my current address? And every other question I asked myself was, "Can I make it?"

I told Annie about the invitation. She asked me what I wanted to do about it. I said that I wanted to give it a try. She said that was our deal—- if I wanted to take off once in a while there was no problem. Just don't do any dressing up around here. Right.

Do I really want to put my buns on the block? Am I ready to do this?

Of course you are. You should know by now that opportunities like this are rare. You also know that you want to go, and that if you keep thinking positively about it, you will find a way to make it work. Besides, you have as much at stake in women's lib as they do.

What do you mean by that?

Well, you are a woman, or will be soon. The essence is there, and with a little nurturing, the flower will bloom. Then when you find yourself in the work place as a woman, you will need support and a fair deal.

Are you for real? Who *are* you anyway?

You can answer that for yourself if you want to. In the meantime just go to the meeting. Rent a cheap motel. Change there. Up and back in the same night.

Yes, but…

Hey! We've been through this indecision routine before. You get an idea then you get scared. Remember San Diego in '71? And remember your first time in San Francisco?

Yes, I do.

Have I given you bad advice yet?

No, you haven't.

Then stop the protests. Do it. You'll like it. Trust yourself.

I felt a little awkward as I entered the room. There were a dozen up-beat, animated women wearing blue jeans and sweatshirts. Keds. I wore a black jumper dress with a flowered silk blouse. Heels. They didn't seem to notice, but I know they did. It didn't matter. To them I was another woman who cared, and that was what counted. I did not speak until I was spoken to. I was unfamiliar with the protocol. Nowhere in my limited experience had I been in totally female company as a female.

One woman approached me, holding out her hand. We smiled. She said her name was Barbara. I said my name was Sally. We shook hands and she began to introduce me to another woman when the gavel sounded. The meeting was being called to order.

I took a place at the long table. Okay, I thought, here comes the moment of truth. I was still a little scared, but I had to know if I could make it. Besides, I wanted to be there to offer my superior leadership and organizational skills for the success of this group of nice women. Well, I had been a leader in the Navy, and I'd been to graduate school where I specialized in organizational behavior. I was so sure I had so much to give.

That evening was my first real experience at being Sally, a person. Until this event I had been a stroller, a customer, a figure in a car. Now I was saying to a group of women that my name is Sally, and by implication, I was a woman too. I was not in a grocery store, nor was I in a safe harbor with my "sisters," or anyone else who knew about me. No safety net this time. I had broken through my 5-Day deodorant in ten minutes.

The first thing I noticed about these women was that they moved faster and with much greater efficiency than any mixed or all-male group I had ever shared a meeting table with. It was the beginning of many lessons for me regarding male egos. I'd chaired meetings as a male and all others were women. But this was really different.

The acting chairperson called us to order and stated the purpose of the meeting. Then she reviewed the essence of several conversations she had with three or four others (also present) regarding the idea of creating an organization of, by, and for women. We all clapped to declare that to be a smashing idea. There were many questions, comments, and new ideas from the group with respect to the services, the scope, and who was going to do what. The enthusiastic ideas of each person began to cause a lack of direction, and a loss of unanimity became evident. I knew what to do to restore order. Before I lost control and jumped in, the chairperson banged the gavel three times and said, "Let's take a moment to find out why we are here. We'll go around the table so that each one can introduce herself and tell us why she is here and what she wants from a women's center."

Brilliant. It was a tactic I had not learned in graduate school, nor seen modelled in the Navy. It was decorum and logic. Even though my male ego suffered a little, I felt good. Several ideas went *clunk!* in my head: Women do this kind of thing better than men; I want to be a member of this gender; I am losing my allegiance to manhood and I like the feel of it; and, I've got to incorporate this tactic in my future meetings. Those were the thoughts that had definition. Other notions were stirring, but not identifiable at the time.

As my mind tried to clarify those notions, I noticed it would soon be my turn to speak. What now, Mommy? Do I blurt out the truth and disrupt this meeting one more time? Do I try to fake it by mouthing what someone else has said? What?

Tell the truth, dummy. You know you are not smart enough to lie and get away with it.

Yes, but ...

Hey! Listen! The truth is your strongest card. Surely a moment of truth is at hand. You will either be loved for what you are and what you want to become, or you will quickly learn that this is not for you. The worst thing you can do is not find out.

My turn. "My name is Sally and I am here for a very different reason than anyone else. I want to be socialized as a woman."

I saw the confusion on some faces and blankness on others. My ed psych professor in grad school would have called this cognitive dissonance. I found my hand reaching into my patent leather purse (that matched my shoes, of course) for The Letter. Unfolding it I said that I had lived most of my life as a male. "Here is a letter from the Stanford Hospital that explains my situation."

Every eye focused on me. As the letter started around, I stated that I was not a cuckoo or a whacko, that I was very serious about becoming a woman, and that I needed help. I added that I needed help from this group especially, and that I expected to give whatever I had that the group could use.

Silence.

By now, the letter was half way around the table. Those who had read it had changed their countenance from confusion to comfort. Those who had not read it yet were reading the body language of those who had. The chairperson was doing some posture reading of her own, and said that she would like an expression from the group. Was there consensus?

Silence.

I never sweated this much over a final exam grade as I sat there, not breathing with any regularity. The letter moved a few more spaces.

Silence.

Was I in or out?

A clear, impassioned voice said, "If Sally wants to be a member of this group and be one of us, I say we should welcome her!"

I was accepted by acclamation. When the applause and words of welcome subsided, the chairperson said that from this moment on I was to be regarded as everyone else and would be expected to carry my share of the load.

I thanked the group for accepting me. I was overcome with gratitude.

The meeting got back on track and continued for another hour or so. A summation of the night's progress was made. The chairperson would send a copy of the minutes to each person who signed in that night. The next meeting would be in a fortnight.

On the way home that night, I was thrilled of course, but it dawned on me that the impassioned voice nominating me came from a young woman who had not read The Letter.

Due to the frequency of the organizational meetings, I was going broke paying for motels. No wonder Superman used telephone booths. I called Brenda, explained the situation, and asked her if she and Lorna would let me do the costume changes at their place. She was amazed that I took such a chance and more amazed that the group accepted me. I reminded her that I've always had more guts than brains. She said of course I could change there. That's what sisters are for.

By early spring of 1974, the meetings stabilized at one per month. We continued to meet at the Jewish Community Center. Suse was the property manager and a member of our group. We had free rent for a year.

Suse and I became friends. She was about ten years older than me. We felt a mutual affinity for some unidentified reason. She lived in San Francisco and did part time work as a translator for various embassies. Her other languages were German, Hebrew, Yiddish, and French. She had been part of the organizational effort to create an Israel after WWII. We had some nice times together. She was intrigued with me and often said so. "How can you be what you are? You are an attractive young woman, yet you have been a male for over forty years. I cannot see any male in you."

But those were later conversations over luncheons (never just a lunch) at her house, or dinners at my place. When she stopped working in Belmont, she also stopped attending the meetings. We did stay in touch for several years, entertaining at each other's homes. Good food and great conversation. She was one of several of my women friends who urged me to write this down. "You must publish your story for others." I am working on it, Suse, wherever you are.

The Women's Center of San Mateo County, Inc. had other treasures for me. The very first one to befriend me was Barbara. Then Michal and I became friends and have remained so since that night of my birth at the organizational table. Ginny was a nascent friend, but like many others, she was distracted by some of her own heavy personal problems.

Of course there were a few who were not in total sympathy with my quest. It was this group that let me know how the larger world out there would respond to me. Some would be very much in my corner and support me and love me, others would smile and accept me, others were detached and indifferent, and… well, the bell-shaped curve comes into use here.

I taught the plumbing and electrical repair classes at night and on Saturdays. Probably a dozen or more groups learned how to rewire a lamp and how to adjust the linkage in a toilet tank, attend to leaky faucets, and general safety precautions. It felt good to teach those things and enable women to show themselves and their husbands what they could do. Everything went well. So well that one of my students asked me to do the class for a Girl Scout troop. I still have the letter of thanks they wrote.

Barbara invited me to her home after the second planning meeting. I do not know why she took an interest in me. It is not important that I know. She was curious about the male me, but more curious about why be Sally. We managed to talk of very serious, personal topics right away. It seemed easy and natural to do that.

Michal has been a continuous friend. She was the real force behind the Women's Center until it generated its own force some months later. She was my mentor and saw to it that I had every chance to be an active member. She was the one who suggested that I not wear mini skirts because they called too much attention to me. Besides, the effort of the center was to get away from the girlie, swishy stuff and concentrate on what was inside. She also pointed out that one or two visitors to the center asked if I was really a woman.

I asked how she responded to that. She said she told the inquirer to ask Sally herself if she was a woman or not. No one ever did. With a nose like mine and an amateur at a lot of the subtleties, I was surprised that more people didn't ask.

The problem of appropriate female exteriors continued. They wore blue jeans, sweats, athletic shoes, no makeup. I had to wear makeup, nylons, skirts, and heels if I was going to be convincing. I had a lot to hide, to mask, to cover up. They were moving in the direction I had left. I was moving into their old space. We managed somehow.

The center did a magnificent job. We had a hotline and resources for referrals to lawyers, banking counselors, doctors, Planned Parenthood, the clergy, a big sister group, … whatever a woman with a problem could want. Consciousness raising groups, of course. It no longer exists as such. After five or six years, the YWCA and other county agencies began to duplicate our services. We turned over a lot of our programs to them. We were done and everyone who was involved had grown immensely for the experience. Annual reunions for the staff continued for a decade after we closed.

The activity at the center placed a new stress on me. A typical week for me consisted of two evenings teaching extension classes as a male, one night at the women's center as female, every day at work as male, two Saturdays a month teaching as female, and every Monday night at school board meetings. And the one Thursday afternoon each month at the Gender group. I was committed to being the male figure at home and at work, yet I was making enormous strides in becoming socially female. It occurred to me that if there really is a universal plan for one's life, then all that stress I endured in my early years, in the Navy, in the marriage—those times toughened me up for what was going on now. Both sides of my life were unfolding quite well, but in opposite directions.

Annie and I were pleased with our living arrangement. We never had a quarrel. Instead of name calling or saving up hurts and irritations to an explosive point, we would simply send an I-message to the other. "Boy! I really felt {angry, hurt, disappointed} when you {whatever it was the other did}." We didn't even use the I-message very often. We loved each other and it showed. We were sure it had a positive affect on Annie's daughters. I think my #3 son noticed it too, but he never said anything to me about it.

A lot of my happiness was due to Annie's understanding of the Sally phenomenon's importance to me. Her position was one of acceptance. She never wanted to know what Sally did, felt, or anything about her. She knew Sally was a big deal for me, but nothing that would get in the way of our relationship. We both believed that-then.

And so it was in the spring of 1974: I was husband/father, school administrator, extension course instructor, and emerging as a woman. Life was not ho-hum. Life is never ho-hum for a Gemini.

In December of 1973 I had applied for a sabbatical leave from the school district. It was my nineteenth year and I was ready for some independent study time. My real reasons were a growing disenchantment with the public school system, and I wanted a less structured schedule to better accommodate Sally's development... somehow. In March the superintendent and the school board approved my stated plan for the leave to begin May first. I was to receive half pay to do the research, write a scholarly paper, and develop a practical plan to implement a new pedagogical technique. I knew I could accomplish everything I claimed in my proposal and do the other too.

My idea was simultaneously bizarre and practical. I would rent a studio apartment in another town, do the research as Sally and devote four-to-six months time to the plan. I had to have an extended period of time as Sally to find out if Sally could make it in the real world. The twelve-month deal I had made with Annie would end that September. As I explained to her, I needed the slack now so that I could make a better decision in September. She was not thrilled with the idea, but she saw some sense in it. I think she was betting on me to fail as a woman, and then Sally would be relegated to the closet forevermore. Life would have been a lot simpler if Annie had won the bet. But is life supposed to be simple?

Chapter 10

From May through August of 1974 I was Sally, exclusively. Sally rented an apartment in Foster City. I was going to find out what life would be like as a woman. I was to be a lady of leisure, but certainly not a couch potato. I had things to do, places to go. This was to be my real test to see if I could survive socially and economically.

The continual logistical problems associated with my numerous turnabouts were a pain, but the payoffs far outweighed the hassles. I left all of my male clothing, except what I wore, at the house in Los Gatos. I packed all my female stuff into my '71 Pinto, drove to the modelling school, changed clothes, and then continued up the peninsula to my new apartment.

The new dwelling was called a junior one-bedroom. The resident could open the vertical wooden slat curtain and have a large studio with the bed on display, or close the curtain and have a smaller living room.

Annie did not want to communicate with me during this time. I assumed she wanted me to be totally independent of her; or she wanted me to stew in my own juice; or both. Maybe more. Regardless, I was on my own. Could I make it in this new context? Could I get a job? While I was about to get answers to those questions, there was always the question, Did I want to become a woman? In retrospect the answer is painfully obvious. Back then it wasn't obvious at all.

My agenda included some plastic surgery, inviting some friends to meet me, look for a job to see if I could get one, attend as many social activities as I could, continue work at the Women's Center on a larger scale, and... oh, yes, start on my research paper. A lot of those things happened. I am glad that I started keeping a journal/diary because so many events did occur, and at a fast pace.

A few days after settling in, I was admitted to Chope Hospital for plastic surgery. At last, my nose was going to be substantially reduced, my jutting chin was to become more ladylike, and my Adam's apple was to be shaved to reduce the big pointy lump. At the last minute, I chickened out on some of that. I told the surgeon that maybe I was not ready to make the total commitment. Could he please do a unisex nose, and forget the chin reduction for now? Yes, he could.

I was wheeled to the operating room wearing the traditional gown and cap. The nurse had given me some kind of pill that set me free so that by the time I was on the table, I really didn't care what they did. The anesthesiologist poked something in my arm and started pumping interesting fluids.

I was totally aware of everything going on. It seemed amusing to me that the surgeon picked up his scalpel, smiled at me, and cut my throat. He had to get at my Adam's apple so that he could use his electric grinder to smooth the barbs and reduce the size as much as possible. Ho-hum. After that was done and stitched, a fresh scalpel was aimed at my nose. The septum was cut, and the soft tissue was pulled back toward my forehead. He was going to trim some cartilage and reduce the width of the bone on the bridge of my nose. After the cartilage got reshaped, I expected another electric tool to do the bone. No. He picked up hammer and chisel... very shiny and pretty, but *primitive*. There was no pain, but there was a lot of concussion. The word barbaric came to mind. I wondered if any splinters were going to invade my brain. To avoid whimpering, I called up my John Wayne script and decided to play The Duke until it was over.

As the surgeon started on the second side, I became aware of the need to urinate, and said so. A pleasant nurse had been holding my hand, and she told another nurse to get Sally a bedpan. I thought: No, you silly goose, that won't work. Then I remembered I had been admitted as Sally and the plastic wristband said I was Sally. Before I could say anything, the sheet was turned aside and the bedpan was poised to be placed under my rump. There was astonishment on their faces when they saw my crank staring back at them. The bedpan was set aside and a flask came to the rescue. The doctor smiled and said that he forgot to tell the nurses about my special circumstances.

Barbara was waiting. She drove the bandaged me back to my apartment and made sure I was comfortable. I took my pain pill and we talked some before she had to get back home.

Lying on my back, still slightly woozy from the trauma, the anesthetic, and now the pain, I began another moment of reflection regarding Who am I?, What am I?, What is happening to me?, and What will I look like after the bandages come off and the swelling subsides?

The only answer I had for myself was that every step I took towards becoming female seemed right. I never had a regret. Not then, not now. I was terribly concerned and troubled by all the confusion, hurt, and disappointment I had caused others. There wasn't a whole lot I could do about the past. I vowed to be a lot more careful in the future. I knew that I was unsure about my future. It seemed that my top priority was to find out quickly.

The bandages came off ten days later. Under the bandages on my throat I saw the black thread, some dried blood, and a multi-colored pelt. Twenty years earlier I grew a beard while at sea during the Korean Police Action. Back then it was all brown. This rectangle was gray and brown, with a little white. The stitches came out easily and I was given permission to shave the unladylike growth. The scar was just a faint pink line. A month later it was gone. The nose was a little shorter and still swollen. It was weeks before the tenderness began to subside. Then I had to get new frames for my glasses. The optometrist told me that the bridge of my nose was definitely of female measure. Yes, I had a unisex nose, but it could have been a little smaller.

I was getting used to a new feeling about my place in the world, and I wanted to redefine myself. I wanted to do what women did. I had no rule book, no operating instructions for the role. I decided to just fake it and do what felt right and observe the reactions of other people to my behavior. Take notes and write my own manual.

One thing I learned quickly enough was that people out there will leave you alone unless you have a problem that they know about. Barbara, for example, was certainly solicitous while I was recovering from plastic surgery. When it became obvious that I was free-flight and able to do my own shopping and other ambulatory activities, she stopped calling. It makes sense. People have their own lives to live.

This was my first living arrangement where I was totally on my own. Not having others around me was a new phenomenon. My conclusion was that if I wanted company, I had to make the move. I could either call people to invite them to my place, or I could go to a gathering where a lot of people were. There was a third procedure for connecting with others that I discovered, and that was to be contacted by someone else. I realize that all this esoteric introspection seems mundane and even somewhat stupid. As I said, I had to re-define myself and that meant starting at square one. Perhaps a lot of previously learned social skills would come into play, but right now I wasn't sure what.

Margaret was one of the women I taught with in the old days—- 1955-1971. Late forties, never married, and a wonderful person. She was always a part of the group who talked of diverse religions, reincarnation, karma, psychocybernetics, the Polynesian huna, autohypnosis, and any other novel ideas that came to our attention. I felt she was simply a superior human. She knew how to handle any classroom of kids, how to tell a story, and how to make other people feel at ease. Margaret knew nothing about Sally. There had been no reason for her to know.

One evening I called her, using my male voice, to say hello and let her know that I was living in Foster City in an apartment by myself and that it would be fun to get together and catch up with each other's news. She asked about Annie, and I told her there was a separation… perhaps permanent, perhaps not. She agreed that we should have dinner soon. I offered to cook it if she would not mind coming to a bachelor's pad. She said that she could handle that. Next Tuesday at 6:00. Great.

My plan, of course, was to cook the dinner as Tom. I would greet her at the door, welcome her in, pour the wine, sit awhile and start the conversation, then let things progress from there. My real agenda was to somehow let her know about Sally. If Margaret could accept Sally I would be delighted. One of my secret ambitions was to be a woman friend of hers. Silly, perhaps, but I never claimed to make sense.

On the morning of the special dinner, Barbara called to invite me to go with her to explore the new shopping mall in San Mateo. I agreed, but said that I was going to entertain an old friend that evening, and gave her a quick summary of the situation. She said that we would be back to my apartment no later than 3:00. Fine.

Barbara and I walked the new mall and saw a lot of nice things. It was my first experience shopping with another woman. We looked at clothes, mostly, and talked of style. The issue of style was new for me. I understood the concept all right, but trying to identify my style was the problem. When you are about six feet tall and over 185 pounds, and your shoulders are wider than your hips, you can't wear just anything.

Then we discovered a wine shop. Lots and lots of wine. We each bought a few bottles, mostly unknown labels. I thought about serving some of that at dinner with Margaret.

We returned to my place around 4:00. Well, there was still plenty of time. Barbara wanted to open one of her bottles to sample it before serving to anyone else and wanted my opinion. We were feeling mischievous-two women drinking wine in mid-afternoon. It had been a fun trip to the mall, and we were just a little frisky, and we both had a lot of talk in us. In the middle of the second bottle of wine my doorbell rang. Oh!

It was not planned to happen this way. Not consciously, anyway. There was no time to wash my face or change my clothes. Barbara asked what she should do? The bell rang again. I told Barbara to just sit there on the floor where she was and we would play it by ear.

I opened the door and saw Margaret staring at me, confused. "Oh," she said, "I must have the wrong apartment." "No, this is the right apartment. Do come in." The confused look stayed in place, and so did she. "Margaret, please come in and I will explain." She entered cautiously, saw Barbara on the floor with a glass of wine, smiling. I closed the door and said in my male voice, "It's me, Margaret."

The poor dear just stood and gasped a little, her face doing the contortions of confusion, surprise, comprehension, and then a big smile. In that order. When I saw the smile that I knew so well, I knew everything was going to be all right. And it was.

Now we were three women on the floor with fresh wine in our glasses. Barbara and Margaret liked each other immediately. I quickly apologized to Margaret about the rude trick, that I had not planned it that way. Barbara dittoed my story of how the plan was supposed to have worked. Margaret waved at us to stop apologizing. She said that after the first couple of minutes, while I was pouring the wine, that she began to pick up on the situation. "I think this is fascinating and I want to hear all about it."

I proceeded to tell her about my lifelong ambition to be a woman, or at least find out if that was what I wanted, how I met Barbara, and what I was doing in that apartment. Barbara added her version of my involvement at the Women's Center, and a few other things to let Margaret know that I was indeed a suitable candidate for womanhood. The phone rang. It was Barbara's sitter wondering when she was going to get back. Time had flown by at incredible speed.

I got dinner started. Margaret sat in the kitchen and we continued talking. She had so many questions. While the chicken baked and the water for the pasta heated up, I made the salad. Talk, talk, talk. I was feeling much more comfortable than I would have guessed, but then again, that's Margaret— a wonderful person. She remarked on my gestures. She said that I seemed to act like a woman, all right. How did I learn to move that way, and use feminine body language so well? And my speech patterns. All I could say was that it all seemed to be natural for me. Sure, I went to Miss Lorraine's girl school and I learned a lot. But mostly, once I get into the space, I slip into automatic. I don't think about what I am doing, I just do it.

We sat down to dinner and I asked her about her. I was getting tired of talking about myself, and I wanted to know what was going on in her life. She told me about her latest romance and some possible employments away from the school district. We had a wonderful evening and we forged a new level of friendship. At 1:30 a.m. she went home.

The first unsolicited reaction to my new status came in the form of advice for a basket of fuchsias I had hanging in my patio. Joe was a neighbor who had more patio shrubbery than a movie set for a Tarzan film. He hollered across the way to tell me that my plant was getting too much sun. I hollered back that I didn't know where else to hang it. I think that was the answer he was looking for. He smiled and said he would be right over. We looked around and found a better place. He removed the hanger and installed it and the basket in the shady place. He smiled, as though he had made his contribution to the universe for that day. He introduced himself, and to express my thanks, I asked if I could pour him a glass of wine.

I found that he liked to talk as much as I do. We talked about apartment life and how it differs from typical suburban home life, why the lagoons in Foster City were so special, and should we open another bottle of wine or not. We phoned a pizza order and started on the second bottle. He said he was in the process of divorce. I said that was the hardest thing I ever did. It was emotionally wrenching like nothing else. He said that one can get used to it. This was his fourth divorce. I gasped. He said that he has been married and divorced four times with the same woman. I had no comment for that.

The pizza arrived. It was getting dark and cool outside so we moved to the living room coffee table to eat. The conversation continued to religion, philosophies, the difference between a religion and a philosophy, speculation on the meaning of the universe, and man's quest for an understanding of his reason for being. We were in the middle of a comparison between the gods of Greek mythology and the twelve apostles of Christ, when he stopped with a strange look on his face. He asked if I had ever been a Jesuit. I laughed and said, " Hardly." He grinned and said that he had not had such a conversation since he left the seminary some years ago. Then he said he never knew a woman who wanted to talk about such things. Or *could* talk about such things. I wanted to call him a sexist bastard, but thought I had better not.

It was almost 2:00 a.m. We decided to call it a night and vowed to do this again. We never did. In a few days, he began dating his wife. In a month, he moved out. I did not get an invitation to the wedding.

I had time to reflect on that conversation in the days that followed. It occurred to me that while I had presented the image of a woman, the speech patterns and body language of a woman, my sophomoric discourse was definitely male. I did not let him control the conversation, nor did I let his remarks go unchallenged. I did my best to intellectually pin his shoulders to the mat. Women don't do that, I told myself. Then the rhetorical question, Why not?

Clancy lived in the apartment below me. We had waved at each other a few times without ever trying for conversation. One evening after the dinner hour, he knocked at my door and asked if he could come in and get acquainted with me. We exchanged names, and I asked if he would like a glass of wine. He said he would take a beer if I had one. I got his beer, my wine, and we sat on opposite sides of the room. He seemed a little nervous. I wondered if he was going to try to put the make on me. I was so new at the craft of living as a woman that I was unsure of the signals and how to read them. I was relying partly on my budding intuition, and partly on my experience as a horny male.

He said that he wanted to tell me about the dream he had last night. Oh oh. I think I know what's coming. He began to describe an orgy that he and I had in my bed and ended the fantasy "dream" by asking if I believed that dreams could come true.

I was impressed with his delivery of the approach, flattered by the attempt, scared, and without hesitation, I used the response I'd gotten the last time I tried that pitch. I said, "No." Then I stood up, signalling that the conversation was over. He got the idea and left, saying that he hoped I wasn't mad at him. I said I wasn't, that it was nice to be asked, but I was not ready for such an invitation. It was all true. We continued to wave at each other, but no more conversations.

One morning in the coin-op laundry room, I saw a notice for a singles and couples party at the apartment recreation room. "Bring Your Sweetie or Find One Here." The details stated that all we had to do was to show up. The landlord was paying for the buffet dinner. We could purchase beer, wine, and ardent spirits. Live music from 9 to midnight.

This was one of many moments in my new role when I was reminded of an old Jimmy Durante song, *"Did Ya Ever Get the Feeling That Ya Wanted Ta Go, Yet Ya Wanted Ta Stay"* I could see that this would be my chance to meet some people and make some friends of my own. The down side was that I might not make it undetected. I could blow my cover. Then I would be in trouble around there for the rest of the summer.

Hey! Why did you come here? You went to all this trouble and expense just so that you could hide out? Not to mention the disruption of other people's lives.

Yes, but I don't want to screw up. I want to feel that I am ready before I go to such a party.

How do you ever expect to get ready?

You're right. I always learn by doing. By getting as prepared as I can, and then act the way I think I should. Observe, and revise as I go.

Atta boy! Oops. Atta girl!

I wore a long multi-colored border print sheath skirt with a navy blue sleeveless knit turtleneck top. White sandals. Strands of shell beads. Not bad for a beginner, I thought. It was one of the more comfortable outfits I owned at the time. It dramatically emphasized the difference between male and female clothing. For one thing, I felt a sense of freedom I never felt in male clothing. At the same time, I felt a vulnerability I never felt before.

I walked into the recreation center, looked around, and saw that no one was taking any notice of me. I relaxed a little, and did what I usually do-I looked for the bar. I rewarded myself with a gin over for getting this far. Because I wanted to relax a little more, I asked for a double, with a single twist. There were lots of empty tables. I picked one close to the window so that I could look at the lights around the lagoon, in case there was to be no one to talk with.

In a few minutes two men and a woman came in. Obviously a husband and wife plus this big hunk. They looked around, found a table and sent the hunk to the bar for drinks. As he stood there waiting for the order, he looked around the room, saw me, looked around some more and then stared at me, smiling. He carried the drinks back to his friends, then brought his drink to my table and asked if he could join me. Sure. The gin had blocked the fight-or-flight syndrome. Besides, I have had this experience before. The first time was at to O-club in San Diego about five years earlier.

He said his name was Andy. I said my name was Sally. He wanted to shake hands. My hand got lost in his. I do not have small hands. Andy said he was a deep sea diver. He had been hired by the Army Corps of Engineers to do a salvage job in the Philippines, and had just returned from two years in Subic Bay. I could tell from this much conversation that he was a very nice fellow, and was not going to be a problem. All I had to do was to act like a nice lady and everything would work out for everyone.

Andy was staying with his sister and her husband for a few weeks. He said that after a week or so it would be time to move on. Maybe Alaska. He had heard that there was a lot of undersea pipe being laid. He asked who I was, where I lived-the usual stuff. I vagued out with a more or less true account: I used to be a schoolteacher, but decided to quit, take the summer off, and look for something else to do.

He wanted to get our drinks refreshed. I did not protest.

To practice my budding skill of directing the conversation, I started asking questions. The system works, but one is obliged to listen to answers to the questions. Not a problem. It was the first time I tried listening to someone else. I was accustomed to paying attention when anyone talked to me. But really listening is different. I mean if you are *really* listening, you hear the content, you read the body language, you evaluate the intensity or emotional level, and you consider the kind of response you are going to make when it is appropriate for you to talk. If your verbalizations are truly congruent with the other person, he or she can't help but continue talking. Women are born with this talent. Most of them use it, but some don't. We student women have to learn it and practice it. A lot.

Andy asked if I was married. I said I had been, but not anymore. His spine got straighter and leaned forward just a little. I asked if he spent much time in Olongopo. His eyes got bigger. He asked how I knew about Olongopo. I said that my brother had been in the Navy and had spent some time there; that there was a big place in the town that had a huge outdoor beer garden with a two-story hotel around it. Andy asked if my brother told me what went on in that hotel. I asked Andy what he meant. He got a big grin on his face, as though there was a secret that only men could understand. I wanted to tell him that we had probably bedded the same whores, but thought better of it. I wanted to tell him that I missed the fine gutsy flavor of San Miguel beer, domestic. Instead, I said that my brother told me about seeing a sunken prison ship in the harbor. He said they had just cleared it before he got there.

We went to the buffet and found that the serious diners had been there, thereby saving us from overeating. "If I can borrow my brother-in-law's car, we could go someplace, just the two of us." "No, Andy, this is fine for me. Could we have another drink? I'll buy." "No you won't." We went back to the table with our meager pickings, and he went to the bar.

I was feeling proud of myself for my performance. I was also enjoying the role. It seemed to me then that the woman's role came to me easier than the male role did. When I was learning to be a male, I had nothing to compare it with. Now the comparison was happening, and I found the woman's space to be so very, very good. Of course, I had to allow for the novelty factor. Would this become tiresome after a while?

I looked around the room and saw Andy's sister staring at me with a slight but unmistakable frown on her face. Oh oh. I think I have been "read." Does she suspect that her little brother is being played with by a... a... I don't want to think about what. The keen edge was now off the evening. I had a problem: Will she tell him? What will I do if she does, and he wants to let me know his opinion? The permutations of possibilities just made me get up, go to the ladies' room, and then come back to whatever was to be. At least I would face whatever it was with an empty bladder.

On my way to the loo, I noticed Andy stopping at his sister's table, listening. Oh shit. When I came back, Andy was sitting at another table, by himself, staring out the window. The word morose came to mind. I saw the drink he left for me, drank some, and tried to catch his eye. When I did, I saw that he was not at all friendly. He turned away. I thought I was lucky not to have to seek medical attention. I took one more sip, got up and walked out, giving the sister a few seconds of blank stare on my way out the door.

It took more than a couple of minutes to evaluate the situation. On the one hand, he had a right to be angry—- he had been fooled into thinking I was a nice lady. He did, in fact feel that way, until she told him goodness knows what. I know that my motives were pure. I just wanted to spend some time with a man as a woman in a polite social setting. If I was a wanton, I would have jumped at the chance to drive off with him when he asked me to. I also would have told him where I lived, or given him my phone number, or invited him to walk me home. No, I did none of those things.

As I walked home alone, I felt sorry for Andy. He was really a nice guy who was being nice to me. I had known a lot of guys like him. Sensitive, yet unable to find the right way to express themselves in standard English. His biggest problem, I imagine, was in dealing with himself. How could he, a tough he-man get interested in a... a... what? What did he think I was? *I* knew what I was, but did he? Probably not. Poor guy. The last thing I wanted to do was to hurt anyone.

There were several lessons for me from that evening. Not all came to me at once, though. The main one was that I had to be very, very careful in the future. I would be a little more standoffish, a little less quick to befriend strange men, and I had better get some guidance from my women friends.

Another big issue that I had to deal with was the morality of what I was doing. On the one hand, I was playing with fire. The situation with Andy could happen all over again. And again, until some morning I woke up dead, or worse.

On the other hand, I needed to learn how to conduct interpersonal relationships with both men and women as a woman. How was I supposed to do that without doing it? Like porcupines mating—-very carefully. For the next month or so I planned to avoid any risky situations with men.

One day I drove up to Black Point in Marin County to the Renaissance Fair. It was a bright and warm July afternoon. Very thirsty outside, that day. As my beer was being poured, an extremely handsome man came alongside and ordered a beer. He was buoyant and lighthearted, just the way one is supposed to be at the fair. He said he wanted to buy my beer for me. I almost recoiled. I said no thanks, and meant it. He insisted. I remained firm in my resolve not to have a repeat of my experience with

Andy. The young man said that it would make him very happy if he could buy my beer for me. I repeated my polite no thank you. He turned sour. He grumbled, as I turned away, saying that it was a downer when he couldn't buy a pretty lady a cup of beer.

I felt good about being regarded as a pretty lady, but very upset with myself for causing a man to be unhappy by keeping my distance.

Well, what am I supposed to do? There is no way in hell that I am going to back off from getting my lessons. You guys out there are going to have to put up with me. I will not tease you, I will not lead you on, but I will keep on trying. When I learn how to read situations better, the problem will disappear. In the meantime I will continue to seek guidance——from friends, and from "out there."

In early August, I saw an ad in the local paper for the Swinging Singles Club. Their "meetings" were scheduled for Thursdays at 5:00 p.m. at the Holiday Inn. What the heck, I thought. I could go there, look around, then decide whether it was safe for me or not.

There was a dues table set up in the foyer. A young woman sat there with her beverage, a cash box, and a stack of stick-on name tags. She saw me come in, smiled and said that they needed me inside. She took my $5.00 donation, asked for my name, wrote it on a tag, and suggested I give it to the first man who asks my name and let him put it on me. A nice idea I suppose, but not for me. I peeled off the backing and put it on my left false boob. The woman did a mock frown and called me a spoil-sport.

I heard the five-piece band doing a fine job of one of my favorites, *Proud Mary*. In a twinkling of an eye, I was ready! I was wearing what I would call outlandish today, but seemed appropriate then: a red, white, and blue plaid miniskirt, the navy blue turtleneck sleeveless top, white sandals, small white shoulder bag, and a long strand of white beads with an overhand knot tied in front to emphasize my cleavage. My choice of wigs in those days was a long chestnut pageboy. I felt good about myself, was pleased by the acceptance of the money changer out front, was turned on by the music, and went inside to one of the more memorable evenings of my life.

Before I could find a table, I had two requests to dance. I wanted a couple of belts of gin before I did anything. I found a large table with only one couple at the other end. As the cocktail waitress arrived, so did Clyde. He told the waitress that he was going to buy this lady her drink. I said no, I would buy my own. He insisted, but I said it was important to me that I buy my own. Seeing the hurt expression on his face, I added that I pay for the first one, anyway. He relaxed and said he would be back. I was learning some diplomacy, I hoped.

The drink came. After two generous swallows, and a few more invitations to dance which I politely declined, a young man in his late thirties came alongside and said his name was Fred, and he wanted me. I stared at him. He smiled and said that he wanted me *to dance*, then. I got up and discovered that he was still taller than me. All right!

The music continued to be fast and loud. It was easy to dance with someone if you were doing the tribal gyrations called for by the music. This was only my second time on the dance floor with a man. I started to move my body to the rhythm and tried a few moves of the pelvis I had seen before and found tantalizing. Fred, my partner, was smiling at me, the way I had smiled at women before. I began to gain some confidence in myself, until the band stopped and Fred got close. The music started again, but they were playing *Moon Over Miami*! Fred's arms went around me. I found my chin on his shoulder. I felt I was in trouble. I did not have the ability to follow. After a few steps, Fred looked at me, smiled, and said, "Okay. *You* lead."

I was expecting conversation, but got silence. I felt something unfamiliar to me poking me "down there." Cripes! I asked Fred what kind of work he did. He said he was a doctoral candidate at Stanford's School of Education. I told him I had a master's degree from there. He mumbled something. More poking. I asked if he knew a professor Turnbull. He stopped and held me at arms length. He said that I wanted to talk classrooms, he wanted to talk bedrooms.

I was certainly flattered, and was certainly scared. By this date, my hormone balance had shifted to predominantly female. I was thrilled to be in this situation, but my brain was telling me I had better get out of it. I told Fred that I did not want to talk bedrooms. He moved back, took my elbow, and silently led me back to my table. At least, he had manners. Being a Stanford person, of course . . .

Clyde saw us return. He came over, sat down, signalled for drinks, and that was when I learned his name was Clyde and he learned that my name was Sally. I felt safe with him. He was a comfortable man. He was about sixty, overweight, balding, and a lot of nice wrinkles around the eyes. He asked if I was married. I said that I had been. I asked if he was married. He hesitated, then said he was. Then I got his story. He had just returned from Africa. He was with a construction crew that built satellite antenna stations around the world. He had been gone almost two years. During that time, his wife had learned to live quite nicely without him. She did not want a divorce, but she did not want intimacy with him either. He said that he needed to build a private life for himself. My heart went out to him. A year earlier, with different chemicals in me, I would have said, "Tough shit, Clyde."

He changed the subject by saying that he was pleased to buy me drinks and to spend time with me. He hoped that I would not think he was a womanizer. No, Clyde, not a chance.

I was learning more about how to converse with men. Clyde was safe to be around. I could relax with him, perhaps experiment a little without fear of penalty. I tried different questions, got answers that were either shorter or longer than I had guessed. Above all, I was thrilled by the awareness that I was a woman with this man. We were talking and drinking as any couple would. That was the space I was looking for. I did not want sex with a man. I wanted to achieve the female consciousness. I had a part of that by having women friends who knew there was another me, never knew the other me, yet regarded this me as a woman. And service people in stores and such who called me ma'am, and used feminine pronouns when referring to me. For me womanhood was something that existed between the ears, not between the legs. Clyde was helping me to achieve my goal of over forty years. How could I not feel kindly toward him?

I was wondering if some essential element was entering my life, or leaving it. I knew that I was not feeling or behaving like a man anymore. Was this new state a gain or a loss? Whichever it was, I liked it very much. Then it occurred to me that I did not have to find an answer just then. Relax, sweetie, and enjoy.

Clyde interrupted my ruminations by announcing that it was after 7:00 p.m. Could he buy me dinner? By now I would let Clyde do anything but try to bed me. I felt we were both gaining enormously from each other's company. I was not hungry, and said so. Clyde said he wasn't either. He said that he wanted to dance with me. This place had cleared out twenty minutes earlier. He suggested that we drive in his new Cadillac El Dorado to the Villa Hotel. There would be music just for us and a food service if we got hungry later. I said that sounded good to me, but I wanted to drive my own car. Lead on, Clyde and I will follow you.

We parked near each other. Although it was getting dark outside, I could see that his car was indeed beautiful. He escorted me through the lobby and into the lounge. It was noisy, but definitely a class place. Clyde ordered our drinks. I was starting to wonder what women see in men. How can a woman get excited about the male body? Maybe they don't get excited by the male body in the way a man gets excited by the female body. Maybe a woman gets excited by something else, and that the male body comes as part of the package.

Quit with the analysis. Enjoy. Behave the way you want to, the way that feels natural. Do the analysis tomorrow.

We toasted each other and smiled. He asked if I was having a good time. Yes, Clyde, more fun than I've had in a long time. That pleased him. He asked why. I told him that he made me feel comfortable, that I had not been out in the bright lights in quite awhile, and that I enjoyed our conversation. He accepted that by smiling some more. Then I got my first clue that he was different. Not weird, but then again …

He asked if I wore panties under my pantyhose. Wild! I should have told him it was none of his business, but that did not occur to me then. I said that I did. He said, "Good! Let's dance." He led a bewildered me to the dance floor. He was not a very active person. We did not last long on the floor. Back at the table, he asked for my address. No. He asked for my telephone number. No again. He said that he wanted to send me flowers in the morning. I was getting nervous. I wanted to see him again, I had never received flowers from anyone before, but I was afraid. I did not know what to do. I could see he was beginning to cloud over. I did not want that. I was getting some insight on male management from the woman's side. Boy, I thought, these guys are tender. Gotta be careful. Later I had to admit that it was natural for the male to be sensitive—ego and all that.

My counter offer was that he give me his office telephone number, and I would call him early next week to set a lunch date. He gave me his business card and made me promise that I would call. Oh yes, Clyde.

We were almost to our cars when he suggested that I try out the seating in his El Dorado. He said that the seats were electrically operated and could move in all kinds of positions. I thought it would be interesting. The hour, the drinks, the newly-found emotional plane all added up to a yes.

It turned out to be my first experience in a car where the driver can control the windows and the door locks. I heard my door go clunk, then my heart did the same. I was trying to enjoy the various motions my seat was moving in. Then I found out how fast Clyde could be. He had his arms around me and his face was on mine. What is a girl supposed to do? Very quickly I realized I was in over my head, socially and emotionally. I had no interest in accommodating his expressed needs. All I could do was to play some of the old tapes from my past. (There was no John Wayne script for this scene.) In retrospect I saw how fast the mind can work in a crisis. Simultaneously, these two events happened: I kept my cool by remembering from the past, and I entered a new dimension by letting him hold me and kiss me. Hard. Deep. I felt his whiskers grinding on my lips. I heard his heavy breathing. I flashed on King Kong holding Fay Wray. I felt that I was a tender woman being conquered by this beast. I remember thinking that I hadn't bargained for this, but I liked it. A new height of pleasure mixed with a new dimension of fear.

He started to touch my breasts. I could not allow that because they were false ones I had hand-crafted for myself. The material was quite life-like, but could not tolerate too much exploration. Because I did not want him to discover that, I gently but firmly pushed his hand away. He misinterpreted my gesture and he sent his paw to my thighs. I got my hand down there just in time to stop him from discovering something more outrageous than false breasts. He mumbled the predictable protest while frenching me. I leaned back to get air and told him that I was sorry that this was the wrong time of the month for me to entertain. Before he could consider alternatives, I made a bid for release and got it.

Several days later I did call him and we did meet for lunch. He really wanted to build a relationship with me. During the days in between, I was a-twitter. I was not having a crush on Clyde as Clyde; I was titillated with the notion that a man wanted me. Clyde was the instrument for this new feeling. Oh, I liked him all right. But I was concerned about our first daylight meeting. Would he still like me? Would he see through the trappings?

We met at the Whistle Stop restaurant in Belmont. It had been a passenger station years ago. It was a nice place. Simple and clean. I entered the place feeling higher than a kite. I was meeting a man, a man married to another woman. Was I discovering something about the female ego now?

Clyde saw me, jumped to his feet, smiled and came to me. He took both my hands, then kissed me on the cheek and led me to our table. I noticed a few patrons watching us. They smiled, possibly thinking that here was a tryst; the older man with a younger woman. We sat down and they didn't look at us anymore. Clyde was beaming. He said that he was so glad that I came. I said that I was delighted to be there and I meant it. I realized I was not nervous. I was being validated as a woman with Clyde and the patrons of the Whistle Stop. I felt like the woman I was meant to be. Meant to be?

Well, sure. Why do you think you have this tremendously powerful drive to attempt to become a woman if you were not meant to become one?

I noticed that I was eating less as a woman. Perhaps that was due to the excitement going on in my head. During the lunch Clyde asked me if I would go away with him for a few days, two weeks from then. He said that he had this almond grove in the valley and that it was almost time to harvest. Although it was being tended by some locals, he liked to be there for the harvest. Usually, he invited his drinking and hunting friends to participate in the annual rite, but this year, he wanted me.

This was overloading my circuits. I even said so. He said that he wanted to work the picking machine during the day and then come in, take a bath, have me scrub his back, and then cook dinner for us. I had to admit that it was a nice fantasy, but it would remain a fantasy. I was concerned about being a captive for several days. I did not know him well enough to feel comfortable with that. I was also concerned about a few other things, such as my privacy and my ability to keep up the illusion of my anatomical womanhood. I said that the idea sounded good, but there was something coming up, planned a long time ago, and I would not be able to give him an answer for another week. He said that would be all right, so long as my answer was yes. I smiled what I thought was a coquettish smile and said that we'll see.

The thing about Clyde was that he had a capacity to be a fine, loving man. He wanted to share that love with me. I do not mean unbridled passion or storybook romance. I mean things like respect, regard, caring, a friendly kind of love. Comfort rather than passion. But I could see that passion had to be a part of a relationship for him. He needed his validation, too. I could see the potential for a symbiotic relationship here. I idly wondered if he would buy me an operation if I asked him to.

Our next lunch date was the following Friday. He wanted to meet at Barney's Place in Sunnyvale. I knew of the joint, but had never been inside.

I had just come from my eighth donation of blood at the Hillview Blood Bank in Palo Alto. The nurses were thrilled that they could take my picture, holding a sign reading: Her First Gallon. I was thrilled to get the Polaroid for my scrapbook.

I parked my little car among the construction vehicles driven by Barney's clientele. I should have been scared shitless walking in to a place like that with all those cowboys. Instead, I decided to play Fay Wray about to be protected by Mr. Kong.

I found Clyde talking to some gents in their Levis, boots, and sweaty T-shirts. He beamed when he saw me and introduced me to his friends. He got me a drink, and we sat at a table in the middle of the room. In my Navy days, the only time I would sit down in a place like that would be at a table against the wall, preferably in a corner. But Clyde's friends were there . . .

I showed him the picture of me at the blood bank. I was wearing my blue and white polka dot seersucker dress, white sandals, white headband, and a terrific smile. Clyde had to show the photo to his friends. They all seemed to think it was O.K.

Clyde said that he had some bad news. He had to invite his buddies along to the almond harvest. They had been planning on it. But he still wanted me to come along. He said there would be three other men. I would be the only woman. Would I mind cooking for all of them? I said if he was there to protect me, I wouldn't mind. Well, that could be a problem. He had been with them lots of time when they had been drinking, and he could not guarantee me very much protection.

Then I told him I had a problem. I said there were some important things about me that he should know. He said that he already knew all he needed to know about me. I asked him to read something. I handed him The Letter. I knew it was a crapshoot to do that in such a public place, but I felt I could count on Clyde to be adult and not overreact at what he was about to learn.

As he read the letter, my eyes panned the room filled with rugged outdoor types, all getting in touch with the T.G.I.F. mood. It seemed to take Clyde awhile to read. I was getting nervous. I looked at him for the first time since I handed him the letter. I saw his lips moving as he read. Only then did I realize the poor dude probably did not know what the letter was talking about.

He handed it back and asked me the most incredible question. "I just want to know one thing, Sally. Are you a Communist?" It was a struggle not to laugh. I said that I was not now nor had I ever been a member of the Communist Party. He reaffirmed his invitation to the almond harvest, but I chickened out.

We never did eat lunch that day. I said that something had come up and I had to be in San Bruno at 2:00. I promised to call him in a day or so. I was no longer worried about Clyde. He liked me, no matter what I was. At the time, and even now, I think the relationship could have developed.

The month of August was almost gone. I had to make some kind of plan for the future. What had I learned? What did I want to do? What did I have to do? And other questions.

After thinking with both hands for two days, I had to admit that the only reasonable course was to return to Los Gatos, hope that Annie would welcome me, decide what to do about the school district, and get organized.

Chapter 11

One can imagine that there would be a time of introspection and evaluation that followed "My Summer Vacation." The review of my four-month experiment began as I drove from Foster City to Miss Lorraine's school.

It was really hard for me to surrender the keys to my apartment. It was even harder trying to convince myself that I was doing the right thing by going back. Oh, there was an overwhelming rationale for me to do so, but I couldn't feel it to be right, emotionally. I had a promise to keep. The old refrain was still with me. *Do your job whether you feel like it or not.*

I had found what I had been looking for: the knowledge that I could function as a woman, and that it felt right to be one. But there were just too many practical considerations to deal with. I had my commitment to Annie. I would never forgive myself if I went back on that promise. There was my uncertain employment future. I would be lucky to get a job for Tom, let alone get a job for Sally.

I did make that one attempt to get hired as a waitress in a Copper Penny coffee shop. I was so nervous that the manager felt that I would not be an enhancement to his staff. I do not know whether he knew I was really a woman or not. Looking at his staff, I wasn't too sure about some of his people.

I pulled into the parking lot of Miss Lorraine's studio, took out Tom's clothes, and went inside. Robin was the only one there. He said I looked like my best friend had died. I said that it was me who was dying. We sat for a while. I shared my cigarettes with him, and he shared his coffee with me. Being the psychologist he was, he knew that I needed some TLC in that hour of transition. If anyone else knew the depth of my desire to be Sally, it was Robin. He reminded me a lot of my father: a man who had some deep regrets about the way life had turned out; that there had been a course of action open to him some years ago, and the option was not taken. Regret had replaced hope. A form of suicide called alcoholism had been adopted and numbed the pain of a lost opportunity. That was my father and that was Robin.

Robin recognized the symptoms manifesting in me. He tried, in an oblique manner, to tell me that I should decide for myself what to do, decide what I wanted, not base my life's decisions on what I thought other people wanted.

Two cups of coffee and three cigarettes later, I took a deep breath, got up, and walked my last steps in high heels to the changing room. I shed the clothes that had become so natural for me, washed my face, and put on my shirt and gray flannels. I looked in the mirror at a tormented face. It was also a face that still had traces of mascara and lipstick. I creamed them again and rubbed some more. Not much better. The skin was becoming raw. I gathered my things, packed up, and walked out the door. I think Robin knew I was on the brink of tears and forgave me for not saying anything, like, Goodbye.

The drive from the studio in Los Altos to the house in Los Gatos normally required about 20 minutes. That day it took well over a half hour. I seemed to need the time to reshape my head for the homecoming. There were so many things to consider and file away in their proper places.

A normal person (whatever that is) would likely be in psychological shambles because of these sudden changes in living arrangements. Be a man, be a woman, feel like a man, feel like a woman, look like a man, look like a woman. Be in the arms of a man, be in the arms of a woman. By now I knew that I could be either one, but I had to be heterosexual, whichever I was to be. All I had to do was to decide. Which way should I jump?

My first thought was poor me.

Hey! Get off that sorry-for-yourself routine. You do realize, don't you, that you have made a major breakthrough?

Yes, but look at me now. I am dressed as a male again. I am on my way back to living as a man again. It is hard to feel good about that. It is an unnatural act.

This is your first setback? Keep in mind that you may have lost a battle, but not the war.

Right. I lost this battle, but I did learn a lot from the situation. I'll know more about survival next time.

I am glad you acknowledge that there will be a next time. You could start planning that now.

All these problems. Then it occurred to me that I was blessed, not cursed, with this obvious duality. I could choose. I was sure that it had to be one or the other. I would not be able to mix the two into one.

Later I realized that I could *not* choose-the choice had already been made, decades ago. I could only decide *when* and *how* I would become the woman I was to be.

I do not think that anyone ever said that life would make sense, would be fair. As a matter of fact, I do not think anyone ever explained what in the hell we humans were doing on this planet, anyway. Maybe it does not matter why we are here, the point is that we *are* here, so get on with it. Getting on with it required action. Action implied there must be some set of rules or guidelines that should be followed.

By what code of conduct, what code of morality should I use to get me through the rest of my life? The ready-made nostrums for so-called good living seemed to lack a base in common sense. Edicts were made, but no rationale to support them. No school of thought gave any attention to one's *inner consciousness*-the desires, the tendencies, the drives-as our *raison detre*. None, except perhaps those religious philosophies from the East. Reincarnation was a way to explain why people did what they did, why disasters happened, why the good did not always win, and why some people marched to a different drummer. I thought I had been through all this over a year ago. I probably had not internalized very much. I had to start all over again.

For one thing, I knew I had to be able to love myself before I could give love to anyone else. Sure, I could try to fake a love for someone else, but the lie would become obvious in time. How do I love myself? The only answer I had was to acknowledge that I was a child of God. Whatever God is.

My opinion was that God is not a man-like person who monitors people the way Santa Claus does when he makes his Christmas list. God is not on stakeout at my house. I believed that Emerson was accurate when he said that *every heart vibrates to the iron string.* It was a remembrance from my English composition class 23 years earlier. The meaning is that every person has a direct link with the Creator of the Universe. I found significance in the meaning of the word religion. It's root is Greek and simply means to reconnect. I had a tough time believing that some other earthling had to serve as an intermediary for me, or be an interpreter. If I really do have a direct link to the Central Intelligence of the Universe, then I should be able to get some sort of guidance by a direct wire if I ask. And maybe that Central Intelligence was trying to tell me something now. Who do I ask? How do I ask? How will I know when I get an answer?

There was no more time for esoteric speculations. I was almost home. I had to have a glad heart and smiling face when I walked through that door. I knew I could do that. After all, I was in love with Annie. She had to be the world's greatest woman. I knew that she would be relieved to see me again, in male clothing, ready to resume my role as husband/father. She would be warm and would make me glad I came back.

Sure enough, Annie hugged me tight and gave me kisses I remember to this day. The young ladies were thoughtfully somewhere else. That was my clue to pay attention to Annie's cue that we test out my equipment. And hers. Everything checked out, but I did have a problem getting started. We agreed that there had been a lot of emotional changing of gears for me. Give it a day or so and it will recover fully. It never did. It recovered enough so that there were good times for us, but I sure did a lot more foreplay than ever. I did that for Annie so that when I did manage to penetrate, she would be ready. I do not know whether the slowness was due to the four months of estrogen pills or due to the new places where my consciousness had traveled. Had my subconscious been altered? Good question.

It was the early part of September. I had to start planning my future. I sure had some things to consider: source of money, identify employment, and make a plan to resume my life as Sally. And try to make it work with the least amount of disruption for one and all.

I was technically still on sabbatical leave to do that research. I would never be able to return to the school district. It would be best if I could find employment first, then submit my resignation. I knew that I would have to repay some money to the district, but I had nothing to pay it with until I got a job.

Annie wanted to know what my decision was on renewing the lease on the house. I said that I thought we should stay another six months. She liked that idea.

There was no discussion about any plans for Sally. Annie never wanted to hear anything about her. I always felt that it was a mistake for her to adopt the ostrich posture. A simple chat about what was going on with me and Sally would have given her a ton of indicators about things to come. I had an inkling of what my future was. Annie was a superior counsellor. If she had listened to me just a little, my guess is that she would have seen all kinds of signals that I was not consciously aware of.

Sally had to go underground, back in the closet. But not for long. There was a way that Sally could have a *shadow* existence in that family arrangement. No dressing up, but at least some of the consciousness would be able to survive and perhaps grow a little. I began to develop my newly-found nurturing feelings. Specifically, I did all the cooking and I set my male ego aside in my dealings with the others in the house.

Now that may not sound like much, but it was plenty for me at that time. Consider the matter of cooking. No one else could cook as well as I could. They loved the arrangement, and there was no competition for the job. When one assumes the total responsibility for putting food on the table at mealtime, a lot of thought has to go into it. Who likes what kind of food? How do they like it prepared? How often can the same meal be served in a month without complaint? Who in the family needs a favorite meal to cheer her up? And so forth. In that light, cooking transcends the mere technique of cutting, combining, seasoning, heating, and serving. Cooking becomes *an act of love*. The cook chooses the foods that will please, that will be nutritious, and generate happy people. Payoffs come in the knowing that you have done something good for someone else, and in seeing and hearing the acceptance of what you have given. Good food at the table can be a facilitator for good conversation. The good conversation can develop a cohesiveness in the family. I was seeing the immense importance of the homemaker. There is certainly a lot of scut work involved, it does lack glamour, but it is a unique employment for giving to others.

The notion of the male ego was something new for me. Of course I had one. Every male has one. Society requires that males have them. Nature turns a girl into a woman; society makes a boy into a man. The newness for me was the realization that I had a male ego, i.e., something females didn't have. What was this thing? What is the nature of my ego and what does it do?

The answers came from my involvement at the Women's Center. By observing the behavior of those adult women, I could compare my feelings and attitudes for any given situation with their actions, reactions, and verbalizations. I saw that what those women were doing was to behave responsibly: to listen to the other person, to make an effort to accommodate someone else's point of view, to achieve a solution or to set a course of action that would lead to the goal. The male ego tends to take the position that says *do it my way*. The male ego is capable creating dysfunctional situations in a meeting in order to do battle with someone else's position, or whatever it takes to *proclaim himself the leader*. When I became aware of all that, I began to divest myself of those aggressive, do-it-my-way tactics and adopt the female way of interacting. I discovered that it worked better for me, even if I was presenting myself as a male. One might call it a "being reasonable" tactic.

I had an unexpected opportunity, then, to continue my growth into womanhood even though I was living as a male. It was made easy because everyone else in the house was female and they couldn't tell what I was doing. I just fitted in a little more comfortably that anyone would have guessed. The wildest part of it is that if I behaved that way, everyone thought I was powerful because I did not have to *act* aggressively.

An old colleague of Tom's had gone into the educational consulting business a few years earlier. He called me one day, said he heard I was at loose ends, and would I care to help him do some work. I took one assignment, then another, and finally made the decision to work full time for him. I resigned from the school district in October.

In November, the divorce from Helen was settled. I got my half of the net, and all of the debts. She had a fine lawyer. I also had child support and spousal support payments to make. Only son #3 was under eighteen, and the support was for a short time. By the time I paid off the bills, made cash contributions, and assigned a piece of property to my son, I had one thousand dollars for myself. Somebody screwed up somewhere to let me have that much. The house had sold for $47,500 and I cashed in my teacher's retirement which came to over $18,000. To have as much as $1 K was some consolation prize.

I boasted this fact to Annie. Her response was that we should go on a cruise. I thought that was a splendid idea, but I could not pay for her. She got a loan from the credit union and made reservations for us on the *Sun Princess*, subsequently called the Love Boat on TV.

I was getting restless being a good boy. I needed to find a way for Sally to come alive once in awhile. My solution was to rent a tiny office space in a small shopping center. It rented for $55 per month. That was a lot cheaper than motels. I moved a lot of my girl clothes and the other necessities for transformation there along with the legitimate props of an educational consultant. Even though I had only one client-the friend I worked for-I set up a business, complete with telephone, checking account, business license, business cards, stationery, and retained a secretarial service, to take calls, do correspondence, etc. My short term plan was to accommodate Sally, and possibly build a business for myself. There was also the possibility I could eventually get Sally to do some of the work. It was fantasy, but why not?

In early January, I received a phone call from Gordon, a man Tom worked with at The American Institutes for Research in Palo Alto in 1970. He had his Ph.D. in mathematics from Stanford. He called to ask if I would be interested in doing some work for him. I said that I would like to talk about it. We set a time for the next day.

I was there in my blue jeans and sport shirt, the required uniform for that think tank. Gordon met me at the reception desk and escorted me back to his office. It overlooked a small forest of oak trees. He explained the nature of the project he had to do.

told me of the people he had already hired, the role he wanted me to play, and asked if I would do it.

What happened next is a prime example of what I mean when I say that I have more guts than brains. I told Gordon that I was very much interested in the job, but there was a letter I wanted him to read. I reached for my wallet, extracted The Letter, and said that I had to go to the men's room and would be right back.

When I returned to his office, Gordon was staring out his window as though he were watching the Second Coming, holding my letter between thumb and forefinger. Motionless. Silent. I was sure I had blown it this time. Then he slowly turned toward me, carefully folded The Letter, handed it back with a poker face, and said, "I just discovered that I have one more interview to conduct, Tom. I hope this does not inconvenience you too much." I said, "No, it doesn't, Gordon." Without any trace of a smile, he asked if I knew how to get in touch with Sally. I said I thought so. He wondered if she could be notified to come for an interview at two o'clock that day. I said that I thought that would certainly be possible.

At 2:00 p.m. Sally, in sweater and skirt, reported to the same receptionist, was announced, and Gordon came out to greet me. It was as though we had never met. Who is this guy? I decided to play my part, taking cues from him. We walked back to his office and had the same interview all over again, except for the ending. When it was obviously time for a summation, he said that he had planned to offer the job to an old friend and former colleague, but that I had the exact qualifications he was looking for, and that I could have the job if I wanted it.

I told him that I would accept. Then I dropped the role playing and asked if he knew how happy I was. He smiled a very broad smile and made the grandest speech I ever heard, "What I am doing, Sally, is hiring a *mind*. How that mind comes packaged is of no consequence to me."

The next day I telephoned my friend to say that I would not be in a position to do any more assignments for him. He was not happy with that news. He said that the business was really beginning to take off and that he saw a great future for me in it. There was no way I could just end it there. I told him about Sally, my hopes, aspirations, and the opportunity at A.I.R. I even told him what Gordon had said about hiring a mind. After a short pause, he slowly said that he wished he could feel that way. The new job was scheduled to begin in February 1975, just two days after the end of the cruise to the Mexican Rivera.

On my way back to my office to change, I had a few things to think about. I would have to tell Annie. But she will not want to hear anything about the job, no matter how estatic I feel about the opportunity. Just the facts, ma'am. I counted on my fingers to verify that my additional six-month obligation would be honored. Then I had a lot of logistics to work out. I had my plan complete before I got back to my office.

I changed clothes, returned home to cook dinner, and later said to Annie, "Guess what happened at the office today."

Well, it was not said quite that way, but I did tell her. And I suggested that she might want to consider cancelling the cruise. Then I got my second big surprise for the day. She said that no way did she want to cancel the cruise. We would go, have a blast, enjoy the whole thing immensely, return home, and then I could go away if that was what I wanted to do.

And it worked out just that way.

In mid-February, Sally reported for work at 9:00 a.m. My mind was reeling due to the frantic moves of the last two days. I had rented an apartment in Pacifica before we left for Mexico. I had to move, leaving Los Gatos as Tom, arriving in Pacifica as Sally. I was getting good at these games; they were a challenge, they were fun, but tiring.

Not until that first morning at work did I come to grips with the reality of what I was doing. What if some of the old timers recognized me from five years ago when Tom worked there? What if someone says they doubt that I am a woman? What if some other thing goes wrong and I have to leave before I can get started?

There you go again with your self-doubts. Be cool. Act like you belong. Smile, be warm, friendly, and gracious.

Okay.

I was introduced to Jeri and Barbara and told that we three were going to share the same office. Gordon left, saying that we should not forget the reception for new employees at 10:00 in the conference room.

The way those two young women fired questions at me was like being interviewed simultaneously by Mike Wallace and Howard Cosell. I did my best to answer honestly, but it was tough. They were lovely women, and they just wanted to be friends. Was I married? Did I have any children? Did I sew or do needlepoint? I think it took them less than five minutes to determine that I was "special," not really a female. They had no problem with that. To them I was a woman, a person of the female persuasion, anyway. We became friends immediately.

At the reception, all of us new people were introduced to the entire company. I was presented by Gordon to everyone as the senior editor for the career education rewrite project. A lot of eyeballs snapped, and those belonged to the other eight women in "my" group.

As I looked around the room, I saw four people that I had worked with five years ago when Tom was a teacher on loan from my school district. There was no flicker of recognition. One of those four was a senior member of the company, and in charge of the massive project I had worked on. I had been a coordinator as well as a writer, and my duties included a planning meeting with him every morning for a year. He never did recognize me.

Dewey was a young Ph.D. in psychology, specializing in tests and measurements. I remembered him as being a self-styled stud. I wondered if he was going to check me out. He was never particular about who he tried to make out with. I trembled at the thought.

Mary, the resource librarian, was the personification of a bookworm. Her office was certainly ample for her needs, except for the books. They were stacked waist-high everywhere. Only two narrow trails existed. One to her desk, the other to a visitor's chair. I think her boss made regular visits to ensure that the trail was always open. She did not recognize me either.

Caroline was the last one that I saw. She and Tom had many arguments years ago. She was the editor-in-chief for all the copy written for that huge project. Everything in print had to be signed off by her. I can appreciate accuracy as much as anyone else, but Caroline used to cavil at everything. I favored *Words Into Type* as the authority for proper usage, punctuation, and such. She claimed that *The Chicago Manual of Style* was the bible. I felt sure that she would recognize me, but no, not her either.

The current project consisted of rewriting seventeen student books, their accompanying teacher manuals, and the test booklets. The theme was career education, and the age group was primary grades through senior high school. There were nine of us women to do the job. We had six months to get it done.

Before lunch that first day, Jeri introduced me to all the members of the group in their various offices. I knew that she knew my true gender, and I figured that she knew that I knew she knew. But there had been no time to verbally acknowledge any of that before she was told by Gordon to take me to the other offices to meet the rest of the team.

I had felt just a little awkward all morning. I was a lot bigger than everyone else. And there was the perennial problem of clothing. I needed a lot of standard female dress to come off as a female. I wore a sweater, a skirt, pantyhose, sandals with a heel, full cosmetics, etc. They wore denims, keds, no makeup, minimal care of the hair.

By the end of the day, I had met everyone in my group, had reviewed the total project, and reorganized the assignments. I felt comfortable doing that right away because I needed to stake my claim as leader, and to let everyone know that there was organization within our group. During lunch it occurred to me that as a male I had been a leader of men. As a male I had been a leader of women. Now I was a woman being a leader of women. Would there be any differences? Probably, I thought, based on my experiences at the Women's Center. I vowed to tread softly in order to observe and assimilate their reactions to my moves. I could not afford to alienate anyone on this first day, especially. I counted on my instincts to guide me. My expectation was that if I really was a woman, I would know how to play my cards just right. I was and I did.

My strategy was to let them know that my appointment was based on my M.A. degree plus some experience. I did not ask for the leadership role, but there it was. I needed their cooperation so that we all could look good. They understood. I did not have to draw pictures for *that* group. I asked a lot of questions about the project that they had begun work on a few weeks earlier. I redoubled my efforts to *listen* with my eyes as well as my ears. It seemed to be a reasonable thing to do. I made decisions when I knew I had consensus. I would never have gotten away with that style in the Navy. But I wasn't at sea anymore. Oh, I might have been *adrift* once in awhile . . .

In a few days everyone was feeling warm and comfortable with each other. That was when the humor started. Jeanette had a sense of the ridiculous that matched my own. Because work like that can become deadly, the humor was a necessity. Sometimes we told jokes or stories, other times we were silly. It felt so good for me to be a part of this group of smart ladies who were first-rate writers, damned good workers, and clever enough to be funny when the situation called for it.

After a few days, Jeri, Barbara, and I had a heart-to-heart talk about me. They had talked it over. Their conclusion was that they were the only two that knew I was new at being a woman. The others had said nothing to them. They decided to keep the information to themselves, let me be what I wanted to be, and to extend friendship to me in every way. My eyes misted and my voice quivered as I tried to say thanks. They jumped up from their chairs and put their arms around me and said that I must be going through a huge adjustment period. Anything they could do for me, I had only to ask.

It was Barbara who said that she did not know why anyone would choose to become a woman. I said that I would explain it to her as soon as I knew myself. Then I said that perhaps it was a better, more civilized sex than male. There was a wider range of behaviors and emotions open to women. "Like this moment we are having now. Men can't do this hugging and feel the warm fuzzies we three feel for each other." They accepted that as a start towards a rationale. Soon I was privy to a lot of personal information that no man would ever hear from a woman. I began to develop a new understanding of a woman's place in the office, in a marriage, in the attempt to secure a marriage, and in not expecting to have a marriage.

The months passed a little faster than I wanted them to. In early May I decided that I wanted to move from Pacifica to Foster City. That move enabled me to invite my colleagues to come for dinner. First I invited Barbara and Jeri. We had a fine evening with more serious talk than at the office. There were no interruptions, and we could follow topics at length. We also had our silly moments. There was also time for comparing notes on our observations of some of the company's leadership. Some people might call that gossiping.

That was when I told them about my involvement with the project I had worked on years ago at A.I.R. They didn't know that I had been there before. Naturally, they wanted to know who had recognized me, and what did they say. They thought it was funny that no one did. Then they wanted to know if I thought those people were the same as before, or had they changed. I told them that the only difference I could see was that men interact with men differently than they do with women. Take Dewey, for example. Around the men, he would come on strong and make sure they knew he was the king of tests and measurements. Around the ladies, he was like a teenage kid trying to flirt or to show off so that we would all think he was wonderful. Jeri and Barbara were fascinated. They thought he was an airhead, a political appointment to the staff. I assured them he was a hot operator in his specialty, and that he could always win his way in any meeting. I pointed out that he had a lot of articles published.

It was a good exchange of information for me: the woman's view of men and other women; my own view of men and (now) other women, as well as how I saw things when I was a male.

Hettie was a graduate student at Stanford. She was assigned to the project, but her hours were irregular. She and I were working past five o'clock one day as the custodians were starting their evening cleanup. One of the guys was kind of a loudmouth, with not a whole lot of common sense. It was getting warm in early April and I wore a sleeveless cotton shift to work that day. The guy came in to empty our wastebaskets. I got up and went to the ladies' room. When I came back, Hettie was fuming. I asked what was wrong. She said that clown asked her if Sally was really a man. *Ouch!* I asked what she said to him. She said that she told him that Sally was a real lady, a real woman, and too smart to be a man. I said that I wondered why he would ask such a thing. She said that he said my arms were too big for a woman. I asked her what she thought, and she told me to not worry about that creep. I had passed muster with her.

In May I began to worry about the next job. The funds for this project and the calendar would run out by the end of July. Would there be any new work there, or would I have to go somewhere else? By now we had the reputation for being fine workers...

as a group and as individuals. If there was something, we would be hired for it. I could tell that Gordon was getting concerned for us. He wasn't too sure about his own future there, but he did have offers elsewhere. A doctor of mathematics who wants to be involved in education is a rare bird.

One time I invited Gordon and his wife to my place for an afternoon and dinner. They came with bottles of champagne. I had bottles of champagne. We really had a fine evening. Cora was an artistic soul. She was involved with theater, with dance, with string quartets, and most recently with *avant garde* films. She was bright and entertaining, but never allowed herself to dominate the conversation. I was fascinated just listening to her, but she kept pulling me back into the conversation. Gordon was silent in her presence. She and I had our own dialog. Of course she knew my history, but had never met the other me. We talked colors and fabrics. She suggested alternate hair styles for me. I told her of the various hair-dos I had tried and what they did for me. I asked her about my style of dressing: What did she think my style should be? She had a lot of ideas, but she was really suggesting her style for me. No matter.

They came at 3:00 p.m. and left around midnight. They enjoyed the *cordon bleu* I had cooked. We all hugged and said goodbye. It made me feel so good when she told me that I really was a woman.

One of the special features of living in Foster City was the lagoon system. Virtually everyone lived in sight of the water, if not directly alongside it. My apartment was less than twenty feet from the salt water. I had my El Toro, a sailboat just under eight feet long. No jib, just a mainsail that made it easy for one person to handle. The boat was about the only object I got from the divorce.

The warm weather in May was an invitation to sail. One afternoon after work, I got home, changed into shorts and T-shirt, grabbed two cans of beer, and rigged the tiny vessel for a cooling and restorative cruise around the waterways. The wind was a bit gusty, and I was feeling gutsy. Working on my first beer, I ran with the wind to the center of the main lagoon. Ah! Peace and tranquillity. Then I decided to tack toward one of the channels that leads to other lagoons. There was only one other sailor, and he was diligently rowing what looked to be a punt... a small, rectangular, flat-bottom craft perhaps ten feet long. Poor baby, I thought as I skimmed the surface, starting to come about for my tack. Too bad he cannot enjoy the exhilaration of canvas instead of those oars. Handling the sheet, the rope that controls the angle of the boom (therefore the sail), was a chore in that wind. Foolishly, I did something I had never done before: I wrapped the sheet around my left hand several times to make sure it would not slip. I have to sail close to the wind or it isn't much fun. However, the consequences of that combination of decisions caused me to capsize.

I knew what hypothermia was, but I had never experienced it before. I could not breathe. It was a terrifying experience. If that were not enough, my boat would not sink, but it would not serve as much support, either. Zero buoyancy, I suppose. My first thoughts were about breathing: It seemed I could only inhale, and there is a limit to that. Exhaling was impossible. My second thought was my wig: Where is it? I was not too sure I wanted to go back to shore without it on. I soon found it undulating alongside my floatation cushion. As I was putting it back on, I realized I was breathing full-cycle again. With breath and a wig, I knew I could make it to shore. I grabbed a line and started to swim back to the closest point of land, towing my vessel with the line over my shoulder and wrapped around my chest. I had earned letters in swimming and water polo in high school, and even though I was a smoker of non-filter cigarettes, I knew I had the endurance to make it. About the time of this resolve, I heard a very loud, "Ahoy!" about ten feet away. It was the man in the punt. He was most gracious and solicitous. He wanted to help. I asked if he would tow my boat back. He did and I swam the rest of the way in my very best breaststroke, interrupting the rhythm only to push my wig back on from time to time.

Oddly enough, I got back to my dock before he did. As he tied up, I came back out wearing a dry terry shift, kept the soggy misshapen wig on for realism, and greeted my hero. I never had a hero before. It was a nice feeling. We drank a couple of beers and talked a bit. He was from Lubbock, Texas, and was out here visiting his sister and husband. Cripes! I've been in this scenario before. I was a little relieved when he said that he was going back to Texas in two days.

The most memorable evening I had in that apartment was the occasion when all nine of us writers had dinner. I insisted on a sit-down dinner that I would prepare. It was just a huge pot of spaghetti, tossed green salad, and garlic bread. And wine. Lots of wine. They chipped in and bought me the largest fuchsia plant I ever saw.

I had a table that was about twenty inches high and three feet wide and deep. The top was hinged and could unfold to three feet by six feet. Plenty of room. We had to sit on the floor, but that was the kind of dinner party I wanted to have. Informal. That was the evening I learned that women can have wild dinner parties and have a lot of fun by themselves. We told stories, we told anecdotes from our pasts, we listened to music, we stuffed ourselves with food and wine, we laughed a lot. And all at the same time. I felt a comradeship developing that surpassed the bonds created at the office. I could see that I fitted in this gender. I would not be losing a thing by not being male again and missing those stag parties. Hen parties could be even better. Specifically, I noticed that women do not try for the one-upmanship games that men do. Women will make an effort to add to someone else's joke or statement, not try to outdo the other.

The metaphor that comes to mind is that men's conduct at parties is like they were playing football to score points. Women act like they were playing volleyball, and maintaining the volley was more important than scoring points.

It was also during this time that one of the students in my plumbing and electrical repair class at the Women's Center called me at work one day. She wanted to know if I would teach the course to her Girl Scout troop. My office mates were amused by that. I could tell that they very much approved of the idea. It was good for me and it was good for the girls.

The other major activity during this time at A.I.R. was the reactivation of my participation in the Gender Clinic at Stanford Hospital. I was permitted to go to the monthly meetings with no disruption to my work. The greatest boon from attending the meetings, however, was to reconnect with Steffie. Some months earlier she said she was going to work a special deal that I might be interested in.

The deal, it turned out was with the Veterans Hospital in Palo Alto. She knew her way around in that place because she had administered one in another state in another gender. What we vets could get by way of service there was general medical care, but no sex-change surgery. The most important benefit was to get psychiatric counselling. At $85 per hour back then, free shrink time was a true blessing. Steffie took me there one day, got me signed up as an outpatient, and helped me to schedule my first appointment.

From 1975 to 1980 I had counsel from a psychiatrist, psychiatric interns, Masters in Social Work, and psychologists. They have their own pecking order, but the one that I felt closest to was an M.S.W. Sandy was a real love. She cared a lot about me. She was a tough lady if she thought I was working a game on her. In fact, I had to reread Eric Berne's book, *Games People Play*, so that I would be able to watch out for the games I had a tendency to play-unintentionally, of course. She helped me get over the game playing, which was a major achievement.

I attended those sessions once a week, then twice a month for a long time afterwards. Those women, regardless of rank were absolutely wonderful. There was only one male therapist I saw. After three sessions, he told me that he could not see me anymore. He said that it bothered him too much to see a man want to become a woman. I think that males have a tough time with that phenomenon. He was one. I felt sorry for distressing him, and said so. I suppose that therapists are entitled to their biases, too.

In June I realized that my tastes in apartment living were overloading my capacity to pay. I had to leave Foster City and find another place with lower rent.

I found a lovely garden apartment in Santa Clara, close to the highway system, but removed enough to seem rural. It was the first apartment I ever had with a fireplace. I love open fires, but the season then warranted air conditioners. One more move. Maybe I could get a job with a van lines company next time I am out of work.

That came in early August. The project was complete, the budget was drained, and the party was over. And it looked like my life was over, too. There was a lot of effort being made to get me another job. The company looked for me, my friends looked, and I certainly looked. I wanted to get another job as Sally, but overriding that desire was the need for a job to get money for food and shelter.

Gordon assumed some responsibility for me even though I assured him he was not obliged to do anything. I was so grateful to him for hiring me in the first place. I owed him, he did not owe me. His view was that I was a woman on my way out of a job. It was a fascinating situation; he had worked with Tom for over a year a long time ago, but for the last six months he knew me as a female, and that was what I was to him. And I had begun to see him, and all other males, as the opposite sex. Gordon was small in size for a male, but he was a giant in brain power and compassion. I let myself feel protected by him. I liked the feel of it. Somebody wanted to take care of "little Nell."...

Two days after I left, a parcel arrived at my apartment. It contained copies of the books I had rewritten. Each of the four had my name as author. Manuals and test booklets too. That was Gordon's doing. He wanted to make sure each of us got full credit for our work. None of us expected that we would get our names printed. Naturally, I still have them.

The next day Gordon called to say that he knew my apartment rent was coming due soon, and asked if I had plans for that event. I said I did not, and that I had been sending out resumes under both names, expecting to double my chances for employment. He said that he had a friend in the Los Gatos hills who lived in a big house all alone. He said he would call his friend to see if it would be acceptable for me to move in for a time. I said that would be wonderful.

Gordon called back that evening to say that he spoke with his friend Timothy, and he would consider taking me in for a short term. I would have to be interviewed. Gordon also said that Timothy was an unusual young man, and his guess was that I had better present myself as Tom, otherwise . . .

No problem. I did not like the idea, but I liked sleeping in the streets even less.

Chapter 12

The meeting with Timothy was scheduled for an early afternoon. I had to dress as Tom, look as casual as I could, and sneak out of Sally's apartment when I thought no one was looking.

I followed the directions that Gordon had given me. By the time I got there I thought I was lost. Hidden Hill, it was called. I imagined it to be just a plain mound, but the hill was actually hidden. It was like a large bump in the middle of a number of other hills.

I rang the bell. No answer. Rang it again. Still no answer. Was I being stood up?

I decided to walk around the place. I saw a young man, leaning over a fence, in communication with a goat. Heidi, I learned later, was the neighbor's pet, and Timothy had developed a fondness for her. I felt like an intruder. I intruded anyway.

We shook hands. I could tell right off that Timothy was not a salesman, not a fraternity man, but perhaps a gentle person, more interested in esoteric ideas than anything else. We moved to a small private garden, sat at a distance from each other on a stone bench. It was a cool, secluded place overlooking the swimming pool. I could tell that he was uneasy with me. People usually like me. I learned later that I reminded him of his father, not in likeness, but in age and style of dress. My scraggly hair saved me from looking like Mr. 1947, which would have stopped the interview cold.

After a confused fifteen minutes or so, he told me that he was reluctant to take me. I pressed for a reason. He said that he lived an unusual lifestyle, that I was from a different world, and that since I had no money, how did I expect to pay him? *Well*!

I was aware of the notion that there are *stated* reasons and *real* reasons. I was not convinced I heard a real reason. I decided to take a chance with the supplicant role. If he cared as much about people as that goat, I should have no problem. It worked.

I began moving my things that day. I returned to my apartment, grabbed as much as would fit in the Pinto, and drove back to unload. Timothy merely watched at a distance. A half hour later I was carrying my second load into the space I was allocated when he approached me with a direct question. "Why do you have all those women's clothes?" Oops!

I countered by asking why was he looking at my things. His response was that he went through my stuff because he wanted to know more about the person who was moving into his home. I could see his point, but I did not want to let him know about Sally right away. Oh, well. So I told him. Gently, but without hesitation, without apology, and with as much dignity as I could muster.

He had a problem believing me. I could see a definite change in his facial expression. My thought was that everything was going to be all right. I pressed on by opening my wallet and showing him The Letter. He read it, handed it back saying, "I don't believe this." I pulled out my driver's license and showed it to him. He stared at it a full minute. Then he said he believed it, but didn't believe it. I asked if he would like to meet Sally in person. He said that he would. I did a quick mental inventory of the things I had brought already, and said that after my next trip, I would let him meet the other me.

It was to be my last trip for that day, anyway. I had not yet begun to move any furniture or kitchen stuff. I was trying to avoid renting a truck, but it seemed I would have to. The problem was that to rent a truck, I would have to show a driver's license and a credit card. Those were all in Sally's name. It was a good thing that I would audition for Tim that evening. I would be out of the closet before I actually got in it.

As I came down the staircase, Tim looked up from his book and stared. Open mouth, too. By the time I walked into the room, he was standing, smiling, and said his favorite line, "I don't believe it."... I told him he could believe it, and that he could please find a glass of wine for a lady.

We sat at the eight-foot dinner table, drank wine, smoked cigarettes, and began a friendship that has lasted ever since. There were a million things to talk about, most of them had to wait for later. We quickly established that I was not his father. Then we got into things like I am looking for work under either name, and I do expect to get something soon, foods we both like, music we both like, and a lot of other getting-to-know-you topics. I put in my bid to do the cooking. He said he never cooked anything. I could see that he never cleaned anything either. I told him I would clean the house, too. His eyes were shining now.

We went to the local supermarket, bought some things, and went back home. I cooked a meal that set my place in his heart.

Over strong black coffee and a decent brandy, we started on more serious conversation. He told me about his job. He was an orderly at the county hospital on the graveyard shift in the emergency room. That meant that he was confronted with any and all disasters that happened late at night or early in the morning. I asked how he came by that job. He said that he had been promoted out of the burn unit. I asked how he got that job. He said that he had been a conscientious objector during the Viet Nam war. He told his draft board that he did not want to kill anybody. They told him to find a job in a hospital and they would leave him alone. I asked him why he felt that way about military service. (See how I can handle questions?) His answer to that was that he had just gotten his master's degree in ethics from the University of Santa Clara. That explained a lot.

The time was creeping up on ten o'clock. He said he had to get ready for work. I washed the dishes while he shaved and showered. I was suddenly aware of the domestic scene that was being played here. I was even more aware of the new feelings stirring in me: *I was feeling like a wife.*

I liked that. Tim came out of the bathroom. He was clean shaven around the neck. He had a wonderful beard and mustache. He smelled of Old Spice. I asked if he were going on a date or to work. He said that he believed that he needed to bring a certain something to the unit. He smiled and started out the door. I asked if he would like a breakfast when he came home. He really had to think about it. Then he said that he didn't know, that he never ate at that time, and not to plan on him for breakfast.

I read for awhile, then went upstairs, made up my bed, undressed, and took a long hot shower. When I came out, I creamed my face, put on a fresh nightgown, and rearranged a few things in my closet. All the male stuff went to the rear. Then I thought that as long as I had made my bed, I may as well lie in it.

I woke about seven, saw lots of daylight, and only the birds were making any sound. I mused over the situation I found myself in. Yesterday at this time I was nervous about finding a place to live, detesting the idea of returning to male status, and wondering what was going to happen next. Now it seemed I had found a new friend, I was living in a house that was really a chalet, in the most expensive neighborhood on the peninsula, and I could be *me!* More than that, I could develop and extend *me* into *the woman of the house*. Would I want that? Is the Pope a Catholic?

As I stretched, the significance of 7:00 a.m. popped into my head: Timothy was just getting off work now. I went downstairs, glad that I had done the dishes the night before, and got the coffee going. Looking in the ancient refrigerator, I extracted the eggs, bacon, and juice we had bought the night before. I scrubbed some potatoes, made home fries, had the bacon, eggs, and toast in the ready position. By that time the coffee was ready. I poured a cup and took it outside, wearing my nightgown and robe. And wig, of course. Sally *always* wore a wig.

I was enjoying the nascent warmth of the early morning, wondering what the poor folks were doing, when I heard Tim wending his way up the hill. I scooted back inside to pour his coffee. When he came in, he looked worn to a frazzle. I handed him the coffee. He said thanks, put it down, and reached for the tequila bottle. He belted down two shots right away. Then he sat down at the table, pulling the coffee toward him. I asked if he would like breakfast. He looked up at me. I saw the tears running down his face. He just stared at me, as though he wondered who I was. Or maybe he wondered who *he* was. Then he simply said in a very hollow voice, "She died."

Without thinking, I ran to him, put my arms around his shoulders, and did my best to comfort him. I could see why this sensitive young man, twenty years my junior, walked into the house at 7:30 a.m. and reached for the bottle. His job was to work with a trauma team to save lives as best they could. It turned out that the woman who died was in an automobile accident. The police had also brought in the drunk driver who caused the accident. He had to be treated for cuts and scrapes.

We talked it out for nearly a half hour. Suddenly he shuddered, seemed to come into the present, and asked what smelled so good. I told him what was on the menu. We ate. He ate like a logger.

After breakfast he went up to his room, changed clothes to shorts only, in anticipation of the hot day, and went out to talk with Heidi.

I washed the dishes and tidied up the kitchen. One more cup of coffee left in the pot. I poured it and sat at the table, alone, thinking. Was I in the middle of a dream? Was all this really happening? No fantasy of mine ever conjured a situation like this. I was still in my first twenty-four hours, and already I had made a connection with one of the sweetest men I had ever met. I had to allow that I had not been interested in sweet men for very long. I was just asking for a place to stay and I found a clear and present need for a woman in this house. I had wanted to be a woman and here was my chance to live the role, in spades. It was several weeks before I became aware of the full extent of the need.

Tim was going through a lot in his life. I will not try to say what that was because it was, and is, his business. The situation called for patience on my part. The role of woman of the house continued, but the role blurred into mother, wife, sister. Not in turn, but an amalgam of the three. There was never any sex or talk of sex with us. We might touch; and there would be kisses, but no passion. Only expressions of fondness and closeness.

In the meantime, reality kept shrieking in my brain: get a job, dummy! It was like waking up on a very cold morning in a very cold house with only a nose poking out of a very warm and cozy bed. Get up, get up! Has that ever happened to you?

Tom had been making calls to old friends announcing my presence and availability. I looked in the papers. I went to the college placement offices. "Nothing right now" was the response from every avenue I could think of. Because I had not yet changed my ID back to male, I went to the state employment office as Sally. No jobs, but there was unemployment insurance money for me. Not much, because I had worked as a contributing member only six months. The checks started to come. I could buy the food, but Tim would not let me pay rent. He valued my services and said they were worth a lot more than the rent he would have charged. That was nice to hear.

My network was seemingly played out. I even called my old friend that I used to work for before I went to A.I.R. He was pleasant, but said that the others in the staff were definitely against me now, regardless of what clothes I wore. Part of the dues I had to pay, I suppose.

Eventually, I called Annie just to say hello. She was cool, but not angry. We had a reasonable conversation. She had been moving on with her life. Yes, she had been seeing someone else. A strange sensation visited me when I thought of her with another man. My own manhood was not dead, but it was not getting any exercise either. My first reaction was a surge of jealousy. In a split second, it turned to something else. I have no term for it, but it included happiness for her, a release for me of any obligation to resume manhood, almost a permission to stay as a woman. She did not seem to need or want me anymore. Whatever the term... if there is one, it was bittersweet. We rambled on. I told her about the new residence I had, the young man who took me in, and my efforts to get a job. She wanted to know which identity was doing the looking. I told her that both of my selves were. She said she had to hang up as her oldest daughter had just come in. She invited me to call again sometime.

September is a nice month in Santa Clara Valley. The weather becomes changeable, offering a cool day now and then. One even gets a hint of fall. Fall meant school was starting up again. I thought of those nice people I used to work with in the school district, and how they must be feeling overjoyed to start one more year with the youth of their community. I was missing out on those exciting faculty meetings that never got anywhere. What a relief! Then it occurred to me that since I had no taste for returning to the ranks of the teachers, how about being a student? Wild!

I read the flyer from West Valley College and found an ideal class: Italian Cooking. The class was scheduled for Saturdays, 9 a.m. to noon. The men were to wear white trousers, jacket, and a chef's hat. The women were to wear a white dress, white shoes, and a hair net. I signed up for the class, was accepted, and went out to buy a white dress.

Strange how the little things can seem so exciting. Every Saturday morning for a semester, Sally showed up for the class. It was taught by the head cook at the original Original Joe's restaurant in San Jose. We were to learn by doing. He divided us, every week, into the salad makers, pasta people, main dish cooks, and the dessert makers. We rotated through those roles. My classmates were insurance salesmen, bankers, an airline pilot, secretaries, and cafeteria workers doing in-service training. We had fun. I assumed they accepted me as a real woman. I was certainly treated as one. We started doing things right after a quick overview. The instructor set us to our tasks, and he was in constant motion around that large kitchen. He gave more instruction as we worked. He joked with us. We had to rush to meet everyone else's schedule. By 11:30, dinner was served. We all gathered around the huge dining table and ate what we had prepared. Semi-revolting squid at 9:30 became a truly delightful calamari by noontime. He critiqued our work as we ate. Then we did some self-critiques as he ate. It was a wonderful experience. Of course, I still have the little paperback cookbook we used. I shared a lot of that stuff with Tim. By the end of September, he said his pants didn't fit anymore. I was gaining, too. It was all right for him to add pounds because he needed it. I did not.

In early October, Jim called to say that they were getting overloaded at Contemporary Ideas, and could I come to help out? Sure, Jim. I can spare the time. This was a novel situation. Seven years earlier, Jim came to my math classroom as a student teacher from San Jose State. He was really a geography major with a math minor. He had to do student teaching in both fields to get his credential. He was not excited at the prospect of teaching math to those kids. I gave him some slack, let him watch me for as long as he wanted, and finally he said he was ready. And he was. Once he got started at the chalkboard he was hooked. It happens a lot. People think it is a terrifying job to stand up in front of a class and teach a lesson. But a transformation occurs. The timid become hams. It is hard to stop them. But Jim was special. In addition to being a good teacher, he had fallen in love with mathematics. By the end of the semester, he asked if he could get a job at my school. It was easy for me to get his application accepted.

We were colleagues for a few years, then he and Dave, another math teacher, went into the publishing business. They formed their own company. They struggled for a few years before they got established. Their wives were teachers in the district, so there was financial backing.

At the time of his call to me, his company had entered into a contract with Prentice-Hall Learning Systems, Inc. It was the only Prentice-Hall subsidiary outside New Jersey. The president had great plans that called for an enormous number of workbooks to be produced in the next six months. I was asked to help in some way.

The other thing about Jim was that he and Sally had become friends. First Jim, then his wife, Jean. We three were pals, and took turns serving dinner parties. Every once in awhile, Jean and I would have our own private dinners.

Naturally, when Jim called me to offer the job, I asked if Sally could do it. He was genuinely sorry, but the others would not understand, and so forth. I was ready to accept a job on any terms.

On my first day, Tim and I passed in the driveway. He was a little late that day, and I had to leave early. He was not happy to see Tom. He understood, but didn't like it. It was to be months before I understood what Sally meant to him.

I found the office. Dave was there. He shook my hand and welcomed me to the company. Then he showed me where I was to sit and what I was supposed to do. I got my coffee, an ashtray, and sat down to address the envelopes using a commercial mail list of school districts. I asked why he did not buy the pre-printed, pressure sensitive labels and just stick them on. Before he could answer, Jim came in, smiling. We all chatted for a while, then I continued to address envelopes. Later, I could hear them arguing about something in their executive offices.

At lunch, Jim told me that he and Dave went round and round about what my duties were to be. I was to do whatever I was told to do, according to Dave. Jim said he wanted me to start editing. They made a compromise. Then Jim told me Dave was angry at me for asking about the pre-printed labels. I asked what was wrong with that? He said that Dave did not think of it himself. That told me a lot about how that job was going to go.

Within a week, I was editing full time. Within a month, I was learning about the printing process from the printer. That opportunity came about by accident. It was the beginning of a new career path for me, although I did not recognize it as such at the time. I learned that I had a talent for production.

The atmosphere back at Hidden Hill was not as gay and light hearted. Tim seemed to think a change was coming over me. He was right. I was getting caught up in my job.

An attendant feature was the resurrection of my male ego. I knew it was happening. I had to have it to survive in my job, and it was not easy to shut it off, if on my return home at night I was still fuming over some dumb thing at the office. I would have to do something about that. I did not want to lose the magic that had been on Hidden Hill since my arrival.

One thing I would do was to try to cleanse my head before I got home. A second thing was to make more of the weekends: special dinners, invite Tim's friends, invite my friends, go out, and the like.

On my next telephone call to Annie, I told her about my new job. She expressed approval, but asked how I could work for those two guys. I said that as long as they paid me on time, I would find it easy enough. As the conversation continued, I sensed a warmth returning in her voice. Finally I asked if I could stop by sometime to visit. She said that the girls would like to see me again. And that was the beginning of our return to a relationship.

As Christmas drew near, the Los Gatos community experienced the novelty of snow. Tim arrived home that morning just before the road to Hidden Hill became unusable. My assessment was that it was too hazardous for me to try to drive to work. I telephoned the office to report my distressing circumstances. Jim answered and said I should not risk it.

Tim and I built a raging fire in the great stone fireplace. He carried in the wood as I slipped into something more appropriate for the occasion. I returned to the nightgown and long robe I had taken off not half an hour before.

We were like a couple of kids. Neither one of us had grown up in snow country. We celebrated the novelty by sitting in front of the fire, the stereo playing *The Great Gates of Kiev*, and eating our breakfast. And talking.

We talked a lot about some very serious things in those days. We had been together long enough by then to know there were no closed topics for either of us. He wanted to be accepted into the Jesuits. I used to ask him why. In five months I must have asked a dozen times *why them*. He had a different answer each time. The responses never conflicted with each other. But it was a good question to ask because that conversation always evolved into something else.

His favorite question for me was, "Why aren't you Sally all the time?" My answers covered a narrower field, and almost invariably got us into a rehash of karma and reincarnation, and speculating on what I was really supposed to be doing this time around.

It may not be entirely accurate to say that Tim was a man for all seasons, but he did have a number of talents and special knowledge. I was glad I had not been one of his university professors. He would have made me work awfully hard.

One thing he used to do to calm himself or to sort out one problem or another was to do a watercolor. He had a desk in one corner of that huge living room set up just for doing his painting. He seldom kept anything after he finished it. And he didn't always finish them, which was why I knew they were pretty doodles, mostly. He did a strange one once. It was propped up for me to see when I came home from work one day. Before he went out, he wrote a note to direct my attention to the watercolor. I do not remember the text of the note, but the artwork became indelibly imprinted in my mind. The background was a dark, drab wash. The center was occupied by a head, in profile. What made it so arresting was the head showed two faces, one on each side. One face was male, the other was female. It was me.

He accepted the male version of me, but he was always uncomfortable with it. Too harsh, too goal oriented, too stiff. He could have been right.

By early January, Annie and I were becoming friendly again. We had been out to dinner a few times, visited some of the old places we liked, and very gingerly talked of futures. We were not trying for a joint future. It was too early for that. I think we both wanted to know whether there was room for the other in our separate plans.

In February, I told Tim I was going to move out. I had rented an apartment two doors away from Annie, in another part of town. He was not especially pleased to hear that. I can understand that very easily. I was a truly novel person for him. Because of his religious career plans, he did not want to get involved with a woman. But then again, he wanted the company of a woman for non-sexual reasons, of which there are many. We were not equal in mentality, but I did give him a run for his money on a lot of topics. I liked him and he knew it. I did not want anything from him except the opportunity to act like the lady of the house when I could. And, it is nice to have someone else around. All this would end. Down deep we both knew it would. He didn't give a damn about the male me, but I could not sustain the female me for him *or* myself.

Why not? My only answer to myself at the time was that I had more items on my male agenda to complete. Or, karmicly speaking, perhaps some other people needed to experience the male me for the benefit their karmas.

I remember saying goodbye that February afternoon. I don't know who was working my mouth for me, but I heard myself say to him, "We aren't finished with each other yet."

Chapter 13

The job at Contemporary Ideas was becoming more and more demanding. It seemed that the more we could handle, the more Prentice-Hall Learning Systems gave us to do. I was managing my end of the business well enough to get a compliment now and then. I even got a small raise. That was nice, but there was a price tag for that modicum of success; whether I felt like it or not, I had to reshape my head toward male consciousness in order to do my job. I know that sounds sexist, but wait.

The mind set I started out with was astonishingly similar to the one I had in the Navy. I had a track to run on then that required a clear organizational structure, detailed planning, quick action, a daring move now and then, a set of contingency plans, and always be ready should someone else to make a change in *my* plans. That mental ability enabled me to be a performer in the fleet, and it enabled me to be a performer in making books.

On the face of it, making books does not sound very exciting. Each book required twenty-three separate steps once the manuscript was declared ready for production. Those steps were done by our own staff and outside contractors. I worked with three outside companies: The artist who designed our four-color covers and all the type for the inside covers, the typesetters and paste up people, and the printer.

I was the ringmaster, scorekeeper, editor, and proofreader. When books were ready to give to the printer, I carried the artwork to them, reviewed the print specifications, made some last-minute decisions there, and eventually did the press checks.

It was fun because the diversity and the tempo played to my Gemini characteristics and kept my pulse beating just about right. The downside was that it required me to reinstate a substantial portion of my male ego to do it. The job, as I saw it then, required that I start pumping testosterone as well as spending a lot of off hours thinking about my job. That meant that Sally got crowded out. Making money for food, clothing, and shelter was taking precedence over anything else. Maslow would agree.

There was a problem, however, that I had never had to deal with before: working with women as a male after I had been a woman.

I had been in all the cells of a four-cell matrix that shows all possible combinations of pairing males and females. A male, for example, can relate to another male, or he can relate to a female. Period. A female can have the same two kinds of relationships. I, however, had been a male relating to other males and females, but I had also been a female relating to males and other females.

I was not unique, because all transsexuals experience those four cells as I did. Not unique, but special. The problem I had was in not being able to relate to the women I worked with as another woman. I learned quickly that the one thing I missed the most in not living as a woman anymore was the female-to-female relationship. Another lesson I learned quickly was that there was *no way* I could have that as a male. The women would not let me. I cannot blame them, because how were they to know that I had been one of them? If I flat-out told any of them, the relationship never would have been workable.

I did the next best thing. It took awhile, but it came to me that I would conduct myself as closely as I could to the ideal male that we women used to wish would come along at least once in our working careers. I was pleased that I could do all the stuff that a typical male could do, but I was doing it as a woman would. It worked.

The most important element for that primo relationship was to acknowledge that the woman was a *professional*, first and foremost. The second point was that we were equals. The third point was agreeing that no problem was too big to solve if we worked together. The final point was that if I wanted a woman to do something for me, I would always ask this question: What do you want from me so that you can do your job? Asking that of a woman in the business community was an oblique and muted way of saying that I care a lot about you.

So that formula for success worked wonders for productivity, but especially it got me as close to a woman-to-woman relationship as I could expect as Tom.

The relationship with Annie warmed quickly. She could see that I was working as male and living fifty feet away from her as a male. We had been in love, and we had developed that shorthand in communications that two people in love can have. One does not need a whole lot of words to say something. Nor does one have to be wondering what the other will think if I do such and such. You get tuned in on the other. The proximity of our apartments enabled us to get close again figuratively as well as literally.

Reconnecting with Annie was inevitable. I left her to become Sally. Sally was on the shelf for now, perhaps forever. Tom was back, physically and mentally. Emotionally? Well, more or less. Just because I wore male clothes, spoke the male talk, did the male things, did not mean I had forgotten those incredibly happy months as a woman. For the foreseeable future those memories would have to be just memories.

On a Saturday in March, I said to Annie that we could take a drive somewhere for the day. Just the two of us. Leave in the morning, go somewhere, have lunch, look around, and see what happens. She liked the idea, but asked where we would go. As a male, I was angered by the question because I just wanted to *explore*, to be *spontaneous*, to create a *surprise*. Most men like to do that for women they love. Having been Sally, however, I understood Annie's question to mean: What do I wear? It is very important to the woman to be dressed appropriately for an occasion. I just said that we should wear grubbies-we won't go anywhere fancy.

This was one of dozens of seemingly trivial examples where men and women do not really think on the same wavelength. As a male, it is perfectly understandable to want to surprise the woman with something special. He thinks it will please her. It is also perfectly understandable that the woman wants to dress appropriately so that he will be pleased with her. But it is not a good idea for the woman to ask the male how she should dress. He wouldn't know. She needs some kind of clue, and will figure it out for herself. Neither sex understands the viewpoint of the other, nor is either especially aware that the other sex *has* a different viewpoint.

We got into the car. It was a glorious day. A balmy morning with a gentle easterly wind that promised a hot afternoon in Los Gatos. It was beach weather. As I turned the ignition key, the inspiration came to me to go to Half Moon Bay. I had not been there since my last party weekend before going to boot camp in 1945.

The memories came with a surge. Half Moon Bay had been the beach town for us in Burlingame. As a little kid, I had been there a lot with adults in summer. As a high school kid, it was the place to learn about girl watching and drinking beer. And so forth.

I said to Annie that I could take her to the *very site* where I had learned the rudiments of girl chasing and beer drinking. She said that she thought I was born with those talents. I said no, they had to be learned and be developed through constant exercise. And that Dunes Beach was where the skill was born. She asked where this shrine was located. I said that she would know when we got there.

In less than an hour, we turned off Highway 280 onto State 92 for the winding two-lane drive to the coast. We approached the first intersection in town, and I had my first experience with the concept of a time warp. It was thirty years since I had been there and nothing had changed that I could see. I said that I could not believe this. I had to drive in town a little to see what changes had occurred. Nothing, it turned out. The same three neon signs, the same gas station with the outdoor lubrication rack made of wood, with a pit dug underneath. The same stores with the same ownership. Maybe a fresh coat of paint or whitewash here and there. The rest of the Bay Area had gone berserk with growth. This place was untouched by "progress."

Annie said that the town was enchanted. She used the term time warp out loud, even though she had never been there. She wanted to know the price range of homes in the area. We stopped at a realtor's office and asked. We met Janet and she gave us the quick overview of prices and locations. In less than twenty minutes we three were in Janet's car on our way to look at houses. That was in March. We never did get to Dune's Beach to see if anyone else had left bottle caps in the sand.

Annie wanted to live there. I had to admit that I did too. In the excitement of the situation, we agreed to pool our poverty and try for a house. In that era, even in California, we had to give thought to the issue of two unmarried people applying for a home loan. After several visits with Janet and some false attempts, we did find a house that would just barely meet the needs of the five of us. Three bedrooms and *one bathroom* for four females plus me. We moved in early May of 1975.

Annie found a job in San Mateo, less than a dozen miles away. I continued at C.I. Even though the drive was considerably longer in miles, it was only ten extra minutes of commuting time. Annie had sold her house in San Jose and used the net as the down payment. Her down payment plus my income and peerless credit rating enabled us to qualify for the loan.

In the third week of August, all the books were done, the book I had to author was done, and guess what... *I* was done. My reward for fidelity, perseverance, loyalty, and a lot of other good things, was to be let go.

I was drained emotionally, physically, and was now given a terrible wound to my psyche. How can they not want me? Well, I did not dwell on that too much. I dwelled on it for several years, actually, but not in a debilitating sort of way. I had to get on with living and that meant I had to find a job.

The search was frustrating. No one in my immediate network had a place for me. The people I asked for work could not believe what had happened. I had their sympathy and moral support all over the place, but no job.

A lot of men in my situation would ameliorate the loss of work, concurrently the loss of ego, by drinking a lot of booze. I did not. I knew I was hurting and so did Annie. She felt that those people had taken advantage of me and that I would be better off somewhere else. Right. I had to admit that I made some gains from that experience: I did a good job, and I learned an enormous amount about the printing and the publishing industries.

In the days that followed, I tried to stay on an even keel, but it was hard. One of the balms for my hurt was to recall some of the good times as Sally. She had to be set aside in order to get a job, get some money, and get some predictable future going. The reason for abandoning Sally was to accept the employment that just now terminated.

The mind can play tricks and games. I recalled that just about one year ago, Sally had found herself out of a job. Now Tom was without a job. What did I do then? I looked for work under either name until I got one. Of course, I wondered where I would have been if Sally had gotten the job a year ago.

On impulse, I called an old friend at his publishing company. Dale had started some years ago as a math teacher. He wrote a workbook and sold it. The success of that book was incredible. He wrote more, and finally quit teaching to start his own publishing house. He was a brilliant man, a sensitive man, and a nice guy to know.

Jim and Dave patterned their company after his. Unfortunately, some of their books were patterned too closely to Dale's books and there were problems. Because I had been associated with the "bad guys," I was reluctant to talk with Dale. I called him anyway, got a welcome reception, and we set a lunch date for that Friday.

During lunch we made small talk, then moved into a critique of Contemporary Ideas, Inc. We soon established that we were allies, having been screwed in different ways. Then we moved into math education. He began to probe me on my notions of teaching the rational number system to intermediate kids. I sketched out my series of concepts on my placement, showing the sequence and developmental steps with attendant vocabulary that I had used in the past. We were really having some fun. Then he asked if I would be interested in editing a couple of books on the hand-held calculator. Rewrite, actually. I said that I would certainly like to talk about it.

We went to his office to look at the bad manuscript. He handed me a sample page that he had done to show what he wanted. It looked good to me. Then he said it would be a contract job, and he would pay $9 per hour. In the fall of 1976, that was really good. The ball was now in my court. Would I accept the job or not?

Deja vu. I said that I would like to do the work, but I wanted him to read something before either of us decides. Out came The Letter. He read it, looked up at me, and said, "I never would have guessed." I told him that it was my goal to become Sally. His response was that it was fine with him.

He told me that he would call his managers together and explain the situation to them. I asked what if some of them do not approve. His answer was that anyone who was still with the company on Monday morning would approve. He was a kind and gentle man, but once he made up his mind.... We stood up, shook hands, and he said he was looking forward to meeting Sally on Monday morning.

Of course Annie was upset with me. She knew I had been going through some tough times, and that Sally was coming to the fore, but she had not anticipated another departure. I assured her I had to do this. I also assured her that I would continue to make my half of the mortgage payment each month. She wanted to give me some slack, but it wasn't easy. She told me not to come back unless I knew I was going to stay put. That was fair.

I telephoned Tim to ask that I be able to stay at his place until I could find my own apartment in the Mountain View area. He was a little uneasy, but did agree that I could stay a few days.

During the course of that weekend, I changed my address, identity, gender, and got prepared for my new employment. Sometimes I think a person has to be a little crazy to have any hope for sanity.

I left Annie early Saturday morning, drove to Hidden Hill, changed clothes, and went out to find an apartment. Before nightfall, I found a delightful place not far from my new job. It was ready for occupancy, but papers had to be processed and it was Monday night before I could move in.

The first day on the new job was very nice, but there were a few surprises. Bill was the man I had to report to. I could tell right away he was having a problem with Sally. He knew Tom. His reaction was that I looked just like any other woman, maybe a little taller, but certainly believable. He said that this was going to be a little difficult for him. I was not to worry, however. Not me. I learned much later that he was hoping I would not look very good, or not want to pursue this path.

Bill took me to my working space. It was a large desk situated in the library. He said that possibly someone else might work in there too. In a few minutes I had all the writing materials I needed.

Duncan came by to introduce himself. I had not known him before. He said that I was in his cost center and that time cards would go to him. "$6 per hour, right?" Wrong. I told him that Dale offered me $9. He said that women editors get $6. I said he should speak with Dale. I got my $9, and that sexist bastard paid it out of his cost center, all right.

Before the day was over, I had my first conference with Dale. He smiled and said that I sure looked different. I said that I *was* different. He said that the old brains had better be part of the new package. We reviewed the task, he gave his inputs, and left.

Shirley came in, introduced herself as another contract editor, and chose another desk. We got on well. All the women at Creative Publications were wonderful. One woman was aloof most of the time. I was told that she acted that way around everyone but Dale.

Jane and Flo were my favorites. They were as zany as any two women I had known. I have a strange sense of humor, an appreciation for the ridiculous, and a love of the novel situation. The three of us got on well from the first day. Jane worked for Flo, who was the boss of inventory. Jane wanted to get into editing work, which was why she introduced herself to me right away. The inventory area was in another building across the street, and whenever a messenger was needed, Jane was sure to make the trip. It was not long before we three had lunch. Then I invited them to dinner.

One night when Jane and Flo were over for dinner, Jane said that some of her people were talking about the woman over in editorial who used to be a man. Jane said that she dummied up and asked them who that was. They weren't sure, but they thought it was Shirley. That certainly made my day.

My apartment was unusual in that it had originally been a two-bedroom, two-bathroom place with living room large enough to be comfortable for that size family. The master bedroom had its own bathroom. That portion had been walled off to create a modest studio apartment. I had what was left: a full sized kitchen, a bedroom and bath, and the oversized living room. The sliding glass doors enabled one to see the pine trees and lawn in back. A very restful and quiet place. I had no television, nor did I want one. I had the stereo system and a lot of candles. In my domain, the visitor had better like good food, a decent wine, good music, candlelight, and be ready to talk. Furthermore, I had a conventional dining table with four chairs, and I still had that foldout table for times when it was proper to sit on pillows on the floor to eat.

I invited Bill and his wife to come to dinner one Saturday night. He accepted the invitation, but when he came, he came alone. He was very apologetic about his wife not coming too. I picked up the feeling that she did not approve of me. We had a fine evening, anyway. He was comfortable around me, but I had a hunch he wanted to say something that he never did.

Burt was an artist from Los Angeles. He had done line drawings to provide illustrations for Dale's books for a long time. Commuting to Palo Alto once or twice a month was no problem for him. On his first trip while I was there, he was introduced to me because I was the rewriter of the calculator books. Dale wanted us to meet sometime to discuss illustrations for the two volumes.

On his second visit a few weeks later, Burt stopped by to ask if I would have lunch with him. We had not scheduled a meeting, so my conclusion was that it was purely social. It was, indeed. We had a pleasant conversation filled with unimportant topics, and I truly enjoyed being treated as a lady. Not since Clyde had I had any kind of invitation for anything. And when I realized that there were a lot of other people he could have invited, but didn't, well, that doubled the pleasure.

It seemed, though, that Burt wanted to say some things that never came out. I was hoping he would blurt out something or give me a hint. The problem was confounded because I did not know whether he and Dale had talked about my past. That could have been what he was shy to talk about. Or he could have figured it out for himself, but was timid to verify his opinion. I will never know.

We did meet in a hurry some weeks later to plan for text illustrations and cover ideas. We had time for business only, and got on it right away. I had some crude sketches for the text along with the dialogs for the cartoon characters who were to help explain certain ideas. For the covers, I suggested a collage of calculating devices used since the dawn of civilization.

He thanked me for the input and left quickly to catch his plane back to Los Angeles. He was polite and friendly enough, but there was no attempt to escalate the friendship.

I did not know what to think. I was too new at the business of being a woman to know how to read men, to interpret meaning from the little things. Not very many males acted the way I did when I was a male. I did not want to embarrass myself by asking questions of my few friends. I did ask Dale if he and Burt ever talked about me and where I came from. Dale said conversation about me was minimal. The only thing said about me was that I was a nice person to work with. I thought that I had been thinking about him too much, and decided to drop it, chalking it up to "This is the way it is with men, honey."

A few weeks later the sketches came from Burt via Federal Express. They were every bit as good as I had hoped for. Dale liked them too. No Burt, however.

I arrived at my desk one morning some weeks later to find a business card on my desk. It was one of Burt's. On the back it said, "I love you." Hmmmm. I asked around if Burt had been around lately, and was told that he had come up the afternoon before for a short trip and caught the red-eye back that night. I was confused. I think now that I should have taken someone into my confidence for a reading on the situation. Back then, I kept my own counsel. I continued to remain in the passive role.

Dale and his wife, Margo, came to dinner one Saturday. They came in the late afternoon because they had to get home early that night. I wanted to have a splendid dinner party for them to express my appreciation for the opportunity for the work. I also wanted to get to know Margo better. I had worked hard all morning preparing the best Italian dinner I could. *Petti di Pollo alla Bolognese*, with rice, broccoli, and a small salad. (Page 44 of my Italian cooking class cookbook.) They had brought wine for the table. I had made an extravagant purchase of Weibel's Sparkling Green Hungarian. It was a sharp, crisp wine that could be felt all the way up to your ears. We started with that, finished off three bottles before and during dinner. As we sat on the floor for dinner, I started lighting the candles a bit early. The transition from day to night could be made better that way.

The conversation went non-stop, and covered topics from the books I was working on, to education in general, to their travels to foreign countries, to the future of mankind. It was a wonderful evening. And a shock when we noticed it was almost midnight.

My contract assignment ended in late March. There was nothing else going on that I could do. Before my last day, I telephoned Burt in Los Angeles to say goodbye. The secretary answered and said that he was not in at all that day. I left my name and a farewell message with her to give to him. And that was the end of that.

On my first day of unemployment, I went to the state office to sign up for a job search program. While I was in line I turned and there was Lorna, Brenda's roommate. We stared at each other a few seconds before I remembered their rule: Once we have the operation, we do not know each other anymore. Okay with me.

After my turn at the window, I turned to leave. Lorna decided to break the rule, a little. We spoke quietly as she stood in line. In coded language, she told me she had not been in touch with Brenda since the surgery some months ago, and that she had been laid off from Honeywell and was hoping for a new job at Fairchild. I wanted to know more, but the rule was about to become reinstated.

I have often wondered what Lorna did for those high tech companies. Before coming to California for the sex change, she had been a forest ranger in Minnesota.

I was back on the streets again in the search for employment. It was really hard for me to accept idleness when I had been working on a challenging task at fever pitch. I tried the usual old network, the budding new network, and they both said, "Nothing right now." ...

Going through my mail one day, I was about to toss out a piece of junk mail until I noticed how badly it had been done. I looked at it to see who would put such a thing through the printing press. It was an informational bulletin from a group called The Interpersonal Support Network. They were going to have an organizational meeting in the Palo Alto area to set up a local family. Oh, yes. Now I remembered those people. They had a table at a Whole Earth Fair in San Francisco several months ago. They seemed so nice and upbeat. Sally had signed their clipboard for more information. Network, eh? I put the meeting data on my calendar.

A week later I was telephoned by the founder and president. He said he was doing a follow-up call to make sure I was going to be there, and I assured him I would.

The meeting hall in Palo Alto was crowded. It seemed that the message of the bulletin overcame the poor graphics. The mission of the group was to create an extended family for adult people who felt as though they needed to make friends and develop mutually supportive associations with others. The times were right for that sort of thing.

It was spring of 1977. The name Silicon Valley had not yet become popular. The electronics companies were bringing in technical talent from all over the country. There were a lot of high quality people who were suddenly displaced from their own families and friends.

California has always been a place where the family, in the larger sense, has not been in evidence. Everyone I ever knew in California had relatives "back East." California is also a place with unusual cultural patterns and social standards... unless you grew up there.

This ISN group wanted the conservative, middle to upper-middle class people to come together and make friends. A noble idea and it was welcomed. We were encouraged to ask questions at the meeting, sign up, and pay some modest dues.

A week later, I was contacted by the president again. He asked me to call him Jim. He also wanted me to know that I had been assigned to Peninsula group #2. A letter would be coming soon to tell me the details of the first meeting. He seemed very friendly on the phone. He asked what I did for a living. I told him. He asked if I would help produce some newsletters and some literature. I jumped at the offer.

The whole idea seemed good to me. Here was a chance to mix with nice people of the same age group, more or less, and of a similar educational background. There was also the opportunity to do something, even if there was no pay. I would get free membership, however.

Jim and I had our first meeting to discuss the projects he wanted me to do. It was pleasant, fast paced, and I enjoyed doing business with him. He looked something like Ricardo Montalban and I think he knew it, and wanted to play the part. I did have some trouble convincing him I knew what I was doing. He was a closet sexist-someone who denies or tries to hide a sexist attitude. Actions, however, ...

My first step was to call Joanie. She was the principal typesetter for the books that I produced for Contemporary Ideas as Tom. She was one of the people who expressed great sorrow when I was axed from C.I. At that time of departure, I told her about Sally, and that maybe our paths would cross again. She was happy for me that I was going to do what I wanted to do.

When I called for an appointment, Joanie asked if she could tell her employees about me. I said that would be a good idea because I thought there would be a number of projects to be done and that we had better set up a new working relationship.

I arrived on time and met the old gang all over again. There were appropriate hugs, then down to business. I explained the two immediate projects, and pointed out that the newsletter had a large press run, perhaps worthy of a web press. Joanie agreed and did the layout for it. I gathered the news from all of the Bay Area chapters of the ISN, some pictures, and got a quote from a local printer with a web press. I fed the cost figures back to Jim, got his approval, and off we went. Before I left Joanie's shop that day, her friend Sylvia came in. It turned out that Sylvia and Joanie had worked together with Barbara (from A.I.R.). This was getting to be a small world.

When everything was ready for the press, I took the mechanicals to the printer with the web. The operator was a young woman named Nancy. She looked at the job and with minimal last-minute decisions, the job went on the press.

It was the beginning of new relationships. Working with women as a woman in the print production business was remarkably the same as working with women in the print production business as a male. It was a little easier as Sally. All barriers were gone. Those women did not mince words with me, they did not try to protect a male ego, they just used plain English to tell me when I was wrong or when they had a better idea. I liked that. And I learned a whole lot more because I felt more comfortable asking dumb questions. I had already learned that asking dumb questions can prevent expensive mistakes.

At the first group meeting, Jim and I passed out the first newsletter, a tabloid size with two colors, and six photos. Everyone was impressed and said so. Jim gave me all the credit. It made my day and gave me some status in the group right away. There were about a dozen or so people. Some were married couples, most were singles. We all got on famously.

Naturally, I wondered if anyone had identified me as a transsexual. *I* wasn't sure whether I was a transsexual or not myself, but *provisionally* considered myself as one. I needed social events such as this to determine whether this was for me or not. I knew that I passed as a woman reasonably well, and in my limited relationships on and off the job, no one had ever challenged me, or acted strangely toward me. I had to admit that a lot of people up to now knew where I had come from and that was just fine. What I did not know was whether I could go into a social group such as this, hang out, participate in discussions, engage in dinners and dancing, be available for the emotional support of others and be accepted as the woman I wanted to be. The one thing that kept the spotlight off of me was that everyone else seemed concerned about their acceptability for their own reasons. We were all birds of a feather. We were all there for the same thing: acceptance and understanding. The first meeting ended with everyone high on life and pleased that we were a group. We could hardly wait for the meeting next Friday night.

Two days later I received a phone call from one of the women in the group. She said her name was Joane and that she heard that I was an editor. I admitted that I was. She asked if I would consider working for her. I asked what the job was. She needed a managing editor for her monthly tourist magazine. We set a time for the interview.

Chapter 14

I had no idea what the job of managing editor was about. I had always thought they were pretty important people. If so, how come I was getting this interview?

I needed a job. Any job. And if this had anything to do with production, writing, or printing, then I would want it.

Joane, it turned out, had not been able to attend the meeting of the Interpersonal Support Network that Friday night. An acquaintance of hers was there, remembered Joane's need for an editor, saw the newspaper I had produced, and ...

That explained why I did not remember Joane from the meeting, but it opened the other question, the too-often-asked question I reserved for myself: Can I make it? Would I ever get rid of that non-productive question?

I had never had an interview with anyone who did not know of my past. Jim, the founder of the ISN did not count. That was not really an interview. I did not know whether I looked convincing or not. I have always presented myself as best as I can. I cannot allow myself to become immobilized by fear and all the "what ifs." I had to remind myself that the action coming up was likely going to lead me to my goal of full employment. My final thought as I turned the corner to the address I was given was, *I am what I am*, folks. Take me or leave me.

At 10:00 a.m. sharp, I rang the bell at the huge three-story, half-timbered house on the fringe of the Stanford campus. Joane opened the door, asked if I was Sally, I said I was, and she led me to the suite of rooms she rented in that very large house. She seemed so cheery and nice. We sat at a small table. She served coffee and set out a clean ashtray. Cozy.

We chatted about our mutual acquaintance who connected us for this meeting. That did not take long because neither of us knew her very well. I had never been in an interview scene like this. We nattered away during the first cup of coffee with small talk I have no recollection of now. Gradually, she steered the conversation to inquiries about my last job, and the job before that, and so on until she had a full and complete history of my last three years. In the summary I gave, I mentioned doing graduate work at Stanford, whereupon my stock went up a hundred points. She too was an alumna of The Farm.

Then came the description of the job, immediately followed by her opinion that I was certainly qualified. My own thought was that I was qualified *to learn* the job, but I did not want to burst any bubbles, for either of us. I asked about the salary. She paused, then said the pay was not much: $575 per month. I agreed and said that my last job paid $1440 per month. I also said that I would accept.

Joane was pleased, but expressed her doubts that a self-supporting woman would be able to make ends meet on that kind of money. I merely smiled and repeated my acceptance. She wanted to know where additional money was coming from. I told her that I lived a simple life, I had saved a little, and I wanted the job. She kept probing. I finally told her I had another source of income, a small stipend from the state disability department which would enable me to find a new career. Now she wanted to know the nature of my disability. When I demurred, she pressed for more details. After all, she had a right to know if I had epilepsy or some other problem that could arise on the job. Cripes! Cornered!

She smiled warmly, a concerned look on display. I knew I had to tell the truth. I did not want to because I knew she accepted me as the woman I wanted to be. And if, further down the road, it became known to her that I was in transition, then I wanted to know where I had blown my cover. I opened my purse and produced The Letter. Handing it to her I said, "I think this letter will explain a lot."

She read the letter, looked up at me, and read the letter a second time. She looked up again with a very sweet smile; beaming, actually. Then she jumped up and came over to me, put her arms around me and said, "Oh my dear, how wonderful for you! I had to read the letter a second time to make sure which way you were changing. Oh how lovely. And I thought you had a disability. You don't!"

Fixed for Life 141

I started the next day, May first. That was when I met Marlene, my predecessor, and Lillian, the advertising sales person. That was the whole staff. They were primed for my arrival, meaning that Joane had told them about me. We never had to talk about my special circumstances. I was just one of the women who was going to keep on putting the monthly magazine out on time.

In May, I started work on the June issue. I had to prepare several principal elements: the standard boiler plate copy describing the glories of the advertisers' establishments, the local points-of-interest column, the up-coming events for the month, choosing the photographs, and writing captions.

One of the women that I made friends with was Sandy, a typesetter. In 1977, typesetting was the only way to make copy ready for a printer. Desktop publishing had not been conceived, let alone developed. It took a lot of talent to set type. Sandy was the best at CBM Type. I invited her to dinner one night. We had so much fun and good conversation, that it was almost 2:00 a.m. before we knew it. She stayed the night on the couch.

Our printer was in San Francisco. The sales rep was a classic sexist named Al. He sure knew his business, though. I knew *some* of my business, and let him teach me the rest of it. Printers will tell you how to make things ready for them. It was Al who explained color separations to me, and what can and cannot be done with color negatives, and a whole lot of other things. During that first month I learned enough to shave some costs of production for future issues.

One of my responsibilities was to do the press checks for each issue. To do a press check, you must stand at the end of the printing press as your job comes off the line. The idea is that the customer must approve the color tones, the registration, the whole enchilada. If everything is all right, you sign off and the press speeds up and in an hour or so you have 25,000 copies. Sometimes the checks were easy, sometimes a nightmare. Problems can occur with color... but this is not a treatise on printing.

On my first press check, I was told to be there at 4:30 p.m. I was, but the press wasn't ready. I was told to come back at 5:30. O.K. What do I do for an hour? I walked outside and down to the corner of Sixth and Brannan St. There was a place called the Flower Mart. I decided to check it out. It was a refreshment emporium for those wholesale flower growers who took their day's harvest to market. I was wearing a sweater and skirt. It was a casual outfit, but so was the neighborhood. I had been in the place several years ago as a male. If it had not deteriorated too much, I would be all right. As I walked in to get a cup of coffee, I noticed a lot of men at the bar. I had forgotten that the bar was just inside the entrance. The dining room was past the bar. I was self conscious as I walked past the growers, or the truck drivers for the growers. I quickly found a table, ordered my coffee, and wondered why it all seemed so different. Half way through the coffee, I realized that the place was the same, but *I* was different. Practically every place that I went to was new. I had not taken Sally to very many places where Tom had been. It was a strange sensation.

At 5:30 I was back at the press. They had someone else's job running. Printers do that now and then. It is a matter of printer economics. The new estimated time for my job was 7:45. I went back to the Flower Mart and ordered a sandwich. I thought I should call Joane to tell her of the delays and not to worry. She asked where I was calling from. I told her. She said, "Surely you have been in places like that before." I said, "Yes, but I have never been in a place like this *like this*." We laughed.

I did the press check at 10:15. Afterward, Al invited me to board his boat that was moored in China Basin. I said I was bushed and wanted to get home. Perhaps another time.

I produced four issues of that magazine. I had an enormous amount of advice, but those issues were *my babies*. No one else touched them until they were delivered to the printer. My pride in those issues ranks with navigating that tanker for two weeks, back in 1948.

My work continued for the support network. There were not very many printing or writing projects besides the monthly newspaper. Nancy at the printers was a great help. We hit it off well. The group at Joanie's type shop and I continued to be friends.

The social side of the network was absolutely wonderful. All of us in that group liked each other. We talked of many things from what clothes Californians wear to which events, to the future of the electronics industry. The couples in the group acted like singles. Everyone mixed as much as possible. Some of us met for lunches or other times in between meetings. There was a slight amount of flirting, but it never got out of hand. It was just enough to keep the spirits up and to gently massage an ego now and then.

I found I had a taste for flirting with men. Nothing serious, because I did not want to be a tease. Nor did I want to be found out.

Larry was a divorced man who took a shine to me. I was flattered and I wanted to be what he thought I was. I had to keep myself at arm's length, lest he find out. The other concern I had was that if I showed real interest, but then put up barriers, he might feel rejected. I certainly did not want to do that to him. The poor guy had been through enough rejection as it was. I was the only woman that he cared to spend time with. He was a sensitive soul, and was a brilliant man in statistics. I wanted to comfort him, pump up his ego so that he could be the dashing, self-confident man he could have been.

I think it was Larry who convinced me for certain that I was in no way a transvestite, but a true transsexual. He evoked feelings in me I did not know I had. Clyde did a lot for me. Casual associations with other men, including Tim (which was not casual), had caused me to realize I *really was* a woman in my heart and in my mind. Between my legs was another matter. My assessment had been that I certainly could feel like a woman, and it was a good feeling. With Larry, the feeling escalated to a new level that told me being a woman was the right and proper thing for me. Anything else would indeed be less.

I was learning that a woman could have a power and a responsibility I had never considered. A woman figuratively as well as literally, can hold her man's testicles in her hands.

Larry was transferred less than two months after we met. We were both saved from the possibility of a bad scene.

There were other things going on during that time. I got acquainted with my next door neighbor. Cathy was one of the prettiest women I had ever seen. Aside from her magazine cover beauty, she had the charm, the energy, the optimism, and the innocence that created a truly lovely three-dimensional personality. She was the only woman in that year who caused me to think about what I was doing. For about five seconds, anyway. Old reactions die hard.

We became friends. We both lived alone. I knew why *I* did, but she certainly did not have to. Cathy was in her late twenties, a graduate student of clinical psychology and was doing her intern work in the rehab department of an insurance company across the bay. Sometimes she would ask for my reactions about her cases. I was old enough to be her mother. I wished I had been. *Anyone's* mother would have been fine.

We first met in the apartment's parking lot. That encounter ended with dinner at my place that night. We surely did talk a lot. I did not tell her about me. I wanted to have as many friends as I could have who did not know my former gender.

We became close to each other. We talked girl talk, mostly. I asked where she shopped for certain things, she would ask how she could get the stain off her aluminum cookware and such. She told me about the men in her life and asked for advice. I took that as some kind of evidence that I was a convincing woman. I learned a lot from those conversations. I asked more questions than she did. Fortunately, the questions she asked of me were such that any person my age could respond. She liked my cooking and thought the candlelight in my apartment was something special. I thought so too.

One evening, one of my old schoolteacher buddies called me up to say that I was a turkey for not telling him about my transition. I apologized and said that I did not think he would approve. He told me that was always my problem: I tried to think. After we traded insults for a bit, he told me that his Ajax Jass Band was going to play some first class Dixieland sound at the Elks Club in Sunnyvale the next night. He wanted me to come listen. I reminded him of who I was at the time. He said there would be no problem. Just walk in, and his wife Bea would be at a table waiting for me. Okay, John. You asked for it.

I asked Cathy if she would like to come with me. I said that the place would be packed with old guys my age, but the music would be peerless, if she could appreciate authentic Dixieland jazz. We arrived about an hour after starting time. Neither of us was dressed to impress anyone. We expected to sit with Bea, drink a little, and talk with John in between sets. I did not know what John expected to see when he met me. Bea simply accepted me as though I were a total stranger whom she had just met and liked. Cathy, of course, was greeted warmly.

We had just gotten our first round of drinks when some old guy came over to our table and asked me to dance. He was a very happy person and I danced with him for three pieces, then asked to sit for awhile. In a few more minutes, some other man came over and asked me to dance. I could not believe what was going on. At the next break, John came over to our table. I think I looked better than he thought I would. He was nice enough, but he did act differently toward me. I asked if he asked those guys to give me the rush. He said most emphatically he did not. He was not even sure I was there yet. He noticed the tall broad with the real looker come in, but he was not sure it was me. Several people came to our table to tell John how well he was playing, and then wanted introductions to his women. Good old John obliged, introducing me as Sally, his old friend and former fellow teacher.

He liked Cathy. Who wouldn't? He got up to get his people together for another set. When the music started, the guys came back. For me. To this day, I do not know why, unless a woman nearly six feet tall is any attraction. Finally, I asked one nice man I was dancing with to please ask Cathy to dance. He said she looked a little young, but he would do it.

On the way home that night, I witnessed the one and only snit I saw her in. She was really ticked off. Not mad at me, I don't think, but she started telling me about being the homecoming queen, being voted Sweetheart of Sigma Chi, and other awards for good looks. Why was she being ignored at that place? All I could say was that they were old guys, and maybe they had daughters her age. Or their wives would not approve.

Later, we laughed over that and other shared experiences. One of those shared experiences was a "chili burn-off." It was a private party to honor *Cinco de Mayo* in

1977. Cathy and I dressed in costume. She wore a peasant blouse over a brightly colored skirt. I wore an authentic Mexican dress of natural cotton with a riot of colored embroidery. I had bought that dress in Puerto Vallarta while Annie and I were on our cruise there in February of 1975. She was not thrilled that day when I made the purchase.

We drove in Cathy's 280Z to Janet's place in Santa Cruz. It was a contest for the chili *aficionados*. Most of the guests there were her old friends from Half Moon Bay. I did not know any of them from my male days, so I was feeling at ease in circulating and introducing myself to everyone.

Sometimes I would feel nervous about being detected, other times I would fret if I was in the company of people who knew Tom, but did not know of my new status. Life can get tedious at times.

That day was Cathy's turn to get rushed. I watched it happen and I saw how she handled the swains, or the flirtations. I learned some helpful hints, should the opportunity ever come my way again to need such skill.

The late afternoon turned into evening. The chili was very good and so were the margaritas. It was fun and a very comfortable time, until Ron and his wife showed up, late. Now I know that horses sweat, men perspire, and women glow. I was doing all of them, and it was not from the chili. Ron's appearance was a shock and this is why...

In February of 1977, Annie wanted to sell the house we had bought and buy the house that Janet had owned before she moved to Santa Cruz. I thought that was a good idea because the proposed purchase would mean I would have a half ownership in a house that was across the street from the Pacific Ocean. To achieve that purchase, I had to dress up as Tom, get fresh documents regarding income, and meet with Annie and the loan representative at Eureka Federal Savings. It was uncomfortable to dress that way again, even if it was for only a few hours. I still had gray flannels and a blue blazer with appropriate accessories. My hair was a little tacky, but you can't have everything. We met at the lending institution, and were soon introduced to our loan officer, Mr. Ron somebody. We were there a couple of hours filling out forms, revising forms that had been filled out, and talking a lot. The loan went through all right, and we sure got to know Ron in the process.

That was the reason for the secretion of moisture when Ron and his wife came to the party at Janet's house that day, a scant three months after the deed was done in his office. He did not say anything, but he surely did look at me a lot. I asked Janet if he had said anything to her. She said no, and that she did not think he recognized me because he wasn't that bright.

One of the events that Cathy and I did not laugh about was the night I cried so loud that she came over to see what was wrong. In the other instances when I made a departure from Annie to be me, she wanted no communication from me. In this twelve-month episode, things were different. Basically, it was the joint ownership of the real estate that called for telephone conversations on an infrequent, but necessary basis. At Christmas time, I called her to see if I was expected to be present for the benefit of her or the kids. She said that she did not think that would be a very good idea because she was getting very serious about another man. I was stunned. I had no reason to be, nor did I have any justification to be either shocked or jealous. But I was. I told her that I was not one hundred per cent sure that I was going to stay as Sally for the rest of my life. I knew I was waffling and trying to hedge my bets, and I hated myself for it. But it was happening.

She very gently reminded me that *I had left her*, and that I had no claim on her anymore, and that she had herself to think about because evidently nobody else was going to. She laid it out for me in a calm voice, measured tones, as though she were explaining to a four-year-old why she could not have a new doll. We ended the call soon after she made sure we had communicated.

I was crushed. Totally wiped out with grief and sorrow. I was unable at that time to know what I was being hit with. All I could do at the time was to cry. And did I ever cry! Of course I knew that *loss* was what I felt, but I had lost things before. I had not cried since I was twelve. I was trying to analyze my feelings when the doorbell rang and Cathy hollering at me to let her in.

She had heard me crying. I was totally out of character. What could she do to help me? I wanted to tell her what had happened, but before I could tell her about the phone call that triggered my waterworks, I had to tell her the whole story-my true status, etc.

For a person that young and somewhat sheltered, she took everything in stride. My "true status" was *not* my true status. She said I was the woman next door, that she was pleased that I had taken her into my confidence, and shared that information with her. The fact remained that I was a woman with a problem and she wanted to help me.

Having redefined the situation to her perception, she became the clinical psychologist and asked questions to get enough information out of the sobbing me, then proceeded to put everything in proper perspective. She was a natural at "shrinking." In a few minutes I began to understand what was really going on. She did not *tell* me anything. Inductively, her questions caused me to tell myself how immature and short sighted I had been. My hurt turned to embarrassment. We had a glass of wine and talked for a while. When she felt sure I was all right, she went back to her place. But I was stuck with myself.

I spent the next couple of days thinking how stupid I had been. How could I have been so dense, so immature? Then it occurred to me that I had not totally internalized the consciousness of a woman. I believed I was a woman, but here was an old circuit that had triggered a male response. It took a few minutes to rewire some synapses, then I began to savor the new awareness that came with the realization that I was now a woman feeling very happy for Annie, another woman. Well, some lessons are more complicated than others. The loss I felt now was a loss of the friendship I had with her.

It was Lincoln's birthday in February when Annie called me. It was her turn to cry. Her new fella had died. Evidently, he was an older man, and his heart gave out. It happens. I was able to console her somewhat on the phone. Then I asked her what I could do. She said that if Tom could come to see her, that she would appreciate it a lot. I agreed to drive over that evening. It was during that visit that I learned about this man she had connected up with, and their plan to purchase Janet's house. The deal was in process when he passed away. She asked if I would be willing to lend my support to close the deal. Why not? It would be half mine, and it was no big thing for me to lend my support.

Annie and her daughters moved in on Saint Patrick's Day, 1977. A week or so later I was invited to come see the place that I owned half of. I found some old pants and a plaid shirt, and drove over early one Saturday morning. It was a nice house, but the back yard was a jungle. The weeds were as tall as me. As I slowly walked through the tall grass, I stumbled a lot due to all the junk that had been left by previous tenants. Bricks, drain pipes, an old toilet, flywheels, barn door hinges-it was all there. Within me, something stirred. *I wanted to clean it up.*

Two weeks later, I drove over again. I spent the whole day hoeing weeds. And picking up junk as I went. Why was I there doing that? Well, it was part mine, and that yard was dangerous. After I got a path cleared to the north side of the house, I saw the wooden siding rotting away due to the moisture from the weeds and lack of sunlight. Every other weekend, I turned into male for one day to go hoe weeds and clear junk. I was doing something nice for them, and I was enhancing my property. Would I ever live there? I doubted it very much. I appreciated the chance to get outdoors and work off some fat.

It was during that spring that Son #3 called to ask why I was so available on the telephone, but unable to meet him for lunch. He and I were closer than any other combination of two people in that nuclear family. I really missed his company. We had any number of telephone calls while I lived in Mtn. View, but no getting together. This was the longest period of being Sally, and I had made no provision for seeing him in person. He finally put it to me; can we meet sometime? I really love the kid. I said that we could meet at Denny's in Mtn. View if he wanted. Let's make it about 10:00 p.m.

As Tom, I got there first and ordered coffee at the counter. As I fiddled with the fresh package of cigarettes to get one out, I wondered what the agenda should be. Was I going to tell him about what was really going on in my life, or was I going to bluff my way through another interrogation as I had done other times? I could be honest and tell him. Only his mother knew what I was up to, and she was emphatic that I not tell any of the boys. Sure, I could buy that. As long as they were boys, but even the youngest was 21 now. Who was a boy anymore? And of course, was I still obliged to follow her admonitions from four years earlier?

He lumbered his way through the door, saw me seated at the counter wearing my plaid shirt and blue jeans. Very scraggly hair. He fitted his six-three frame on a stool next to mine and said that I needed a haircut. Did I think I was a hippie or what? We always liked to trade gentle insults with each other. And I had always been particular about haircuts. I was a Navy-trained man, and the boys knew it. He ordered his coffee, and before it came, he turned to look me straight in the eye and asked, "What in the heck is going on with you?" I asked what he meant by that. He just said that I was not around anymore and that I seemed different in some way. He repeated the question.

I had to decide whether to tell him the truth or try to create some new lie. But if I really love this person, how can I keep the truth from him? Besides, we might be able to redefine the relationship to include the new version of his father. So I told him.

I simply said that all my life I thought I should have been a female. No matter what I did, no matter what success I had as male, no matter how hard I tried to be the man everyone thought I was, I could not extinguish the need to want to live as a woman. Furthermore, I did not know whether I could or should be a woman, but I had to give it a try. I had made some earlier attempts, and they were successful so far as the experience itself, but the timing and the economics were working against me, and I had gone back to male status... not out of desire or because I had failed as a woman. So now I was at it again, and I expected to have a whole year to do or die, as they say.

He sat like a piece of stone during my halting, yet impassioned discourse. Then he opened his mouth without disturbing any other features on his face, and quoted the last line from the film classic we all had seen as a family years earlier, *Some Like It Hot*, "Well, nobody's perfect."

That was my son. He was bright, perceptive, and always with a sense of humor as well as an appreciation for the ridiculous. I was startled by his response then, but later I realized that it was probably the only thing he could have said.

The rest of the conversation included things like I was not a homosexual, I was not interested in having sex with men, that there was no logic to this, that I had been seeing a psychologist for years, that there seemed to be no cure or any way to turn it around. Sure, I could return to male living anytime I wanted, but I didn't want to. I was getting payoffs living as a woman, and that was the way I wanted it to be. Could he adjust to that, and could we be friends on that new basis? No.

He was polite. I could not sense any damage to the old relationship, but he would not be able to be around me on any new basis. He was holding on to the old me. I was holding on to the new me. We declared it a standoff. No hard feelings. We respected each other's stand.

Subsequent conversations were done on the telephone. If he wanted to get together, he knew what he was asking me to do. If I was unable to meet with him, he understood that the logistics were too much at the time. It felt good that I did not have to lie anymore. It felt bad that my needs alienated the one I loved.

Chapter 15

September of 1977 was a time for an assessment of my situation. I had already informed Joane that I would not be able to continue as Managing Editor at *Discover Magazine*. The pay was too far below my living expenses, no matter how frugal I became. Also, I had learned that the job was traditionally held by journalism majors at Stanford who wanted some real experience prior to graduation. I knew that a certain young woman wanted the job, starting in the fall. So my departure from there was all right with everyone. Elizabeth would do the October issue.

The manager of my apartment house had informed me that the rent on my apartment was going to escalate from $250 to $315 for the next lease period.

There were no other jobs in sight.

My financial position was tottering, soon to be a disaster.

A decision had to be made by mid September on the apartment.

I had a few weeks to consider my options. There weren't many to work with.

There were three notions that revolved in my head: I have been truly in love with only one person ... Annie. Second, the kinds of work open for me as Sally all required skills and experiences that I did not have, e.g., typing 65 WPM. Nor did I have any qualifications for service jobs like hairdressing and such. A lot of jobs I would have been pleased to do called for schooling or preparation that I had no time to acquire.

My third notion was that I had a lot to offer as a male. That was where most of my experience and track record had been built. How poignant the issue of sexism was for me. All the talents I had to offer an employer were necessarily classed as men's work, not open to females. Then, anyway.

The three notions revolved, ever changing their hierarchy of importance. I missed not having a person to love, I missed the kinds of challenging work men could get, and I missed the financial rewards open to males.

I telephoned Annie to say that my world was crumbling around me, and I wanted to have a place to stay until I could find a new job. She reminded me that the house was half mine, but she was in charge. I could certainly return anytime, she said, but I would have to do it as a male. The tenor of the conversation was unemotional, matter-of-fact, and maybe a little bit cordial. After all, I had done a lot of work in that yard. It gave me brownie points that I never expected to cash in.

A week before move-out time, I made one more round of calls to those people who might want Sally's talents at any price or any terms. Nothing. Everyone was certainly sympathetic, but sympathy gets you nowhere at the grocery store.

I told Cathy that I was going to move out. She was unhappy. We had grown so close to each other in those last several months. I reviewed the situation with her so that she would understand. She understood right away, but wanted to check around her place of business to see if there was something for me. There wasn't, it turned out.

During my last week in apartment #6, I started moving my stuff back to Half Moon Bay. I would make my trips as Sally in the daytime. No one was in the house week days during the daylight hours. I did not know what the neighbors thought, seeing a strange woman unloading her things, several days in a row, but not seeing her any other time.

There was a weekend in the middle of the move. That called for special arrangements. I had to put on a cotton shift, wear my wig, and a light application of lipstick in order to leave Mtn. View with a car load. At the summit on Highway 92, I would pull over, wipe my mouth, remove the wig, shinny into some pants and a sport shirt, removing the shift in the process. Now Tom was driving the car, unloading stuff into the house. On the return trip I reversed the process. Oh, the games we play.

The night before the last day of moving, I told Cathy that the male me was going to take the very last load. Sally was going to check out with the manager in the afternoon. From then on, Sally would be back in the closet for... who knows how long.

She and I had dinner that night as our grand farewell. I was not interested in her meeting Tom. At dinner we did a lot of reminiscing, a lot of laughing, and shed some tears. I continued to marvel at how much she liked me. Our ages were so different. I suppose she liked me because I liked to have a good time, was almost always upbeat, and I did lead her into a few situations where her world opened up to a little more adventure than it would have otherwise. And I certainly liked her a lot. We never had trouble finding things to talk about. We were close, we were fond of each other. I considered it to be an ideal woman-to-woman relationship.

At the end of that dinner party, she said that we had to stay in touch. I asked, "Like pen pals?" She said that would be fine. Then the bombshell. She wanted to meet the other me. She was adamant. O.K. with me Cathy, if that's what you want to do. I told her that during my very last moments in the apartment, I would bang on our common wall to let her know.

The next evening I had everything loaded, not one thing left in the apartment, and I made the signal. Soon there was a familiar knock at my door. Wearing my blue jeans, red plaid shirt, and loafer shoes, Tom opened the door. Cathy stood there with no real expression on her face. She asked for Sally. I said that Sally was gone. She asked who I was. I said that I used to be Sally. She was non-believing at first. "How could you two have the same body?" was her first question. She said that she needed a few minutes to get herself together. I suggested she go back to her apartment to get two wine glasses, and I would go out to my car and bring in a half bottle of wine. She said I *sounded* like my old self.

We sat on the floor and leaned up against the wall with our wine. I flashed on the last time I did that when moving *into* an apartment several years earlier. Cathy and I talked of the departure neither of us wanted, although "I" had already left. (Personal pronouns get a little confusing sometimes.) When the wine was gone, we stood up, hugged, and I closed the apartment door for the last time. End of an era.

The drive back to Half Moon Bay was made a little difficult because of the tears that would not stop. They were *not* sorry-for-myself tears, although there was a sadness. A sweet sadness. I cried because everything that year had been so beautiful. Now it was over. I think any woman would understand the tears. Men would have a different expression for a similar emotion stirring in them. I believe the difference in expression is due to a difference in hormonal balance. And I was still pumped up on estrogen.

I had made many new friends, and there were several old friends of Tom who became friends of Sally. I got to do everything as Sally that I wanted to, *and a whole lot more*. Especially, the remembrances of the men I met in that year.

It was incredible that I could only think of them in a distanced, abstract way. I could not feel anything for them. I remembered everything in acute detail, but there was no feeling, no emotion, as though it did not really happen to *me*. It was then that

I realized that there must be two of us in the one body. Two different kinds of consciousness, was my guess. Or consciousness compartmentalized, perhaps.

I thought of a lot of things that night, but the drive was only about forty minutes. I had to start reshaping my consciousness to become the long-lost male returning to the old family, in a new house. And I had to lay off the estrogen pills, too. After a year's regimen of Estinyl and Provera I was going to walk into that domicile of four females with the same chemicals prevailing in me that were their birthright. I would have to work hard at role playing until my suppressed testosterone could resume dominance.

Annie and I shared the same king-size bed as we always did, but if I should happen to touch her accidentally, it was as though she were zapped with a cattle prod. I knew I did not have sex privileges, nor was I looking for any. I was a poor waif, choosing an arrangement that was better than sleeping in the streets, or worse.

I was treated politely by the girls. They did not know where I had been, exactly. Nor did they know anything about Sally. My arrival was not a big shock for them as we had all pitched in on the work in the back yard on the day gravel was spread.

The second day I was there, I volunteered to resume cooking. That was met with enthusiasm. I also agreed to keep the kitchen clean, but we would all take turns washing dishes.

Life went on. I looked for work as male, exclusively, thinking that would provide a stronger financial position. Nothing turned up right away.

In November I registered with the local school district as a substitute teacher. I felt I earned a thousand bucks a day, but the district pay scale was only $30. Being a substitute teacher is not the same as being a regular teacher. Regular teachers walk into a classroom to make some learning happen. Substitute teachers walk in to provide an adult presence. That is "the code of the hills." If the substitute teacher tries to teach something, he or she is in for trouble from the kiddies, who instinctively believe that the regular teacher's absence means a holiday for them. But this is not a treatise on public schools. I was pretty good as a classroom teacher, but I was a rotten substitute.

It was a tough time for me. I had to find regular work. It was going to be difficult to strengthen my male consciousness unless I could have some kind of work association with others as a male.

The corollary was the difficulty in letting go of the female consciousness. Intellectually, I knew I had to if I was going to be of any worth as a male. My chief obstacle at that time was dealing with the only role I could perform: housewife for four females. I loved it, but it was counterproductive to the new person I had to create.

My head was a mess. My emotions said to build a nest and nurture those in the nest. My mind said to get a male job and win some bread for the ladies of the house.

My mind was far from being idle, but the devil's playground beckoned for me to dress up and look like the lady of the house. Annie would have freaked out if I had done that. I cried a little, and *this time* it was because I did feel sorry for myself. I had been a woman and it was beautiful. Now I had to be male again, but nobody would let me work as a male. If a man does not have a job, his ego and self-esteem are in jeopardy. If a woman does not have a job, there is no such threat. It was shaping up as a no-win situation for me.

I tried selling life insurance. It was easier than being a substitute teacher. The company that took me in paid me to learn. After five months of learning, getting a license, making cold calls to get appointments, and not selling anything, *we* decided that I was not an insurance man. The last conversation I had with my manager was something like this:

Me: You mean that if I want to sell life insurance, I have to gain emotional control over someone?

Him: Well, sure.

Me: I would not do that to anyone, even if I could.

Him: Goodbye.

The first year was ending and I still had not found anything secure yet. Just as I was leaving the insurance company, old Jim from Contemporary Ideas called to invite me to lunch. We met at a Velvet Turtle restaurant. It was about as low as Jim would tolerate. We talked b.s. mostly, as we ate. Over coffee and a cognac, Jim explained that he bought Dave's share of the business, and that now he was the sole owner. He and Prentice-Hall had entered into a new contract, and they had placed a very large order for books to be produced. He needed my help and asked if I would be willing to come back. He said that he would give me free reign to do the job as I wanted to do it. He also said that the leadership at PHLS would be very supportive of my coming back. Then he told me the salary. I saw the specter of the unemployment line dissolve. I told him I would be delighted to return under those conditions.

The end of 1978 was infinitely better for me than the end of 1977. The season's parties, open houses, and dinner invitations were enjoyable because I could hold my head high in the company of other males. One of Annie's women friends at work invited us to join her and her husband one evening for champagne and smoked salmon. We sat around their Christmas tree, sipping, nibbling, and listening to fine German lieder. Erv and Betty were both from German families. Erv was also a manager of a Radio Shack store. He was a salesman, and that meant there was no lapse in the conversation. It was a most enjoyable evening, the first of many times together for the next decade. We had such a fine time at that pre-Christmas evening that I suggested I do a sauerbraten dinner for the four of us on New Year's eve. It turned into a tradition, and lasted until 1987.

In mid-summer of 1978, Erv announced that he had been selected to be a manager of the Radio Shack Computer Center in San Mateo. It was a real honor for him, as only fifty such stores were to open in the entire country. We celebrated his success with a few bottles of *fume blanc*. During the occasion Erv asked me if I would work for him on a part-time basis to teach people how to use the TRS-80 microcomputer. I almost choked on my drink. But he was serious, and said that it was a requirement for all computer centers to be able to teach regularly scheduled classes. It was a marketing effort.

Only a tiny fraction of one percent of our population knew anything about computers of any kind, other than computers that screwed up people's telephone bills and department store charges. Radio Shack was one of only six companies that manufactured microcomputers that year. Tandy wanted to sell them, but nobody knew how to make them work. Not regular people, anyway.

I was one of those regular people. I demurred. Erv, the salesman, came on strong and made some good points. I continued to resist, saying that the publishing business kept me busy, and that not only did I not understand computers, I didn't care, either. I was the kind of guy who had to interact with people, not mechanical devices. I was adamant, but there was a soundless whispering in my ear that said Erv was going to get me on this one.

I continued to resist until early fall when I became convinced that I had to help out my buddy, Erv. He was unable to find anyone else. He really wanted me and needed me. I had been wistfully thinking of the joys of teaching *anything* again. I admit that I am a ham. I did miss the classroom, although I did not miss the public school system. Here was a chance to teach in a commercial environment. All I had to do was to learn the instrument, then figure out how to teach it. I could have embarked on an effort to learn molecular physics with the same chance of success, it seemed.

I saw the victorious smile on Erv's face as he loaded the cartons into my car. He said I should take the system home, use the manual to teach myself, then let him know when I was ready to teach classes. It sounded simple and straightforward enough. After all, one of my mottoes in life is

If you can read, you can do anything.

Of course, that motto is valid if the copy you read has been written with a vocabulary you can understand, and the writer employs the rudiments of standard English grammar.

The manuals are a *little* better a decade later. People who write them seem to be oblivious to the vocabulary level of those neophytes they write for. Has anyone ever complained about a manual that was too easy?

Erv said that Tom, his son, would answer any question I had. And he could. The problem was finding him to get answers to my questions. He was a busy kid.

I think I discovered a new level of frustration when I began my self-education on that system. At Halloween time, I had it packed up in the cartons, ready to return. A week later I unpacked it and tried it again. I made a little progress, but mostly I was learning how much there was to learn. Staggering.

The unit was in and out of those cartons at least four times, with a firm resolve to return that device to hell, where it came from. The only thing that kept me going was the silent voice of my deceased father giving me the familiar admonition, "Try it *one more time*."

By Thanksgiving I had my breakthrough. I could make some kind of sense out of it. At Christmas time I told Erv that I was ready to teach a night class. I had reached the point where I knew some things, but I did not know what I did not know. Only a class could tell me that. We scheduled the debacle for the first week of 1979.

It was sort of a disaster, that first class night. By the end of it, I learned what I didn't know. We held an extra session to complete the course.

I was hooked! I loved it. There was something in BASIC that captured my imagination, and it took awhile before I discovered what it was.

Actually there were several elements that I liked. The "machine" was really just another electrical appliance, like a toaster, vacuum cleaner, etc. The structure of the *language* of the computer is a curious version of English or algebraic equations. I had undergraduate minors in English and mathematics, so the computer system was really an extension of something I already knew. Other aspects included the need for absolute accuracy, and the encouragement to get creative. Quite a combination there.

It had been a hard fight, but I won. My ability to teach math was built on my childhood failures with math. My ability to teach BASIC and disk operations was built on the same frustration. Because I knew exactly the ways in which a person could screw up, I was prepared to identify the learners' problems, and offer alternate ways of presenting any topic or concept. The hotshots who wrote the books never understood how a person could not understand right away.

I tried to get my boss, Jim, to take a look at the microcomputer as a new market for educational workbooks. He and PHLS thought it was a waste of time. The microcomputer was not going to become a popular item, so why waste money developing materials that no one would use? O.K., guys.

Life lurched along from winter to spring, and the other seasons, in their predictable order. Once in a while, I would pack up some of Sally's stuff and head out for a weekend by myself to recapture the glories of being a woman again. It was never the same. The social network was gone, the excitement of a future was not there, but it was better than nothing. Just barely. Like masturbating when you would rather have a partner. I knew I was a transsexual, yet I was trying to get release as a transvestite, a part timer.

A transvestite gets a rush by dressing and acting like a woman for short, infrequent intervals. For me, dressing as a woman was an *enabling activity* to get me into another level of consciousness, and to explore and enjoy a social and psychological parity with other women. *And stay that way*. The occasional weekend was like taking aspirin to stop a toothache, or drinking to forget.

Sometimes Tim would see me at his place. I learned that it was hard on him to see me as male, then female, then male again. It gave me a strange feeling to know that my on/off mode troubled him. I had to accept the fact that he really cared about Sally, and that I was just screwing up some good memories for him. What was worse, I learned later, was that he was greatly troubled that Sally was on the wane. He believed that Sally was superior to the male counterpart, and it was a waste of time, or even a blasphemy that Sally was being supplanted by Tom.

My situation in the summer of 1979 was comfortable on the economic and social fronts. Sally was not causing pain because I was so busy at work, at the computer center, and enjoying the renewed, loving relationship with Annie.

The thaw with Annie began about a month or so after I moved back in. The pattern was the same as in early 1976 when I moved to the same apartment complex as Annie's. Proximity, interaction on a daily basis, utilization of communication patterns developed years earlier. We were destined to be together. For awhile, anyway.

I really loved Annie. I still do. I regard her as a truly superior human being. She never walked on water, she had to use underarm deodorant like everyone else, but there was a string of qualities that, in the aggregate, placed her at the top of my list of people I would choose to be on a desert island with. If you have ever been in love with someone else, you know what I am talking about. My life has been enriched enormously by being in her company. If I had to live my life as a male, then I wanted to live it with Annie. I used to think about that a lot: Did I have to live the rest of my life as a man?

That was a frequent topic for consideration while driving on the freeway, or walking on the beach. It called for a review of my understanding of the universe, the role of people in it, the name of the game we are all playing, and what are we supposed to do with our lives. Sometimes those issues produced dreary thoughts, but mostly I was heartened by the knowledge that *I could decide*. It was Annie, actually, who helped me to understand that. Of course, I had to acknowledge that there is a price tag for everything one acquires in this world, and that by choosing one course of action, you automatically reject the other options. You can't have it all, but you *can* have what you want. I believed then as I do now, that if you really want something, you can have it. Maybe not an hour from now, or even next month. In some cases it may be years before your heart's desire becomes yours. So what did I want?

I knew that I wanted to stop fighting the Divine Order for me. Yes, I believe in reincarnation, and that has *everything* to do with day-to-day living. I have to accept the notion that all of us are born into this world to learn... to grow... to develop... or to evolve into whatever we are supposed to become. My life's agenda is not the same as yours. My agenda this time around was tailor made for me, probably by me, before I was born into this life.

It is my soul that needs to grow, not my persona. My persona is the vehicle for me to interact in this world. I am supposed to use it to get those lessons for the growth of my soul. So what are my lessons? How do I know what I am supposed to do on Earth this time around? What is my agenda? I dearly wish I had simple answers, but I don't. The complicated answers are still coming to me, becoming a little more clear as the years pass. Even though I do not have all the answers I would like, I am delighted that at least I can ask the questions, and if I keep listening, *sometimes* I get answers. They come in the form of a hunch, an inspiration.

There is another issue, often overlooked by those who subscribe to reincarnation, and that is that part of each person's agenda is to have some impact on other people's agenda. This is not a private planet. We are a family, and as we learn from association from others, they learn from us.

In the summer of 1979, life was improving for me in several ways. I was still unsure what Sally was doing way out on the periphery of my consciousness. The pattern of my life was beginning to get some clarity. For one thing, every time I declared my male life to be more fulfilling, more comfortable, more genuine, than anything else, I would get a whamo of a jolt from you-know-who, saying, *"Don't forget about me!"*

I was very much in love with Annie, and I used to tell her so a lot. Likewise, she would say. So, one Sunday morning in bed, I asked her to marry me. She asked about Sally. I said that I was beginning to think the need to go off and be Sally was at an end. Why Sally was still around at all was a mystery to me. I said that she would need to get out once in a while, but the real love of my life was her, Annie. I added that I had already internalized so much of Sally into me, that there was no need to develop her any more.

It was getting close to two years since Sally packed it in, and the male resumed control. During that time several of Sally's friends wanted to maintain contact with me, whoever I was. Annie accepted them easily because they seemed to like Tom as well as Sally. Michal and her husband, Dick, were guests at our dinner table, and we were guests at theirs. The relationship continued comfortably for years.

Cathy, from next door in Mtn. View, came for dinner within a few weeks of my return to Half Moon Bay. We had a fine evening, the three of us, not counting Sally. Cathy and I did correspond when she returned to Idaho to marry an old sweetheart. She would write to Tom. At that time, I was so desperate for female communication, Sally would write back to her. She said that Sally was not around anymore. We got a little heated over that issue, and soon there was no more communication. I consider the loss of her friendship as one of the casualties of my life. At the time she quit writing me, I was really in bad shape. Later, I could have communicated on her terms, but by then I got no answers to my letters.

Al and Florence from the Interpersonal Support Network were regular visitors for almost two years until a transfer took them out of state.

Viana and her husband became frequent visitors too. Neither one knew anything about Sally.

Once or twice a year, Annie and I would throw a big party. All of those friends and a lot of local people would come together. I would see Viana and Florence talking, and maybe Michal would join them. Florence and Michal both knew Sally, but from different contexts, and neither knew that the other knew. Erv, Al, and Ed were becoming pals. Al knew me as Sally, the others did not. It took some time for me to get comfortable with that.

Once or twice I did some reintroductions for some of the women. I derived some pleasure from saying to Florence that Michal and I met at the women's center. Eyes would register interest. Now there was a shared secret. The three of us could now talk on a new plane. It helped and it bothered me a little to find that such a practice felt good. To feel comfortable about it was one thing. To feel *good* about it was something else. I was unable to see it as a warning signal at the time.

The wedding was attended by almost a hundred people. We were married in a little church that had been a railroad waiting room sixty years earlier.

My cousin, Bill, and his wife, Pat, drove up from Los Angeles to the wedding. No other relatives deemed the occasion to be of enough importance to respond to their invitations. Did that bother me? Yes. A number of my childhood friends from Burlingame came to see me get married for the second time.

Annie and I were very happy. I was in love with her because she really was the world's greatest woman, as I mentioned earlier. I would have continued to love her if she weighed 300 pounds and had warts all over. It was her mind and the love that she radiated. She was smart and had a wonderful sense of humor.

She loved me for reasons I may never know. I can guess at one or two of my traits that she approved of. First and foremost, I really and truly tried not to be a jerk. I kept my male ego in check pretty well. If her idea on something was better than mine, I said so. We never called each other bad names because we listened to each other and were always sensitive to the other. We respected each other. Once in a while, a friend would say to me that Annie and I were more like friends, or brother and sister than lovers. I think that is accurate. The essence of the relationship was not sex, although it was there. The essence was a love based on the things I just mentioned.

If there was one aspect of me that probably had more to do with our love, it was my experience as a woman, brief as those months were. I learned a lot about caring, about how a woman's mind works, but most of all, I found that head space much more comfortable for me. In plain English, I felt I was a woman even though I dressed as a man and created an acceptable male veneer for the general public.

Chapter 16

Annie and I were in love, and now we were married. We had often said that marriage for us was not necessary. Our love would bind us, not a legal contract. We were old enough to know that people change. Growth means change, and we expected to grow together. Should the love wane to the point where we should separate, a divorce would only create another round of pain and unhappiness that we had both experienced before with others. For over six years, we had dated a lot, lived together and separated a couple of times, and always seemed to feel as though our destinies were really one destiny. We really felt that way for a long time. What was so special about that love?

Our ability to communicate, our mutual respect, our continuous willingness to be honest with each other, our comfort level with each other made our love possible. We felt that neither of us owed the other anything. Each of us felt good about ourselves. The goodness we felt was something we wanted to share with the other. Most people come together to get fulfilled or completed by getting something from the other. We already felt good about ourselves. Our individual need was to give to the other. We were both like cows full of milk, and would feel good only after giving. Therefore, we gave of ourselves to each other because we needed to. We demonstrated the notion that giving and getting are really the same thing. If you do it right.

It was impossible for me to give something to Annie without getting an equal amount simultaneously. For example, a seemingly small thing: The Foot Rub. After dinner, most evenings, we would either watch the tube, or read, or listen to music and read. Depending on our energy level, we might talk. Otherwise, we were comfortable not talking. Regardless of the situation, I would reach over, remove a sock, and start to massage her foot. It meant so much to her; therefore it meant so much to me to provide that service.

We had to deal with all the tribulations of middle class life, such as paying bills on time, getting someone to come fix the washing machine, deciding what to do with the yard to make it as labor free as possible, whether to paint the inside of the house this year or next, and so forth. And there was always the awareness that either of us could lose our job.

And we did that too. Sometimes both of us had jobs, sometimes only one of us did. We managed without any stress to the relationship, although I had my private, male stress when I was out of work.

What we had that no other couple seemed to have was the undying optimism that comes from knowing that as long as we were together, back-to-back, the world could not harm us. We would be able to triumph over any adversity that life could manifest.

Months would go by without me ever thinking about being Sally. I was beginning to see that Sally was really in two principal parts. One part was the persona, dressed and ready to interact with others as a woman in social situations. That part could be fun, stimulating, and rewarding for me. It had been my passport to the realm of womanhood. Logistically, it was a lot of trouble to accomplish now.

The other part of Sally was strictly internal. Of course I had a lot of memories "on tape" that I could replay anytime, but the awareness of my developing female nature continued. I was getting a glimmer of the difference between being female and being feminine. Perhaps that helps to distinguish the transvestite from the transsexual: the TV wants to be feminine for a short interval, the TS wants to be female forever. It seemed to me back then that I could continue to develop my female nature without acting or appearing feminine or presenting a womanly appearance. I had my opportunities to nurture, to phase out my male ego, to establish a parity with Annie, to be sensitive to the needs of others. It was this developing internal component that caused me to believe that I could become the person I was supposed to become without having to display the *person* of Sally. Armed with this conclusion as *my reading of reality*, I proposed marriage.

But why get married when the love bound us together? I have no winning answer for that question. It just felt right to me to ask, and it felt right for Annie to agree. After the ceremony in 1979, we complimented each other on our decision for quite some time. It did make a better relationship for us, though neither of us could explain why. We just continued to live happily ever after in our home by the sea.

My job at Contemporary Ideas/Prentice-Hall Learning Systems was doing well. The books moved along on schedule, I was promoted from Production Manager to Vice-President for Production, and received a raise in pay.

The classes at Radio Shack Computer Center were gaining in popularity. The requests for more classes were beginning to crowd my free time. I loved the teaching because I could not help but learn more as I taught. Some students have a way of making a teacher work harder, and I loved the challenge.

In April of 1980, a rift developed in the relationship between CI and PHLS. It was contract renewal time. The two presidential egos squared off and everybody lost. CI, by definition in the previous contracts, was permitted to have only one customer... PHLS. When that customer evaporated, CI had no time or enough cash to reestablish itself as an independent publishing house. In plain English, I was out of a job. PHLS did offer me work as a production person, but due to a loyalty to my boss, Jim, I declined the offer. Besides, the dynamics of their side of the house constituted an unfavorable environment for me. A year later, they were out of business. Male egos can do wonders.

Being "at liberty" was good for Erv at the computer center. I was now available for day classes as well as night and weekend classes. It was fun for me, but anyone who has ever worked for the Tandy Company can tell you, there is no money in it. The paychecks I got were great for a high school kid still living at home. For me, they represented a fraction of my former pay. It was subsistence, and Annie and I had to economize more than ever to keep afloat. I had been out of work several times by this time in my life, and I knew that any job was better than no job. It is so much easier to maneuver one's way to better employment if one is presently employed.

I didn't see it right away, but the devil's playground was under construction. The daytime classes were not very popular. Perhaps one or two classes per week were requested. Nights and Saturday classes were booked several weeks in advance. I found myself at home a lot during the day.

Annie's youngest daughter, Linda, was still living with us. She was a lovely little person. Smart, mature, very good looking, a fantastic sense of humor, and a remarkable set of values for a high school kid. On the down side, Linda had to endure the physical torment and social discomfort of cystic fibrosis. At age nine, the doctors said she might make it to her twelfth birthday. She was well established in her teens by now because of the medical advances in treatments, but it was my unexpressed opinion that the kid was too stubborn to succumb. She was a very private person. We hardly ever had private conversations, but there were some sterling moments at the dinner table on many occasions. Sometimes we debated social issues, but mostly we played one upsmanship with puns. Making funnies seemed to be the way we kept in touch and expressed our aloha for each other. It was a safe device. I was not her father, and that blocked any chance for a normal, healthy father/daughter intimacy. We settled for an intellectual intimacy instead. It was good for us both.

Linda's attendance at school was irregular. Everyone understood. They understood that every year of her life was a precious gift, and that she needed some slack now and then. Invariably, she would make up her work, rekindle her friendships, and be back on the track for another few months. The idea was to make her life as normal as it could be.

Most days Linda would go off to school, Annie would go off to work, and because I had no classes to teach until 7:00 p.m., I would wash the dishes, have more coffee while I scanned the want ads in the *San Francisco Chronicle*. Other activities included tidying the house, making up the bed, making an occasional telephone call to the old boy network to inquire about jobs, maybe some yard work, and so forth.

At first, the "and so forth" meant writing in my journal. Because of my reduced circumstances in the work place, the vestige of my ego was taking some lumps. If one's self-image is tied to one's occupation.... In my male days, my self-image *was* tied to my occupation. No amount of mental gymnastics could assuage my need for self-actualizing employment. It was fair to say that my teaching was fulfilling, but the monetary rewards from it dampened the benefit. It was difficult to feel good about going from vice president of a publishing house to a teacher who made $3.50 per hour.

The journal writing was therapy. I would write about the dream I had the night before, but I rarely had (or remembered) any dreams. I usually had some kind of scenario or mental picture of something as I reentered consciousness. I would write about them, and sometimes extend, those thoughts. It wasn't long before recollections of Sally and her heydays started showing up in my writing.

I am not qualified to evaluate the dynamics of my subconscious mind when I wrote about the meaning of Sally. I can say with great authority, that Sally was coming back to my conscious mind, and I was pleased to renew the relationship, whatever that meant. Writing about the good times seemed like a safe thing to do. A release. Wrong. I soon realized that the stage was set for a modest, short-time reappearance of Sally. Where were my things? Oh yes, in boxes out in the garage.

The morning routine continued as before, except that after everyone was gone, I got up, put on some things, and Sally poured the coffee, proceeding as before. The journal writing took off like a shot. Maybe twenty pages of yellow pad each day. I was now feeling a lot better. Why? It didn't matter at the time. If wearing a nightie, robe, and a wig made me feel better, why should I waste time and energy in self-analysis I was not licensed to do anyway? After an hour or so, I would take my shower, get dressed in regular clothes for a housewife, and maybe a touch of lipstick. After all the chores were done, I settled down to write what was going on in my head, which seemed to be quite a bit all of a sudden. When I look at some of that stuff now, I am repulsed by what I read. Back then, it was a release for a lot of pressure. Period. There could be some grist for the clinician's mill in that garbage, but I have no stomach for it now. The writing exercise enabled me to be more relaxed and upbeat when others were around Tom.

One of my questions to myself was, Why was it so important to dress up as Sally when I had already decided that the persona was not important because the internal woman was developing secretly inside? A clumsy question, but what the hell. The basis for my proposal of marriage to Annie was predicated on my not needing to dress up as Sally anymore. My only answer for a long time was that it felt good to dress up. Not a sensual feeling, but a psychic feeling. *I sensed a change in my vibration rate.* I really did. I had no way to explain that terminology at the time. The notion popped from my pen to the yellow pad. I had a *very scary* feeling when I read it from my yellow pad before I thought it. Was this the beginning of automatic writing? Yes and no. It depends on one's definition of automatic writing. I will admit that stream-of-consciousness is a simple thing for me. If I can make the pen move fast enough, I am sometimes amazed at what I have written. I am convinced that everything I write comes from me, not some outside spirit in the ether. I don't give channel.

We lived on a very quiet street in a very small town. There were no visitors, no door-to-door salespeople, no delivery trucks. There were neighbors on both sides. Across the street lay the Pacific Ocean. The only woman on the block of four houses who didn't work outside the home was Frances, next door. She was a wonderful person, but usually very shy, and the last person who would pop in for a visit or to borrow a cup of vodka, or whatever.

Peace and tranquillity reigned on my block. I had my space, I got my work done, I did my writing, and life was looking a whole lot better. And of course, just as Mother Nature abhors a vacuum, She doesn't like it when things are going too smoothly for any of Her children.

It was early in June. I had just sat down after the chores to have coffee and plan the rest of my day until Linda came home from school. I had dressed in a cotton circle skirt, tank top, hose, and sandals. Complete makeup and polished nails. Once the camel gets its nose in the tent, you see.... . I had the front door open, with the screen door locked, to get fresh air. If anyone should come to the door, I hoped that they would think I was in the back yard. Sally was not about to answer the door.

The Cosmos saw to it that on that day. Frances would have a clear and immediate need to borrow something from Annie. She rang the bell. I did not move. She knocked on the door frame and hollered that she really needed to borrow something. Right now. She was one of the two neighbors who could tell whether or not anyone was in the back yard. I got up and answered the call. I approached the screen door and stood there. She introduced herself and said that she needed to borrow one of Annie's hats. There had been a death in the family, and she and her husband had to go to a service that night in Oakland. I could only croak, "Hat?" She said that she knew where they were in Annie's closet, and that she had permission to borrow anytime. It was firmly suggested that I let her in so that she could get a hat. My mind usually goes from zero to sixty in twelve minutes, but on this occasion, I deftly unlocked the screen door, stood back, and let the woman in.

She zoomed down the hall, followed by me, into the bedroom, and sure enough she knew where the hats were. She found the one she was looking for, smiled, and said, "Who are you? A cousin or a sister?" I suggested we go back out to the kitchen and have some coffee. As we went up the hallway, she said that she really didn't have time for coffee. She stood stock still at the door, waiting for an answer. I said, "I am pleased that you don't recognize me, Frances." Then she did. Her face made all kinds of movement, then she threw her arms around me and said I was beautiful. She wanted to come back tomorrow and hear all about this. Would I please dress the same way again? Oh yes, Frances.

She asked for tea. The word had gotten out in the neighborhood that I made a very strong pot of coffee and had the audacity to call it normal. That was a gross canard. We sat at the dining table that was half way between the kitchen and the living room. Her eyes were larger than usual, and they sparkled. This was going to be good ... the two of us who had already established a friendly relationship as male and female neighbors. Her questions tripped over each other and finally she just said, like any good shrink, "Tell me about it." Before I could start, she interrupted to say how good I looked. I gave a demur thanks, and began relating my highly abridged version of my saga from childhood to date. It took maybe twenty minutes. During my monolog, I noticed a wider range of emotion on her face than I had ever seen before. When I finished, she said that I should be Sally all the time. I, of course, at the moment, was in agreement with her. I also pointed out that it was folly to consider such an idea in these surroundings. We lamented that fact for a minute or so. Next she wanted to know what she could do for me. I said that what we were doing right now was all I could hope for. I told her that I was thrilled that we could act as two neighbor ladies having morning coffee together, and to talk about topics women usually talk about.

And we did. I was amazed that she was able to consider me as another woman. She shared a lot of information about her family that only women will share when they want input or confirmation from a trusted woman friend. I was honored, of course, but I found two disquieting results from such confidences.

First, I felt too comfortable in the role. It seemed natural for me to listen to intimate information, and to be able to dialog with it. The second aspect of this relationship was that my input seemed to be helpful to her. I was able to empathize; my consciousness was on par with hers. My experiences at the Women's Center, my long talks with women friends in my several apartments in the last couple of years, were all coming up front for me and I really was a woman again during those conversations.

I realized how much I missed these woman-to-woman conversations. The final zinger was the realization that all this elevated, estatic mental state was possible because *I was dressed as a woman*. Sally was back. She had come in a side door when I wasn't looking. I was thrilled and horrified at the same time.

Frances and I met two or three days a week, for a time, to talk about serious things and to just have lighthearted banter. I could tell that she felt a lot more comfortable with me as Sally than Tom. Sometimes she wanted me at her house, though she suggested I bring my own coffee. She wanted me to meet her visiting daughters and nieces. I did. We all felt warm and cozy with each other.

One day, while sipping my second cup of coffee in my nightgown and robe, the front door was flung open, then slammed shut. Linda had gone to school, but decided to turn around and come home because she was feeling poorly. Linda did not know there was also a Sally in the family.

In a heartbeat, I raced down the hall when I heard the door open, my pink robe flying, and into my bedroom as the front door slammed shut. I did not think I could move that fast. If I had to think about it, I could not have moved that fast. Terror moved me down to hall. Oh damn! What do I say or do now? I took a long hot shower, dressed in my regular male pants and shirt, and went out to deliver the speech I had composed in the shower. Linda was in her bedroom, door closed. I knocked gently and asked if I could talk. She said, "Okay."

I delivered the speech. The essence of it was that she was born with a problem that manifested in her body. I was born with a problem that manifested in my mind. We were both a little different from most people, but in obviously different ways of being different. I apologized for my appearance when she came home, and said that I did not think she would return before the normal time. I added that my problem seemed to flare up whenever my employment situation was not good, or nonexistent.

Her response was enigmatic. She was used to keeping her own counsel, and she was also not feeling well or she would not have come home. The look in her eyes and the tone in her voice seemed to indicate that she was surprised, not hurt or angry. She wanted to know what her mother thought about it. I said that her mother thought it was not a good thing to do, and she did not want her daughters to know about it. Linda smiled wanly and said that it did not matter to her if I dressed that way or not. Then she rolled over and went to sleep.

Linda's reaction did not amaze me. Based on my years of knowing her, and knowing my place in her heart, I expected something like that for her response. I had been trying to develop a field theory that would allow me to predict anyone's reaction to the female me, should they learn of it. My hypothesis was that if the person loved me *and* the relationship was contingent on my manhood, then there would be a problem gaining acceptance. The hypothesis has had a very high hit rate. Nowadays, however, it is all academic. The relationship with Linda did not change for the next several years. We interacted as though the event did not occur. The event was replicated a few times thereafter. She gave no indication that it mattered.

In early June, Sally was waxing the kitchen floor. Nice, quiet idiot work and a labor of love. The sun was presenting its maximum drying power through the kitchen windows. I was waxing my way out of the space into the living room when the same locked screen door separated the surprise visitor from me. It was Debbie, the neighbor on the other side of Frances, home on maternity leave. She wanted to know if "the man of the house" was present. I responded that he was not here right now, but asked if there was anything I could do. I said I was his sister. She said that she wanted to buy a pack of cigarettes from him, and save herself from making a trip to the store right then. I said that I would get her a pack, and did. She wanted to pay for them and I said no.

At that point of the interaction, she remarked on the similarity between me and "my brother." She said it was incredible. Were we twins? At that moment I had the urge to tell her that it was not at all incredible because we shared the same body. So I said that to her, out loud.

Her reaction was about the same as Frances'. She tore open the package of Pall Malls, and wanted to sit and talk about it for awhile. She was in her mid thirties, a career woman with Pacific Bell in San Francisco, and possessed a sophistication level that easily accommodated this "new woman" on the block.

Of course, she wanted to know if anyone else knew, and I told her about Frances. We agreed that the next morning we three would all get together for a hot beverage of our choice. We did meet, and had a fine time talking about general neighborhood topics and about my situation. It was pleasant. One thing I subsequently learned was that their husbands did not approve of me as Sally. Tom was still all right with them, but neither had any interest in meeting or talking about Sally. Fine with me. I never wanted to push anyone. You either like it, are neutral, or you don't like it. Nothing I can do-or want to do-to change anyone's mind.

Occasionally, I would teach a day class at the computer center. It was a pleasant thing to do because of the people who enrolled. They were almost always women who wanted to know what the big deal was with these computers that were taking their husband's time and attention. I was pleased to be able to provide them with some insights. First, I liked the idea of them gaining a level of competence and comfort with the device. Word processing was just getting off the ground in the early eighties, and many of them would be able to transfer their hands-on computer experience to a word processing system. The second good thing they were getting was a common vocabulary with their menfolk. As a result of the class, they were gaining useful knowledge for home and for possible employment.

Another boon to the day classes was that I got to be friends with Rosie of Rosie's Corner. She owned and operated a women's ready-to-wear store next door to the computer center. Before or after class, I would drop in to say hello as a good neighbor, and sometimes I would ask about things for Annie. Annie used to shop there on occasion. Rosie's stock was all factory seconds. Only the most minor flaws were present. Perhaps a loose button, or a garment without its belt, or some such trivial thing. Rosie would visit the computer showroom once in a while.

One day I asked Rosie if she could help me find something for myself. I casually told her that I liked to wear women's clothes now and then. It was a big secret, of course, and I had to be discreet. She was not shocked in the least, and said that she would help me find something, and she would also look for things especially for me on her buying trips. She gave me a few things to try on to establish my size in the Koret line of ready-to-wear. We concurred that I was a 16 and my best style was a town and country look. I bought a sweater and skirt, paying about half the price of department stores selling the same labeled garments.

A week later, I stopped by to show her the complete outfit on Sally. I had parked in the parking lot in view of her window. As I walked in, she was staring hard at me. Then she smiled and said, "I saw you walking in from the parking lot, recognized my inventory on you, but I didn't recognize you. I couldn't figure out how you could have my clothes if I didn't sell them to you."

If it hadn't been for that, she would not have recognized me. That made me feel comfortable. My visit also told her more about me and what I could wear. From then on, I was one of her regular customers. She asked me what I was up to that day. I told her I was on my way to the Wig Palace to shop for a new wig. She asked what was wrong with the one I was wearing, but we both knew it was not in good shape.

If I had to name one place that was my security blanket for my years of frustration, confusion, and indecision from 1977 to 1988, it was the Wig Palace in San Mateo. The owner, her daughter, and a series of hired stylists were there to help me find the right wig and to keep it (or them) cleaned and pressed. I might see them on a regular basis for several months, or there might be an interval of a year or so between visits. After the first few trips in, I was able to loosen up and level with them regarding who the wig was really for. I started off as male, then as Sally, then it could be either. Whichever me was handy. Only Sally tried on wigs because of the clothing and the makeup. It really did make a difference in deciding whether a style was going to work or not. The women were wonderful. They were interested, they liked me, and we spent a lot of time talking about me and about them. We were women friends.

Evidently, I was the only male customer for female wigs that cared to acknowledge that I was a male who wanted to appear in public as a woman. They said that they had a lot of male customers who were very uptight and would not admit who the wearer was to be. They lamented the customers' lack of honesty because they could have served them so much better if they had been as open as I was. They asked me an enormous number of questions about transvestites and transsexuals. I did my best at providing qualified answers based on my own experiences, which were considerable by this time. I suggested they read some of the experts, and furnished them with bibliographical data. They never read them. They said my answers served their purposes. Sometimes I would just pop in if I was in the neighborhood. They were always pleased to see me no matter how I was dressed. I felt like family. I could always walk in, go into the back room, pour some passable coffee, and sit a spell to visit. It was the longest single commercial relationship I had. Sometimes, life was almost too much for me, and they served as sidewalk psychologists once in a while. I think we all gained from the relationship in many ways. We still write to each other a few times each year.

Mary F. was a woman I met during my last full year as a school administrator back in the early seventies. We found ourselves on the same committee to develop the curriculum and the standards for the A.A. degree requirements for Teacher Aide. She was a librarian at the local community college. There were probably a dozen or so educators from various disciplines invited to participate in the task. My first surprise at the end of the first meeting of the group was to learn that this live-wire, animated woman was a librarian.

At the end of the second meeting, I asked her if she had time for a drink at the Hacienda, a local upscale motel, restaurant, and lounge. She looked at me as though the stereotype of a public school administrator was as blown for her as the stereotype for a librarian was blown for me.

It was the beginning of a friendship that has continued since we first clinked our beer glasses. We felt a *simpatico* from the start. All of us know someone in our lives like that. Right away, you know that you are friends. By the time we had to get on to our homes, I had told her about Sally. I gave her just enough to let her know I was not really whacko, but felt alone in all of it, and wanted some kind of friendship for Sally. She was fascinated and said that she would be glad to meet with Sally sometime, have drinks, and see what happens. That was in the fall of 1973. We did meet a few weeks later in a nice lounge, had a lot of drinks, and reestablished the friendship on a new basis.

For years afterward, we would plan to meet for lunch somewhere. She would ask who she was going to dine with. I would say Tom, or Sally, depending on which one I thought I would be. More often than not, I was what I said I would be, but I was the other if last minute circumstances changed my plans. I was pleased that Mary was amused by the lack of predictability. A few times she would get there late and ask the headwaiter for Sally's table, but I had to be male that time. The reverse situation happened, too. After awhile, she just asked for a large, tall person with glasses,...

Mary took a great interest in my duality. She said that I was the same, but then again, I was different. She felt that the male was a little tense, serious, and restrained. A nice guy, but not the kind of man she would date very often, if at all. Sally was animated, a lot of fun, a little zany, indeed a woman, and a lot like her. After a few years of intermittent lunches, she made the observation that she acted very differently around Sally than around Tom. She said she tended to be protective of Sally, opened doors for her, spoke to headwaiters on our behalf, and so forth. When I was Tom, she sat back and let him take charge. She said that all this had been going on for some time before she realized it. I hadn't noticed the pattern until she mentioned it.

During those times when I lived alone and worked as Sally, she and I got together a lot. There was predictability in my costume when we met for lunch or dinner. One late afternoon, Mary and I met at the Hacienda for drinks. We were prattling along on some topic when somebody's pro football team came in for refreshment. Evidentially, the team was staying at the Hacienda for a few days. Mary recognized them right away. I had no interest in reading the sports pages, and didn't recognize any of them. Mary said that they would be all over us in a few minutes, and what did I want to do when it happened. I was excited and I was scared. I told her that what I wanted had no bearing on the situation; we had better get moving. They did come over with beers for us, chatted us up while we drank their offering, then Mary said to me, in a loud voice, that it was time for us to go meet our husbands. We moved out quickly.

Some years would roll by with only an occasional telephone call to keep the friendship alive. It became obvious to me that Mary liked Sally a lot, but not much use for the male edition. It was fine with me.

In 1985, I think, Mary called me to say that she had been transferred to another campus in the community college district. We met again for lunch and she told me... but I am getting ahead of my story.

In late summer of 1980, I was about to come apart in my head. Annie and I had been married for a year, the marriage was absolutely wonderful, and everything was fine... on the surface.

Classes at the computer center were going well. I had been reading a book that dealt with systems selling as opposed to commodity selling. I thought it was a brilliant concept. So I translated the concept into a plan of action to sell the microcomputers to a public school district, where there was no way for them to get a return on their investment, which was one of the key features of systems selling. I gave my pitch with hands-on demo. They bought $105,000 worth of computers, printers, and the network controller. I received zero commission for the effort. Tandy's Rule, you see, says that only salesmen can receive commissions. The salesman of record elected not to share "his" commission with me. He was not obliged to. The lesson I learned from that was there was no way I could win financially at Radio Shack.

I knew that I was in need of a more demanding, better paying job if I was going to maintain my balance. The world out there had nothing for me. I was in a tight spot regarding Sally's resurrection. I liked it too much. I was spending too much time dressed, I was taking too many chances coming and going. During the day as Sally, and I still loved Annie and our marriage. Between a rock and a hard place? Yes.

I searched through my dresser drawer and found my outpatient card for the VA hospital in Palo Alto. It was Sally's card, and I had used it a lot in the middle seventies to satisfy the Gender Dysphoria Clinic's requirements. The therapists were wonderful and they helped me see a lot of things I had been blind to in the past. Perhaps they would be able to help me now. Annie never wanted to talk about Sally, and I can't blame her for that. Annie would have been the best counsellor, but Sally was a closed topic in our house.

One morning I got up, dressed in my latest purchase from Rosie, and drove off to see the wizard. I went to the desk I used to report to for an appointment. I was told I had to go to another department because it had been so long since I had been in. I needed to be screened by Alma before any appointments could be granted.

I was the only one in the waiting room. An orderly came by, saw me and asked if I would like some coffee. I said yes, I would. He asked if I wanted anything in it. I said I would like a little brandy if he had it. He chuckled and said that it was good I still had a sense of humor. The coffee came, and so did the nod from Alma.

We sat in her small cubicle, both of us smoking. I sensed she was from New York City. Maybe Jersey. She said crisply, "What is the problem, Sally?" I said that the problem was with my sex. She said, "Too much, too little, or the wrong kind?" All the tension left me as I roared with laughter at the misunderstanding. Alma was not amused at what she thought was a reasonable question. Then I told her my story. She was now a most concerned listener. I thought she was actually going to cry. I will admit I was in a tough spot. I loved my wife and felt good about the marriage. I loved being Sally and felt good about developing her for permanent residence on the planet. Alma had no trouble being sympathetic. She assigned me to a lovely therapist for treatment. Her parting comment was that she thought she would never say to anyone that it was too bad the marriage was so good.

Ann was a psychiatric social worker. It was a curious title for a bonafide therapist without a degree in medicine. What's in a name? We had appointments weekly for about six months. I felt good as a result of having someone to talk with, someone qualified to listen to detect any contradictions or inconsistencies in my blathering. Whatever was going on helped me considerably. It could have been the attentive ear, the non-judgmental other, or it could have been a legitimate way for me to turn out in public as Sally. It does not matter now. It relieved me of some pressure, and kept the self-doubts to a minimum. She even referred me to a staff psychiatrist to check me out for severe personality disorders, e.g. psychoses. I did the Rorschach test and some others. A week later, the doctor told me I was not crazy, not psychotic, I had a true grasp on reality, I was a goal-oriented person, and a lot of other stuff I felt to be accurate. On my way home that day, I wondered how come a medical man can give me paper-and-pencil tests and an interview, and come up with the same personality description as my astrologer did when she worked my natal chart?

In October, Erv was promoted to corporate level work with the Tandy Company. He said they appreciated his success with the missionary computer center, and they wanted him to help the next generation of computer store managers get on the right track. He was replaced by Dan, who was a hot dogger. In November, Dan said that there would be a new center opening at the foot of Market Street in San Francisco. Would I like to be a part of it? Sure, said I.

San Francisco has always been my favorite city. I've already made that point earlier in this epic tale. What it meant now was that on top of everything else, I would be closer to the sophisticated fashions of the big time office workers. At lunch I could girl watch to my heart's content. Embarcadero Square was across the street where the best restaurants were. And a Hyatt Hotel. On my side of Market there was an office building with about twenty-five stories of finely-dressed female office workers. Every day I had my own fashion show while eating a piroshki and drinking a Watney's ale. Even the restaurant coffee was just right in my new neighborhood.

Oh yes, the computer center was better too. I had an invitation to specify the furnishings and appointments in the classroom. A second reason for wanting to work in S.F. was the proximity to more jobs. Surely, I thought, someone would come into my classroom and say I should come to work in their company, and make it happen. No.

I did have one student who was a financial reporter for the *Chronicle*. A few weeks after he finished the class, he came back to ask if he could interview me. He wanted to do a story on the increased popularity of the microcomputer as being a result of the classroom opportunities for learning. Sure, John, do your interview.

The article was printed in a computer magazine a few months later. He made me out to be one of the good guys in the world of microcomputers. Evidentially, there were a lot of charlatans claiming knowledge when they did not have it. I photocopied the original several times and used it as an addendum to my resume. It was a nice ego stroke, anyway.

Another advantage in working so close to the financial district and the Ferry Building was the proximity to Ed and Viana. Ed worked in the Ferry Building as an engineer. Viana was frequently downtown to meet with stockbrokers. It was fun to meet with either of them and we did get together, never a threesome, about once or twice a month. It was interesting to see the kinds of places Ed liked, and the places Viana preferred. I liked all of the places, but wondered who decided when the two of them were together.

Neither of them knew about Sally. There was no reason to share that information with either of them. Viana said that of all the people she knew, I was her oldest living friend. It was important to her that we remain friends. Viana is, and always was, dramatically different than anyone I have ever known. I think she is a wonderful person, and I was glad she wanted to stay in touch. Ed and I hit it off well, because we had both been in the Navy at the same time and had a common vocabulary. And, any friend of Viana's,...

1981 clunked along. I was working three days and nights at the computer place, and every other Saturday. It was a good schedule because it accommodated both of me, paid better than San Mateo, and my commute was economical. In June, Erv told me he was fed up with the higher echelons, and expected to find a better opportunity in another company. Could he use me as a reference? Of course.

The reference check came by telephone one day between classes in July. The personnel man asked a bunch of questions, and I told him enough about Erv to convince him Erv could walk on water. Before we hung up, the man asked me if I wanted to work for his company. I was surprised and said so. He replied that he had never heard such a convincing sales pitch. I could *certainly* sell his product. I told him I was not pleased with my past as a salesman, that I like what I was doing, but perhaps I should learn more about his opportunity. He said that he would have Erv work on me. Okay. Every female knows that it pays to play hard-to-get, if you can.

By October, Erv had me convinced that I was in a dead end job, which I had already figured out, and that the office equipment rental business was booming. In early November, I was in a training program designed to enable me to sell or lease word processing hardware and software.

The problem with the training program was that nobody knew how to teach us the software. We had the Xerox 860 with its software, and it was magnificent. The Xerox 820 was probably a fine machine, but WordStar was new to everyone. Even the company reps ran into surprises when giving us our lessons. The recollection does remind me, however, of the joke: What is the difference between a used car salesman and a computer salesman? The used car salesman knows when he is lying.

I learned enough about the 860 to give demos and try to sell it. No sales. By January of 1982, I was fed up and so were the bosses. Erv was not happy with anything. I had reported the early warning signs to Ed several weeks before. He called one day to ask if I was ready to leave that no-sales job and come to work for The Port. I said, in a nanosecond, yes. Then I asked what he wanted me to do.

He wanted me to be an Industrial Engineer and help him get information into and out of the new computer system purchased by the Port of San Francisco. An industrial engineer and a systems analyst? Sure, Ed, right up my alley.

Chapter 17

We sat at a small table in a neighborhood restaurant less than a mile from Pier 46. Ed had given me the tour of the maintenance facility, which housed thirteen shops of diverse crafts. At lunch he was going to talk about my duties. After lunch, we would have a tour of the property that Harbor Maintenance was responsible for keeping functional, tidy, and rentable. Streets, too. Harbor Maintenance was essentially a construction company.

Ed told me at lunch what he would expect of me if I was going to work for him. The casual, comfortable Ed of the social scene did not join our table. This was Ed, the Captain, and I would be one of his junior officers. We both understood the meaning of that kind of relationship. I preferred that basis for my own sake.

He said that I would be classified as an industrial engineer, and assigned to the Head of Maintenance, because that was a budgeted position they had not been able to fill. Evidently the City and County of San Francisco Civil Service system had not established a high enough salary range for that job description. He would be able to hire me on as a temporary. If a real industrial engineer came along, my job would be gone.

My actual engineering duties would consist of writing a report now and then. He said that he would do the finer points of industrial engineering, and I would do some inspections, condition surveys, and write the reports. And some lightweight statistics. His opinion was that because I had enough time in the Navy, and had been to damage control school, and knew enough general seamanship as a Boatswain, that I was certainly qualified to do that kind of field work. True.

It was the new computer system that had a lot of people confused. Maintenance had trouble determining the cost of doing business. The software was not written to meet the needs of anyone but the finance office. I was being offered the job of figuring out what was really going on, and make the system work to his satisfaction. *That kind of task really was "right up my alley."*

I told him that all my computer experience had been on microcomputers, the TRS-80 and the Xerox 860 and 820. He said that a computer is a computer. I asked if a Honda was the same as a Mack truck. He said if I knew how to drive one, I could learn how to drive the other. I appreciated his confidence, and I told him I would accept the job if he would give me some slack and let me learn the system in my own way. Sure.

I worked at a terminal that had been installed in a small, private office above the nerve center for Maintenance activity. It had been named "the bird house" because it was a mezzanine room, higher than anyone else's office. There were two windows, facing east towards Alameda Naval Air Station. I saw the USS Enterprise go aground one day.

Once I felt comfortable with that computer system, I felt a lot better about myself. My ego was coming back. I had to have ego in that environment. A lot of what I did involved getting information from the electricians, or the blacksmith shop, or any of the others. To do that, I had to present a strong masculine countenance in a milieu of men who worked with their hands, heads, backs, and were proud of it. It was not difficult for me to become Willie-the-Actor again to get my job done. But I was painfully aware that I was acting.

I received a phone call one day from a woman who billed herself as an information systems specialist, and would I please make an appointment with her? Why not?

We met in my office. In three minutes I knew that what she had to offer was not applicable in my area of concern. It took another half hour for her to reach the same conclusion. Then she said that she was going to meet an old friend for lunch. She felt that Anna Belle was someone I would like to meet, and I should join them at McGinty's Bar & Grill. Why not?

We drove in separate cars. I got there first and decided to go in and get us a table. There was a mob of financial district people in there drinking their lunch. That was just before the world went cuckoo on its health kick. I saw a young woman at a table with no one else, the most likely place for me to sit. I asked if I could sit there until my friend arrived. By then there might be another table freed up. She said not to worry about that. She was also waiting for a friend to come. It was the kind of place where strangers could share a lunch table in comfort. We began a lightweight conversation, and I sensed a strong woman under that very pretty exterior. She had a tattoo on the back of her right hand. It was the now-popular circular symbol for *yin* and *yang*. I first saw that symbol in Korea in 1946.

I figured her for a Berkeley person, probably an MA in art from the university. She sparkled. A warm, friendly, animated woman. I was getting more interested in her than I had a right to. Ruth entered McGinty's, saw me and came to the table, saying that we two had already met. I had been talking with Anna Belle and did not know it. On our way out to our several cars after lunch, we all exchanged phone numbers so that we could do this again sometime. It had been fun to engage in lively conversation.

A week later I called Anna Belle to invite her to lunch. Sure. We met in a small place in an alley off Brannan Street. Cozy. We did a getting-to-know-you routine. At one point, we even remarked that we were interested in forming a friendship, but we did not know why. We had no romantic interests in each other. She was happy with her mate, and so was I with mine. This was to be platonic. We found that we both had a belief in reincarnation, karma, and astrology. Our conclusion was that we were supposed to get to know each other. One day we would know why.

Having lunch with Viana was always a treat. We would meet at a place of her choice, and those places had at least three desirable features, such as elegance, quality of food, and value per dollar. After the first date, she saw to it that all future lunches would be outdoors, or in an extremely well-ventilated place. It was her need not to be subjected to my cigarette smoke, yet she knew that my "filthy habit" was important to me. I appreciated the compromise.

Viana and I had met in 1946 in Tsingtao, China. We had lost track of each other until that coincidence in 1968 in San Francisco. Now we were reconnected, and would remain so forevermore. She attached great importance to the fact that our friendship was the oldest one she had. So many of her old friends had perished due to age or to Communist bullets in China.

I have always been fond of Viana because she was so different from other women I have known. Anyone would be different if they had grown up in China, raised by parents of two different European nationalities, had playmates from other parts of Europe as well as local Chinese. And superimpose that cultural smorgasbord on the constraints of World War II on mainland China, followed by the Communist rise to power after the war. Her adolescent years were lived in a time of war, shortages of food and other necessities, and controlled by Orientals of one political persuasion or another.

She read a lot, even as a child, and understood a whole lot more about life than I did when we first met. A very intelligent young woman. She had a wonderful sense of humor, but it was seldom on display. Deep down, she knew that life was not very funny. Tragedy had spent too much time with her, laying one unhappy event upon another. She never had children. The "why-not?" was an uncomfortable topic for her. I never did probe, but one day she told me about it. I am still wondering if not having children was a blessing or a curse for her.

Viana had established herself as a consultant or advisor to people who wanted to make investments in stocks and bonds. She was incredibly accurate in her predictions. No crystal ball for her. She just did her homework by studying the annual reports of a lot of companies, reading the news magazines, and papers. Once, she admitted that a little bit of hunch crept into her analyses. She made good money helping others make a lot of money.

Viana was a lady with a European mindset, very much like Suse from the Women's Center. No nonsense, but sensitive, gentle, compassionate, and strong. She was one of the few people I knew to change her mind about the acceptability of the gay population in San Francisco. At first she thought of them as a blot on the earth, then came to know them as humans like the rest of us. I regarded her ability to revise her position as evidence of a healthy, adult mind.

It seemed that 1983 was going to be one of the great years. I was learning new skills at the Port. I was making a fine salary, and I was without a desperate need to dress as Sally. My developing female consciousness could only come out on weekends, but it was enough for the time being.

Another benefit to working in the big city was the opportunity to meet with Timothy for lunch now and then. He had taken a job with the California School for Professional Psychological as a temp, back in 1980. Evidently, his job at the county hospital in San Jose had become too much burden for him to handle. A case of emotional burnout. He moved from the Hidden Hill chalet to San Francisco to get a fresh start.

He had been nearly broke, and had signed up with a temporary agency to do clerical work, or anything else. He was sent to CSPP to do something with file cards for the Director of Admissions. In a month he was hired to work there full time. Within a year, his boss lost favor with the board of directors, and Timothy was offered the job as director, on a temporary basis. A few months later he was the permanent Director of Admissions. The man was smart, all right. And he had a lot of energy and creativity to offer. He was credited with producing a large quantity of qualified students.

We had stayed in touch over the years after I moved out of the Hidden Hill residence. He regarded Tom as the custodian of Sally. We talked on the phone once every month or so. There were times, back in my Radio Shack days, when I was able to manifest as Sally and meet him for lunch. He liked that better, of course. So did I.

On one such occasion, he asked me if I felt better as Sally than as Tom. I said that they were really two people: Tom and Sally. They had to be distinct persons. Each one had a chance for feeling good, but in different ways. Then, with his incisive mind, he lodged the dual question: What made Tom feel good, and what made Sally feel good? I asked to defer my answer until I had a chance to think it through. The questions were too important for me to give a top-of-the-head answer. He was not satisfied with my stalling. He asked if I, Sally, felt good right then. I said yes, I felt estatic being out, and walking up Union Street with him, arm in arm. He asked if I could describe the good feeling. I found myself giving him a metaphor without really thinking about it. I told him that being Sally was like the mental sensation one experiences in orgasm, but stretching it out for hours. He smiled. That seemed to satisfy his curiosity. He never asked me again.

Annie and I received an invitation to a cocktail party in Oakland. One of my old high school friends, John, was celebrating thirty years as president of his boiler company. We were not as close as we used to be, but managed to exchange Christmas cards in some years. And of course, there were the high school reunions. He and his wife were guests at our wedding a few years earlier. Annie and I were pleased to be invited. There must have been two hundred people there, occupying three very large meeting rooms of the Oakland Women's Center. Virtually all of the "old gang" from Burlingame High School were there, plus John's other friends, plus all the customers he did business with. Quite a crowd.

It was a thrill to see Pierre again. He had dropped out of the insurance business to open a printing shop with one of his sons. I was able to talk with him as a former buyer of print, and the friendship was indeed renewed. So many times, one sees an old and dear friend, asks the obvious questions—How have you been, Where are you living, and What are you doing now? Then there isn't much to say after that.

We talked of various kinds of paper and how one could do half tones and printed copy using a screen tint to achieve certain results. Soon we were joined by others of our mutual past. They must have wondered what we were talking about to have such a sustained conversation. I asked Mary Lou, Bruce's wife, if Carolyn was there. I had not seen Carolyn since the wedding reception in 1950 when Helen and I were married. There was a sudden change of expression on everyone's face. Mary Lou said, "No." Naturally, I asked what she was doing, how she was, and did she still live in Oregon? Mary Lou and Carolyn had been the closest of friends. She said that Carolyn was dead.

I have never been hit with such force with any kind of news before or since. My knees became weak, and I almost fell down. I thought my drink would fall to the carpet. I was truly stunned. Then I asked what happened. I was told that she died by her own hand. She had been unhappy. Then there was no more talk of Carolyn.

The group slowly dispersed, leaving Annie and me staring at each other. Annie knew that Carolyn and I had a loving relationship in high school; that it was more than a casual crush. She did her best to comfort me, but I felt the loss of Carolyn as a deep personal loss. My cavalier attitude toward death was punctured by the news of her demise. Why? I was not sure then, nor am I sure now, but my feeling is that I really did love her. I was hurting because she felt so unhappy with life that she decided to end it. The pain she must have felt!

Could I have been of any help to her? Probably not. We had been out of touch for over thirty years. Did we know each other anymore? The other old pals were just barely acquaintances now. Could I have helped her understand that to end one's life by choice was counterproductive in terms of the Cosmos? Could I have helped her to see that there are other things one can do to build a new life? I do not know. What I do know is that the news of her departure hurt me deeply, and let me know that a lot of the love I had for her was still alive in me. It may have been only an adolescent love, but maybe that is the most powerful kind; unsullied by the apparent realities of so-called adult life. The love was based on much more than sexual attraction.

It was weeks before I stopped thinking of Carolyn every day. I went through a lot of the what-if type questions. What if I had been more patient with her and the condescending attitude she displayed to me in 1948 and 1949? What if I had not rushed into a marriage with Helen, and waited until I was a little more mature? There were a lot of questions that went unanswered. Then, of course, What if Carolyn and I established an adult relationship, and she ultimately had to come to grips with Sally? What would *that* have done to Carolyn? I do not presume to know the answer. What I do know is that Sally would have won out over her.

In May of 1983, I was informed that a bonafide industrial engineer had applied for my job at The Port. All he had to do was take an oral examination at the civil service board and pass it. Because I was temporary, my job was up for grabs. I asked to take the exam and compete with this interloper. My request was denied because I did not have a state license to be an industrial engineer. I kicked and screamed for a time, but

I knew the game was over. I had no job prospects. I got as far as the Assistant Port Director with my resume and a personal interview to see if there was anything now or in the near future that I could be considered for. He was very nice, but the answer was no. I was given two weeks notice. Everyone seemed genuinely sorry to see me go. There was a small beer party in my honor in the sheet metal shop. I regarded that as a true expression of aloha.

Thus began another tough period in my life. I was out of a job for ten months. It hurt me because I knew I had a lot to offer, but nobody seemed to want any of it. My male ego does not turn on and off like a light switch. I had been pumped up as an important man doing an important job on that computer that no one else had been able to do. Ego? Oh yes. The lack of response to my resumes and award-winning cover letters for advertised jobs was killing me emotionally.

Guess what I did when I was not writing letters and revising my resume? Right. I knew how to put the balm on my wounds with the return of Sally. I really tried to make myself believe that Sally was only an escape mechanism. I could never convince myself that it was true. I even asked my therapist at the VA hospital about it. After some fine questioning, she concluded that she could not see Sally as a hiding place. "Quite the opposite," Ann said one day.

Upon leaving the Port in May of 1983, I wanted to have the best looking resumes possible. I let my fingers do the walking through the Yellow Pages of the San Mateo County directory to find word processing services in Half Moon Bay. I called each of them until I found the one with a Xerox 860 system. It had the best printer of them all at that time. Val became my secretary.

She was as tall as I was, and that made me like her right from the start. Besides, she was a very friendly person and a remarkably good typist. She seemed to know what I wanted her to do before I had a chance to explain. After a few visits to her office, she remarked that I had a lot of diverse experience on my resume. She also questioned some of the stuff I gave her for typing. It seemed that I had accidently given her a copy of an old marked up resume for Sally. She was somewhat curious to know what that was all about. My mindset at the time made it easy for me to casually tell her that I had worked and lived as a woman for almost two years. I felt that the truth would be better than making up a story that would not be believed anyway. She found the idea to be fascinating, and barely believable. I said it was true, but I was now married and happily so. She, like so many others, had a ton of questions. I answered them as truthfully as I could, and as briefly as I could. She said that she would like to meet Sally someday. I said that perhaps someday she could. Then she asked me if I would be interested in talking with one of her customers about a job? Yes, Val.

That was how I met Al. His company had the contract to write the operations and procedures manual for the *La Petite Boulangerie* restaurants. He needed more writers, and asked if I would like to do a chapter. I did one, then four more. By that time the total manual was done, and I had established myself as a good writer for his kind of contracts. We also developed a personal friendship. One day at lunch, Al asked if I had been in the Navy. I suppose it was some expression I had used that triggered the question. I said that I had been, and reached for my ID card. He looked at it and then pulled out his ID card. He was a Captain in the reserves. The friendship improved even more, but there was no more work for me to do.

In the fall of 1983, Linda, Annie's daughter started into a decline she never recovered from. It hurts to recall the details of it, but there were some bittersweet memories. She did graduate from high school with her class. That spring and summer we saw a Linda we had not seen before. She was radiant. Her face filled out to become more round and soft. Her eyes were almost on fire. Her spirits soared. She had beaten the odds on longevity.

In late May, while I was unemployed, she wanted new shoes to go with her graduation dress. Annie was able to buy the dress, but shoes were too expensive. I volunteered to drive Linda to San Mateo one afternoon to shop for shoes. On the way over the hill, I told her that I would buy her a pair of shoes that she really liked, not something that only fit a meager budget. She was pleased. I reinforced my offer by saying that I had an appreciation for the need to have the right shoes for the dress she was going to wear. She gave me a knowing grin on that pronouncement. My final offer was to take her to as many shoe stores as she wanted to visit before making a decision. We only had to go to two places to find what she was looking for.

A new problem emerged: She found two pairs that she wanted, and could not decide which ones she should buy. We started to discuss the situation. I will admit that I was getting vicarious pleasure from this conversation, but that was only a by-product. This small person had a lot to celebrate, and I felt pleased to be able to help her. After several minutes of explaining the total wardrobe situation to me, there was only one course of action: buy both pairs. My private thought was that this time was never again going to happen in her life, and I wanted to help her make the most of it. She was happy, of course. In the weeks that followed, she seemed to live in those shoes. The senior ball, naturally, and a lot of other social events before and after the ball. I felt good, and so did Annie.

In late summer, as the social season ended, and her friends drifted off to colleges and universities, Linda began to feel less than tip top. By Halloween, she needed a lot more treatments than ever. In early November, she had to return to the hospital for intensive treatments. At Thanksgiving, we spent the day with her and had dinner, but Linda was not too cognizant of our presence. She rallied around Christmas time, and we were so happy that she seemed on the mend. Then there was a sharp downward trend that never changed. In the first week of 1984, she left the planet. No more pain, no more discomfort. Without her knowing it, she taught me something about living. I saw her as a kind of role model. My feeling of loss did not even come close to the anguish Annie had to deal with. I felt helpless in trying to console her. Only time could do that.

In late March of 1984, I had an interview with the manager of marketing communications at US Instrument Rentals, a subsidiary of US Leasing. It was the company where Annie worked. I had met Claudia several times at company parties, but had never spent much time in conversation with her. I was told to bring my portfolio of things to the interview. The position I was being considered for was marketing communications specialist. I did not know what that job was, but what the hell. I had been out of regular work for ten months. I had sent out over a hundred resumes, and had two interviews. In both of those cases I was not acceptable to the interviewers. I was too old or overqualified for them.

Claudia was very cordial and made all kinds of nice comments on my portfolio. I had never been asked to bring such stuff to an interview before. I gathered up everything I had done in print, divided it into logical piles according to type of material, and put it all into folders. One problem was that my strongest cards for the job were things that Sally had done, and had her name on them. I took them anyway because they were good things. If she focused on Sally's name, I would just have to level with her. It would have to be the reverse of the situation with Gordon and Dale when they offered the jobs to Tom, but hired Sally. Claudia would have to hire Tom on the reputation of Sally. An interesting possibility. It turned out that I was able to dazzle her with footwork, moving pieces around as I talked. She saw the stuff, but not the name of Sally. I got the job, and started in April on Annie's birthday.

That evening, Al called to ask if I would do a manual for the installation of a quartz furnace at AMD in Sunnyvale. The furnace was capable of reaching 1400 degrees Fahrenheit and was used to bake silicon chips for computers. I told him I had just been hired at USIR. He was happy for me, but he wanted me to do this manual anyway. It would be a night exercise, and he was sure I could fit it into my new schedule.

It took only one night to observe. Two days later I had the manual done. It was a rare experience because the retrofit meant that an old furnace had to come out, and be replaced with the new unit. A *very* technical thing to do. I had to wear a white smock, a hat, and a face mask as did everyone else. I took copious notes, verified some of the steps with the technician as well as the correct spelling of his strange vocabulary. I had never seen or heard of a thermocouple before. He handed me a used one to look at. I put it in my pocket as a souvenir of this experience. Later, as he was picking up his tools and used parts, he asked if I still had the thermocouple. He wanted it back. I said I wanted it as a souvenir. He said there was a thousand dollars worth of platinum in it, and please hand it over. Okay.

The assignment I was given by Claudia included trade show coordination, proofreading of other people's writing, and a minor amount of print production. She had grown into her present job from the ranks of secretary, then an administrative assistant to one of the three product line managers. Her knowledge of advertising, public relations, and all the other facets of marketing communication were learned by doing business with the vendors of those services. It is probably the best way to learn, but Claudia allowed herself to become hoodwinked by the ad agency into believing that only they could do a decent print job, and that most all of the big ticket items should be purchased through them. It took a while for me to convince her that I could get things printed faster, cheaper, and better than the ad agency could. She was pleased, later, that her departmental costs were looking better, but I think she was unhappy that *I* showed her how to do it. I suppose women have a capacity for a male ego, too. Or maybe I just didn't explain it to her properly.

One day Claudia told me to go up to the Data Systems sales department to see the manager. He had a special project in mind, and perhaps my creative talents could help him. My office mate, Cathy, said that I was about to walk into the lion's den. I asked what that meant, and was told that he was a crotchety old man who gave everybody heartburn. I put on my new silk tweed jacket, and ascended the staircase to the second floor. I got directions on where the ogre's cage was, and entered it. That was how I came to meet Ralph.

He shook my hand, welcomed me to the company, and then got down to business right away. He explained what he wanted, and asked if I could do it for him. Sure, Ralph, when do you want it? "Next Thursday," he said. On Wednesday of the next week, I had the specially-printed checkbooks for his new sales contest. He was impressed. Later, he told me that I was the only one in the Marketing Communications department who knew how to get anything done. I told him that he was the only manager who knew how to say what he meant. It was the beginning of a beautiful friendship.

Chapter 18

Full employment was a boon to my psyche and my wallet. Perhaps an even more important feature was that I found myself working for a large corporation. The culture of such an organization was new to me. All the places where I had worked before were small potatoes compared to USIR, a subsidiary of US Leasing, member of the Big Apple's stock exchange.

The only analog I had was from my Navy days. As I was transferred from harbor craft to tankers, to a destroyer, to a heavy cruiser, and finally a battleship, I saw that bureaucracy increased with the size of the organization. And so it was in my new place. Of course, in the Navy everyone on board knows that everyone depends upon everyone else for survival. Not so with landlubbers. The rules for corporate survival required that I recall the principles of *The Prince* from my days in European lit classes.

I never did like the corporate culture. I was able to understand it after awhile and act in conformance with it, but it was phoney, and it had the capability to destroy people subtilely, and in the meanest ways possible. My principal reasons for staying were the regular paycheck and the opportunity to learn some new skills. Side benefits included making a few new friends, and I had to acknowledge that my work was fun as long as I did my job through the efforts of companies outside my own.

It took some time and a few false moves before I learned how to make it in this corporate culture. Evidently, one or more of those false moves caused Claudia, my manager, to recommend that my probationary status be extended for another three months. She made that declaration in writing during the last hour of her last day in the company. There was never a specific reason cited. I could only conclude that there was something about me that griped her. With her gone, more responsibility would fall upon me and my 22-year-old-teenager colleague. That was good, but the downside was that the manager designated as our non-resident supervisor was a posturing fool. In the Navy, success was measured by what you know and how well you perform. In the civilian world, it seemed to be not what you know, but who you know, and *what you know about who you know*.

I took great consolation in the fact that I had an opportunity to redefine my duties and responsibilities. I saw to it that most everything I did for the company was done by outside contractors, such as printers, typesetters, trade show people, and so forth. I had only a few in-house people to deal with to do my job, and that was fine. There were three managers that I had to serve: the posturing fool, good old Ralph, and the general manager of the analytical instruments division, who was a very polite and well-educated man. We got along just fine.

After another three months, the probationary period was lifted, and I became a permanent employee. What really mattered to me was that the managers I worked for gave me clear instructions for what they wanted. I had no problem getting it for them. My attitude towards work is that I am on probation every day... not a fearful attitude, it is just that I believe in working as effectively as I can whether anyone is monitoring me or not.

After my first few weeks on the job, I began making plans for the return of Sally, on a new basis. What that meant was that I would be able to rent a motel room somewhere, and spend a week end as Sally doing this and that. Of course I would tell Annie that I was going off to be Sally for a week end, and that if she needed me during the course of my absence, she could reach me by phone using the number I gave her. She did not like the fact that I felt the need to leave her for a week end, but if I had to do that, it was better to go away. No problem. My re-entries on Sundays, however, were a bit cool for the first few hours.

What can a person do on a weekend that is ladylike, cheap, and satisfying? I would like to know the answer too. What I did was a lot of exploring and trying out several ways of using the precious time. Generally, it would all begin with a phone call to reserve a motel room for Friday and Saturday nights. There were a few in San Mateo County that were clean, with helpful appointments, and reasonably priced. Another feature I looked for was for the line of visibility between the manager's office and the room I wanted. In some motels it is easier to do than in others. I would have to register as Tom, but no one would see him until checkout time. I did not want the manager asking me what the hell was going on. It took me years to learn that they didn't give a damn as long as I paid and I didn't trash the place.

A typical scenario was to make the reservation for the room a week or so in advance. Next I would call the ladies of the Wig Palace to alert them that I needed one of my wigs ready for pick up on that Friday afternoon. Then I would mentally inventory my things so that I would have what I would need. If there was someone I knew, I would call ahead of time to see if he or she would be available for visiting, or going somewhere. If not, I would explore on my own. There were advantages to being alone, as well as being able to talk with someone.

On the special Friday morning, I would load up my car with my stuff, go off to work, and during the noon hour I would drive to the motel, register, unload my things, and go back to work until quitting time. After work, I would drive to the Wig Palace to get my plastic hair, drive to the motel, take a shower, and shave those areas of my body that should not have hair, set up my travel steam iron, remove the wrinkles from my dress or skirt and blouse, or whatever I was going to wear that night (if I could get out in time), and other things for the rest of the week end.

In the early days of doing this drill, it took all of Friday night to get ready. I was a little slow at ironing until I learned that one can request an ironing board from the manager of the motel. That was faster than trying to iron on top of a bath towel on a dresser top. The other thing that took a lot of time was the gluing on of the false fingernails. It took only a few minutes to glue them on, but they popped off very quickly whenever I used my hands for buttoning a blouse, pulling on pantyhose, or anything else one does with one's hands. Eventually I discovered crazy glue. It is not good for the nails, but for short periods of a day or two it seemed to cause no harm. Getting them off became a problem until I realized that regular nail polish remover would do the trick. Most of the times, in the beginning, it took all of Friday night to get ready for the next day.

I would wake up at 6:00 a.m. on Saturday, take a quick shower, get my underthings on, shave my face extra close, do the make up, put on the outer garment for the morning, inspect myself critically, take a deep breath, and open the door to adventure.

My first stop would always be the Wig Palace. I was too timid about combing or brushing the wigs myself. The styling was always ornate, like I was going to a wedding or a grand ball. The ladies were glad to see me again. They would fool around with the wig to fit it to my face... something they could not do too well on their block.

Then we would have coffee and rap for a time until the customers started ganging up on them later in the morning.

My next port of call would be Rosie's Corner to see what was new and waiting for me. Rosie was always happy to sell me something, and would have a few things set aside for my approval. I still have a couple of things I bought from her those many years ago. One belt, in particular. And a scarf I still treasure. Eventually, Rosie closed her business to sell automobiles. It was good for her, but I had to find other places to go for trendy stuff to wear, at reasonable prices. She told me that her mother and sister had a place like hers in San Francisco. It took some time to get there, but they were as nice as Rosie, and had a larger stock. I still have some of their skirts and sweaters.

By mid afternoon I would be ready for something to eat. Any coffee shop would do. I just walked in, sat down, placed my order, ate, and left. Just like real people do.

In the late afternoon, I would consider what to do or where to go for the big Saturday night event. The world reminded me that women do not cruise the bars alone at night, especially on a Saturday night. It is done, but the staff and the clientele of any establishment will give closer scrutiny to a single woman at that time. It was during those moments that I knew I was being read, and was being watched very closely. I did not like to be in that situation because it was a constant reminder that I was functioning as a man in drag. Counterproductive at least. No one ever said anything to me, but their looks and countenance did all the communication.

There was a Saturday during summer when I went to a nice Italian restaurant early in the evening. It had been a very hot day, and I wore a sleeveless blue dress. It was the most comfortable thing I had. There was plenty of daylight outside, and I considered it early, and that I would probably be able to have a pleasant dinner despite my single state. Wrong.

I had been seated at a table for two by the maitre d', when the waiter came by to give me the menu and ask for an order from the bar. I said that I wanted wine with my dinner, but perhaps I could start now. Just after he brought it to me, a young man came over to my table and asked if he could join me. I was scared and somewhat uncomfortable. I asked why he wanted to join me. I could tell that he was a little tipsy, but functioning quite well. He sat down anyway and told me to relax, that he was not going to cause me any harm or trouble. He just wanted to know why I wore a sleeveless dress with such heavy, masculine arms. I could only stare at him, wondering what was coming next. He accepted my silence as a signal to say some more. When he did, it was to tell me that I really looked good, but I should keep my arms covered. He, it turned out, was a transvestite, but because he looked like a lineman for the Forty-Niners, he had no way of making it in polite society. He only dressed at home, or on

Halloween. He wanted to be a friend if I would let him. Then we got comfortable and started communicating. We exchanged fem names. It was not easy for me to call him Linda. In time he told me his name was Charlie. He continued to stay at my table until I finished my veal picatta and coffee. He wanted me to be his date for the rest of the evening. In his fantasies, he wanted someone to take him out on a date, but, well... So it would give him pleasure to escort me for the evening. We went to a couple of bars for drinks, and finally to a pancake house for end-of-the-evening coffee. I assured him that he had fulfilled one of *my* fantasies by being a date for me that night. We exchanged phone numbers and agreed to stay in touch. We did, but it was a long time before we talked with each other again.

One evening some years earlier, Annie and I had been invited to a banquet at a place called El Rancho Motel in Millbrae. It was the oldest motel in northern California. The restaurant was downstairs and the banquet room was upstairs. The special feature was that the motel's swimming pool had a glass wall on one side so that patrons of the bar and restaurant below ground could watch the swimmers in the water.

In the evenings, a senior citizen would come in to play the organ. There was a bar built around the organ for those who wanted to act like groupies. Annie and I had finished off the banquet that evening by moving downstairs to drink and to listen to the old tunes we remembered from the thirties and since then. Bill could play anything. It was only a matter of time before it occurred to me that Sally could probably go to the El Rancho on a Saturday night for dinner, be accepted as a traveller needing nourishment, and listen to the good old tunes of yesteryear. It was a wonderful idea that worked beautifully for a few years.

The first time Sally went there alone, the maitre d' smiled and escorted me to a table. He asked if the table was satisfactory. I said that it was, and was seated by him. I was getting the royal treatment, and did not know why. The young waiter came to take my order, and asked if he could tell me about the specials of the evening. Of course. I chose the poached salmon and the spinach salad. I was smiled upon by the young man. It was an excellent dinner, well served, and with a lot of kind and sincere attention by both the waiter and by Rudi, the owner-manager-maitre d'. After I had finished my coffee and paid the tab, Rudi asked if I would like to have a stool at the organ bar to have an after dinner drink and listen to Bill play. "A wonderful idea," I said, musically.

Rudi continued with the ladylike treatment by carrying my remaining dinner wine for me and helping me onto a stool. Bill looked up from his keyboard, smiled at me, and asked if I had any requests. I gave him some oldies and he played them all. In less than an hour, more people came in and sat at the organ bar. The joint started to jump, if you can jump to old Broadway show tunes, the popular stuff of WW I and WW II, and music older than that, like *Barney Google*. Everyone was so friendly. We all introduced ourselves during Bill's break time. It was then that I learned that the bar at the El Rancho was, in fact, a neighborhood bar for those locals who liked the old music. I stayed until closing as did everyone else at the organ bar. On my way out, Rudi said I should come back soon.

It was over a year before I got back there. Spending weekends as Sally was something that happened two or three times a year at best. The next time I went back to the El Rancho, Rudi beamed with pleasure at my presence. I was flattered, of course, that he remembered me. I thought there must be a catch to it somewhere. It turned out that there never was a catch. I was treated as a polite woman who visited northern California a few times each year, and that I was a good customer and behaved like a lady. If they knew what my trip was really all about, they never gave a hint. I had found a home away from home. Our brief chats grew into conversations.

It was this situation that caused me to compose a cover story, the kind that Maude told me twenty years earlier I would have to have. Rudi was being friendly, not nosey. I put together some facts that were real, but the collage came out as me being an instructor for a computer company in Irvine, CA. From time to time, I would have to do a special training session for an important customer in San Francisco. And that I would not *dream* of spending my free time anywhere but at his place. I suppose that I was there five or six times in three years. It was always the same drill. Rudi would light up when he saw me enter, graciously escort me to the table I liked the most, chatted me up a little, and stopped by a few times to see that everything was all right. The food was always great, the service impeccable, and the ambience unsurpassed.

Bill and I became friendly. If he saw me come in, he would play my theme song, *My Gal Sal*. There were so many people who wanted to be his friend. The competition was keen among the groupies, but I was not a competitor for his attention. All I wanted was to be regarded as a nice, quiet woman who liked the quality entertainment. And the stout coffee drinks. Now and again he would ask me what I would like to hear. I would say, "How about *Shuffle Off to Buffalo*, or *Nola*, or *Big Rock Candy Mountain*, or *What Kind of Noise Annoys an Oyster?*" I can't remember them all now, but you can get the general idea of the man's musical database. And of course, I was playing one upsmanship with the other groupies who requested *Jeanine, I Dream of Lilac Time, Over There*, an such. It was good natured competition and we all loved it.

There were moments during and outside those times that I asked myself what difference did it make whether I enjoyed those moments as a woman or as a man. The only answer I had was that it *did* make a difference. It was then that I created the metaphor of television to describe the two lives: The same drama is unfolding on the screen, but there is a difference if you watch it in color as opposed to black and white. If one begins to list the differences in viewing color vs. black and white, one will begin to state the kinds of attributes I would use to describe what is so hot about being a woman. It *seems* better. There is *more life* in it. The color *enhances* everything. *More senses* are being brought into play. And more. The reasons are all subjective, and if one asks *why* to every stated reason, eventually there is no rational answer. Try it sometime with anything you have a passion for, and see how much sense it makes when you try to analyze it.

The best part of my job at USIR was my involvement with print projects. Catalog covers, direct mail pieces, inventory sheets for customers, and a lot more. All of my experience at Prentice-Hall/Contemporary Ideas, and my job on *Discover Magazine* was used here. I also learned a lot more about printing because the requests for pieces were limited only by the imaginations of three managers. So I learned how to do a lot of off-the-wall jobs from the printers who ultimately did the work. Because I could spend more time with the printers than seated at my desk, I learned a number of production tricks to enhance a piece, yet lower the cost. I also learned a new meaning of PMS: Pantone Matching System. It was a color matching system similar to the color chips you get at a paint store. The color tones will change, however, when printed on different paper stock.

Trade show coordination was a minor nightmare. Our booth was heavy and expensive to move around the country. We had three divisions in the company, all wanting to use the booth with their own graphics on display. Working out a shipping schedule to accommodate all the field offices was a tough job. My first year, I logged 39 trade shows. It would have been easier if I had been allowed to go to the shows, to see the problems first hand so that I could be more effective when planning a show for a field office.

In the summer of 1985, my real mentor, Ralph, was canned. His boss was concerned with the ledger sheets. Ralph was trying to establish solid business relationships with our suppliers and our customers. They argued and Ralph lost. Or maybe he won in the long run. He left the company, and I lost a good lunch buddy. He knew all the great Italian places in the county. He was a well-educated man and considered reading books a terrific thing to do. We talked about a lot of things. Our ages were close, so we had both experienced the Depression years as kids, and had an appreciation for the good things in life. He could tell a story like no one else. But he was gone and he knew that I was sorry to see him go.

In early September, he called me at work one morning and asked if I would like to meet for lunch. Hell, yes! We met in Woodside, about halfway between San Mateo and where he was calling from. At lunch, he told me about his new company where he had a free hand to do the marketing. Then he asked if I would come to work with him again. I said that I certainly would. I gave my two weeks notice after lunch.

By mid September, I was commuting to another job. I was made the manager of marketing services, and my salary escalated to almost double the amount that USIR paid me. Ralph apologized for not getting me more money, but there would be raises in time.

The new job was the best ever. I noticed I said that about each new job I had. I had responsibilities that were new to me, but easy enough to do. One day, I counted the number of outside vendors I needed to work with to do my job: 49. Inside the company, there were three. I liked it that way.

It was one of Ralph's edicts that I be present at every trade show that the company attended. Fine with me. We attended all of the COMDEX shows, and a few telecommunication shows. I loved the crazy business of making a trade show booth ready for show time. The logistics were complex, the timing was dicey, and the possibility of changes two days before show time were real probabilities. Managing a trade show for a company is really a Type A job, but I was a Type B person. All of my experience of being a hot operator in the Navy, all of my experience in attending to last-minute crises at the printing press, and a few other jobs I have done, all enabled me to put on a good show, *no matter what*. It was thrilling. Besides, there was the travel, and the fine dining that came with it. And meeting people that would turn out to be business friends.

Trade shows took me to Washington, D.C., Denver, Dallas, Anaheim, and Las Vegas. The shows were hard work, but the payoffs were great. After doing them between other chores for a year or so, I began to see that possibly Sally could travel too.

Sure, it was chancy, but experience had taught me a few things about reducing risks. As I started to plan for the Fall COMDEX show in Las Vegas in November of 1986, I saw my big opportunity. The huge convention center was located a few hundred yards from the Las Vegas Hilton, an institution in itself. During COMDEX shows, rooms were impossible to get without prior registration, like about six months prior. With Ralph gone, it was hell trying to get approval for a lot of the planning. Ralph had been released from the company by a new president several months before this show. The new president had been an executive with IBM, and it was like pulling teeth to get him to make a decision if he was going to be responsible for the outcome.

He caused a lot of delays that cost us extra money later on. One of his hangups was committing to the names of the company's personnel to attend the show. By the time he decided on the names, he had a list too long for me to place everyone in the standard hotels approved by the show management.

I had seen to it that I had a room at the Hilton, but the rest of the company would have to bunk somewhere else, and it was part of my job to find them all lodgings. Using a secret maneuver, too complex to describe here, I found very nice rooms for everyone and at a lower cost than I thought possible. I also saw to it that their hotel was on the other side of town. That meant that I would have to be in the Las Vegas Hilton for nine days in a room all by myself. The stage was set.

I was obliged to arrive three days ahead of everyone else to get the booth set up. That meant organizing the labor crew, the electricians, the telephone company, the carpet people, the furniture people, and the florist to do their jobs in the proper sequence. We did it in one day without a hitch. My planning had paid off. That meant that I could afford to unpack some of Sally's things and wear them in the hotel room.

On the first evening, I just wore some things in my room. A skirt and blouse over the standard underpinnings, and a pair of shoes. My wig was a disaster when it came out of my suitcase. I applied my makeup and attempted to bring order out of the plastic hair. I found that I could do something with it, but not good enough for prime time.

I just wanted to sit and write, anyway. There was no shortage of yellow pads, it seemed. I began writing about isolated events. My first was the hiring interview as a managing editor for *Discover Magazine*. Next, I wrote about the night I was accepted as a charter member of the Women's Center in San Mateo. After that, I don't remember the sequence of my anecdotes. As I finished writing those first two, I felt hungry.

I looked in the mirror and decided that the image looked good enough to do business with room service. I called down, placed an order for a sandwich and a pot of coffee. In less than two hours, my order came. The waiter was cheery, and when I asked why he brought two cups, he said that no one person could drink a whole pot of coffee. I smiled and signed the tab and included a tip large enough to encourage room service to move faster next time. I hoped.

That was my first day in Las Vegas. There were two more days in which I had no assigned responsibilities.

I woke up at six, although I had placed a wake-up call for seven. I rolled out, peeled off the nightgown, did all the first-thing-in-the-morning stuff, and started to apply my makeup. I called room service for breakfast. The rest of my paint went on easily, then my clothes. I was counting on a fresh person to bring my tray. A young woman delivered my omelette and coffee. This time, there was a small red rose in a vase with breakfast. It delighted me to have a flower in my room. That was a new feeling.

The writing continued. By eleven o'clock, I remembered that there was an invitation to attend a luncheon in one of the tower suites. *PC Magazine* was famous for their parties, and besides, I had to do some campaigning for free PR with those guys. I washed my face, changed into Tom, and rode the elevator up to the *soiree*. After eating and meeting "the right people" and scoring a few points for the home team, I rode the elevator all the way down to the lobby. Cabs were hard to find, but I got one and went to The Broadway, one of the better department stores in town.

The store was located in a huge shopping mall. I went straight to the ladies' sportswear section and started to look at some sweaters. A pleasant saleswoman came over and asked if she could help me find something. I said that I wanted a sweater. For me. Her eyes got big, then they smiled. She was about my age, but she was cool. She asked if I wore women's clothes often. I said that I did whenever I could, which was not very often. I said I had the opportunity now, but did not have many things to wear outside. She said that she would help me. I ended up with a bulky knit sweater that would be a perfect match with my black knit skirt. It was one of those long ones, so that a skirt was almost optional, and it had ragland sleeves. Then I saw an incredible top. It was a shell, all sequins in front, and in the colors of the neon lights seen in Vegas after dark. It was too outrageous to pass up. I asked her when and where I could wear it. Her answer was that I could wear that thing anywhere, anytime in Las Vegas. As I was paying for my stuff, she asked if I would come to see her when I was dressed as a lady. I promised to try. But I never got back there again.

My next move after returning to the Hilton was to stop by the beauty shop on the ground floor. The businesslike receptionist asked if there was anything she could do for me, just as though I had lost my way in the hotel. I asked if there was an operator who could style a wig. She said, "Of course. Just have the lady wear it in, and one of our operators will do it on her head." Then the jackpot question. "I am the lady. When I am dressed, I think I look good enough not to be an embarrassment to you or to myself. Would that be all right?" The stoney silence lasted only a moment. Then she asked what time I would like to come in. I booked Sally for ten o'clock the next morning.

I went back to my room, changed from Tom to Sally, and commenced writing about the day. After that, I started writing more events from my past. I called for dinner, and it was delivered by another person. I concluded that roses came on the breakfast tray only. And that I would not see the same person twice. By midnight, I realized that I was running out of yellow pads. I put in my morning call, and went to bed.

At 10:00 a.m. sharp, I entered the beauty shop and announced that I was reporting for my appointment. It was a delight to have to tell her I was Sally. She escorted me over to Mabel and introduced me to her. Mabel, who was about my age, smiled and said that she was expecting me. I was seated in her chair, and asked what I wanted her to do. I said that I wanted to look like a woman. "No problem," she said.

She talked as she worked. She told me that she thought it was a wonderful thing that I could dress up, and go out. I agreed, and said that society had not always been so accepting. She allowed that I was right. She had grown up in Idaho, and any man who did what I was doing would have been run out of town, if not seriously maimed first. We agreed that the world has come a long way since we were kids. Then she told me about the days when she worked across town at the MGM Hotel. One of her favorite customers was René Richards, whenever she came to town to play tennis as Richard Raskin. In her pre-op days, Richard would play on the courts during the day, and be René at night. Then I heard all about René's fabulous wardrobe. By this time, my hair was done. Mabel was a magician. I looked good. Really. In fact, I felt so good about myself, I decided to go to the hotel's gift shop to buy a new yellow pad. I thanked Mabel, tipped her double, and walked out. She ran after me to warn me not to solicit. I was stunned. She said that I looked pretty good, and I would be all right anywhere in town or in the hotel, but the place was drenched with plainclothes cops. I assured her I had no interest along those lines.

I went back up to my room, without a yellow pad, to get a better look at myself. I *did* look good. And of course, I felt outrageously great. Once again, I sat down and began writing about the day thus far. I was now writing on the back sides of my yellow pad. That would hold me for a time, but the sequence was getting confusing.

I checked the clock, and saw that it was indeed lunch time. In my spangled torso, I went to the elevators to ride down to the coffee shop for a modest repast.

I was nervous. Why? I was not convinced that I was good enough to convince everybody. The hotel accommodated people from all over the world, and of all ages, etc. As I waited for the elevator to stop on my floor, I wondered what would be inside the cage waiting for me. Would it be mercifully empty? Would it have those teen-aged soccer players? Before I could think of any other possibilities, the doors opened. There was a middle-aged couple, smiling. Great! I entered, smiling at them. The woman was wearing a T-shirt and tan cotton slacks. She asked me if I was early or late? It took me a moment to realize that she accepted me as a woman, or she would not have spoken to me. I reveled in the thought, and said something like, "You can't tell in this town." Then we all chuckled. The doors opened and we went our separate ways.

I was pinged on in the coffee shop by some old coot at the table next to mine. I was scared out of my gourd, and said nothing. He gave up in a few minutes. Then I could enjoy the rest of my lunch. When he got up and left, I relaxed even more, and began to feel pretty good about being of interest to the opposite sex. Sally has always felt that men were the opposite sex.

After lunch, I strolled around the lobby of the hotel, watched some crap games, and participated in a lesson on roulette. After I lost all the free chips I was given as a reward for being a good listener, I walked on. And on.

The main floor of the Hilton is incredibly large and offers the finest people-watching opportunities of any place I have ever been. And I knew I was being watched, too. Anybody would be watched, especially a six-foot blonde in that sequined top.

At this time, a lot of the ballrooms were receiving exhibit crates. The world's largest tradeshow building was a few hundred yards away, but it was not large enough to accommodate all the exhibitors. I watched the other guys do what I had done on my first day in town. It was fun to see somebody else do it. I saw a clock and noticed it was almost seven in the evening. I decided to go to the Oriental restaurant for an early dinner.

No problem getting a table right away at that hour. As I ate, I thought about what was going on with me. It became a time for reflection, or introspection. Who was I and what was I, *really*? Could I make it as a woman? The answer seemed to be a provisional yes. So far, I could make it. And I had made it years before. But I also conked out on the role three times.

Did I *want* to be a woman? To answer that question, my thinking took two directions: The logical, and the emotional. I like to be as logical as I can because things tend to make sense more easily. But the dream of being Sally was purely emotional. Then I thought about my edict of some time ago: In a contest between the conscious and the subconscious minds, the subconscious will win out every time.

I was not comforted by that reminder. I was trying to solve my duality in the simplest way I could. I admitted to myself that I wanted to be Sally for the rest of my life, but I did not think that was the time. I came to that conclusion, but did not know what to do with it. If not now, when? What has to happen first? The rational, conscious mind said that I was out of my head to seriously think about being Sally for the rest of my life.

I hardly remembered eating the food on my plate. The waitress came by to ask if everything was all right, and I lied when I said everything was fine.

My post-prandial coffee came. I debated with myself about ordering a brandy to go with it. As I gazed into the distance for my answer, I saw two of my company's engineers talking to the hostess about getting a table. Swell. Their eyes swept over me, no recognition, and then they left for a less crowded restaurant. I ordered the brandy.

I went back to my room. It was the day before showtime, and I had to be up early again, but not to be Sally. I did not consider the lads' appearance in the restaurant to be a worry. They were only the harbingers of duty calling, nothing more.

The show lasted four days. I was given compliments on the appointments in the exhibit booth. Even the president allowed that it was a pretty good job. We got a lot of sales leads, and the show was declared a huge success for us. There was no problem when I told the president I would have to stay another two days to get everything packed up and shipped out.

The next day, everything was ready to ship, but because I expected more time would be needed, I had changed my airline reservation to a later date. Now I could not change it back. Too bad. A real pity.

My last day was the best and the worst. *Best* because I was feeling so good about being Sally, and the *worst* because it was ending. I had called the front desk to ask if I could stay in my room until four o'clock, instead of checking out at noon. Sure.

I was up early. The breakfast tray and the little rose came swiftly. Wearing my new tunic sweater outfit, I took a cab to the Federal Express office to ship something to the company. The cab driver was chatty and he carried the box into the FedEx office for me. The woman behind the counter complimented me on the sweater, and asked where I bought it. We talked a little, then the cabbie and I drove away. I asked him if he knew of a place where I could buy a yellow pad.

He took me to a new mall. I paid him and then disappeared inside, like Alice going down the rabbit hole. It was like another city in there, but without automobiles. In time, I found my yellow pad. On my way out I walked past a specialty lingerie shop. Then I backed up and entered it. Nervously. I browsed a few minutes before a saleswoman came alongside and said, "You are a 36-D; right?" I nodded that I was. She dragged me over to the section having merry widows on display, and asked if I had one of those. I said no, and that I was not ready for one just yet. Then I split.

I returned to the hotel. It was early afternoon, a very warm day for November, and I was thirsty. I crossed the lobby, into the casino, and headed for the peripheral cocktail lounge. I took out the yellow pad and began to write. (I will now type the piece I wrote in the lounge, exactly as I wrote it then. I think it reveals my state of mind at the time better than a summary of it could.)

Sitting in the downstairs bar at the Hilton. The rowdies are on the other side of the lounge watching football and hollering. I really feel the need for this drink. I signed into this hotel as T.—, so I will sign the bar tab that way. I hope no one wants to play me. Just the drink and a moment to breathe and off I go. I'm writing on my knee.

I think my trip out there today was better than average for believability. Mabel did a magnificent job on my hair. The new sweater I'm wild about drew compliments from the woman at Federal Express. She believed me for sure.

Three loudmouths just came in and sat one table away. Their egos spilling out and all over the floor, drenching the cocktail waitress. She's used to it I guess. My drink is nearly gone. It is ten past one. I've got three more hours til reentry. I don't want to quit. Not ever. "Fred" just told "Barney" to watch the game, not the blonde (me). Good.

I'm sitting at a table facing the deli... a table formerly occupied by Tom, Ralph, Alice, Jim, Richard, and others. I like the way I am now better than then. "Sheldon" and "Irving" just came in and sat down close by. Seltzer and lime. Plenty of lime. What's Notre Dame doing, they ask. Their wives are out shopping. They talk about them. Irving has a handsomely-trimmed gray beard and smokes cigars. His wife had better not stray too far, or Irving might stray... in my direction. Today, men are the opposite sex. Sheldon is an asshole and Irving knows it. He tries to help Sheldon, but it is hard work for him. Poor Irving, 152nd fastest gun in the West. All the way from Atlantic City. I drink my greyhound through a straw, ladylike. I will buy no more drinks. Two men are leaning on the railing twenty feet away watching the game that is being played over my shoulder. Are they watching me too?

A preponderance of men out now. If I don't get a tumble.... Of course, I seem to be so intent on writing that they may be put off. I don't know. Or the game. Sheldon does not know football strategy. Where are the women? Irving and Sheldon just left. The loudmouths just told the cocktail waitress they are glad she kicked them out... that Jewboy with the cigar. That donkey! I like Jews.

I feel my ankles swelling, but no one can see them in here. I'm in the most flattering light possible. The cocktail waitress just asked if I wanted another. No, says I. Not right now. So many men. Where is my tumble? Where is my free drink? I would like some recognition of my attractiveness. Wantin' ain't gettin' said Grandma. These clothes are so comfortable! I'll wager that some men here would want someone like me but are too timid.

Back in my room now. No observable reaction to my departure. Just up, up, and away. That's fine. I just called room service for coffee.

It is now two fifteen, and I should start packing soon I suppose. I'm **not** ready to disappear! All of me feels so good right now. So gooood. I suppose no moves were made on me in the bar because of the absent wives and the football game. My femi-

nine ego wants some attention once in a while. Probably my constant writing put some of them off, though I did look off into the distance from time to time. There was no man by himself there, either.

In retrospect, I think the faithfully reproduced copy above says some things between the lines. I was attempting to do a stream-of-consciousness piece of my reactions to events around me, as well as give some opinions and feelings. I wonder now about the shift in my attitude toward the men in that bar. My first thought was that I wanted to be left alone, then I was piqued when I was. What caused the shift? I don't know.

The last event for Sally that day was to carry the small rose-of-the-morning, in its vase, to that sweet lady, Mabel. I just entered the beauty shop, walked over to her, and said, " Here, Mabel, this bud's for you." We hugged and said goodbye.

I managed to catch my plane several hours later. I felt like an imposter as a male until I boarded the plane and started to talk with the guy next to me about the trade show.

In a couple of hours, the plane arrived at SFO. I called Annie from the airport and said, in my best tremolo basso voice, "The eagle has landed."

Annie, in her best Bronx style, said, "Great. Now get your tail feathers home, Mr. Eagle."

Chapter 19

It was always an upbeat experience to come home to Annie. Yes, I have said many times that having to change from butterfly to caterpillar was a painful, unnatural act. But once the uncomfortable transformation was complete, I was rewarded by being able to be with her again.

By now you must know that my mind is capable of managing feelings in the way that other people manage facts. My emotional thoughts get relegated to appropriate mental spaces, or file drawers, and there they sit until called for. It was a survival skill I had to develop years earlier.

Annie had the champagne chilled, of course. I plopped the load of luggage in the living room. "Put that stuff away later," she said as she kissed me and did a light tattoo on my rump with the uncorked bottle of bubbly.

We sat on the floor in front of the fireplace. Had it been afternoon, we would have been in folding chairs out in the sun. As I lighted the kindling, she said, "Tell me about the trade show later. What we've got for dinner is an unordered pizza from Round Table. You phone in the order, and I'll go pick it up while you unpack." Annie was an organized woman. We did the first bottle. Then I phoned the order for the large Italian sausage pizza, with extra sausage and extra cheese. Annie went to fetch the health food.

The half hour I had alone to do my unpacking may have been planned by her, maybe not. Even though I was officially at a tradeshow for nine days, I am sure Annie figured that Sally would tag along with me. She was a smart kid. I think she knew I had diverse articles of clothing to deal with. Only three kinds, actually: mine-to-do laundry, dry cleaning, and Sally's stuff. I always did my own washing, so I started that right away. Boxer shorts, bras, socks, pantyhose, all of it. I stashed my wig, cosmetics and the few accessories, and folded up my suits to take to the cleaners. By the time she returned with the pizza, all of my things were as dispatched as my emotions had been a few hours earlier.

There was only a token discussion regarding the disposition of the third bottle of champagne. The pizza was internalized, the warmth of the living room was becoming internalized, and certainly the wine was internalized. The conversation drifted from whatever it was to the predictable intimate issues. It was a great way to return home. It was always like that with us.

I knew what was going on inside my head; that the duality was there, and that both Tom and Sally were dynamic and evolving entities. Annie never gave a hint that Sally could be a problem. She never wanted to see Sally or hear anything about her. It seemed to me that she regarded my time away as Sally to be roughly equivalent to my visits to the bathroom: She knew I did it, she knew it was something necessary for me to do, but there was no desire for her to participate or to hear about it.

The weeks and months lapsed as they always did, until early April of 1987. Spring was pure enchantment on the coast. Bright sun, warm days, cool nights, and no tourists. On weekends Annie and I did yard work or walked on the beach. We drank a little, ate well, and enjoyed each other's company indoors as well as out.

Ralph had been gone from Dynatech for nine months by this time. Sales figures were falling since his departure, and our new president was in trouble with the board of directors in Boston. It was no fun working for a scared man who can't make decisions. Most of my work required that I spend company money on such things as trade shows, printing, advertising, and more.

A young woman in customer service wanted to learn the marketing communications business. Anne had a degree in English and was bright, but unsophisticated in terms of corporate life and how to succeed in it. The Sally in me said that she needed help. Perhaps Tom could get her assigned to my department, teach her fast, get her a better salary, and I could be her mentor. Why not? We women have to stick together, don't we?

I made it happen, but $17,500 was the best I could get for her. I felt wonderful that I was able to get her launched on a better career with more pay, but I was unhappy that

I could not tell her that it was simply a case of one woman helping another. (I'll bet you think I am crazy.)

Three weeks later I was let go. The board of directors in Boston rejected my president's budget. Among other cutbacks, marketing got slashed $850,000. My severance pay was slim, but the letter was gentle. Essentially, it said that there was no money for me to spend, and they did not need me to not spend it. Sure it hurt. I always had an emotional involvement in everything I did. No matter the reason, it hurt to be zapped at 6:45 p.m., and not allowed to finish the dozen or so projects I had been working on.

I had made it Anne's job to shadow me on everything I did. That was critical. She needed to know the scope of the job, get a feel for the task of juggling ten to fifteen projects simultaneously, and cope with the diversity of projects. In one hour, I might give specifications to get estimates from two printers, dicker with a trade show company to get a better space assignment, place an order with a sign maker, do business with three magazine advertising sales people, cope with a nervous president, and explore ideas with a retail box maker. Anne had to have the ability to deal with all of that and end the day with a smile, not an hysterical giggle. I hoped that she would be able to do my job, for her sake.

The next morning, a Thursday, I telephoned four guys I knew to let them know I was at liberty: Al, my former tech writing boss; Paul and Leo, trade magazine ad salesmen; and Sam, a headhunter.

That afternoon, Al called back to tell me I should call a certain man at Moffett Field. Moffett Field *Naval Air Station*? Yes.

He and I played telephone tag until Friday afternoon. After the usual introductions, he asked me what my background was. I gave him a quick overview of experience in Navy, education, publishing, and marketing. He told me I was grossly overqualified for the job. *Arghhh*! I hate it when someone tells me that I am overqualified for a job.

What I said was, "Harry, are you over fifty or under fifty?" A pause, then he said he was over fifty. I said, "Then let's cut the bullshit about being overqualified." There was another pause while he got the point, then he roared with laughter.

On Monday we met in his office for a brief overview of the job. The employer was the Federal Civil Service. The job title was Educational Specialist, a GS-11 position. The mission he described was to be a pedagogical consultant for aircrew training. I could see right away that my lack of knowledge as an airman would be a strong point in my favor for being successful, although I would have a problem convincing the Civil Service of that. I mean, the students in the training squadron and I knew the same amount about Naval aviation. Who was better qualified to identify blank spots, non sequiturs, and other anomalies in their self-study coursewares and lecture notes? Nobody else.

We went on a tour of the hangar and classrooms. At lunch Harry asked me what I thought. I told him that I was nowhere near being overqualified for the job if it was to be done right. I did, however, feel I could make a contribution and that I wanted to make my application and be interviewed for the job.

By the end of lunch, he knew that the other two who held that job had not really been qualified for it. Airmen, yes. Educators, no. The squadron already had a ton of aviators. When he asked me how come I knew so much about their highly-specialized program, I told him it was just Project PLAN from AIR warmed over, but focusing on flight stations instead of academic studies. He was amazed that the hottest thing in Naval aviation training was known to me for over twenty years. I wanted to say tut, tut, but didn't. I wanted that job.

The curious part was that clear, silent shout, saying, "*Go for it*! *This is Sally's big chance. You don't see how that can be, but this job will enable you to make the transcendence.*"

Uh huh.

There was a lot of on-the-surface-rationale for wanting it, too. We walked back to his office to get some blank forms, and "meet a few people."

I had never filled out an SF-171 form before. It is only four pages long, but page 2 has space for one's last two employments, blocks A and B, and a lot of information required for each block. If the applicant has had more work experience, they need to be listed on continuation sheets. One must not leave out anything or falsify any information. My jobs went all the way back to block P. A lot of employment history had to be shown. The real concern I had was the front page where they asked for my name and *any other names used*. Hooboy!

I would have to write Sally's name because I had been paid by several employers as Sally, and my Social Security card had been changed a few times. I was in the Fed's computer as Sally *and* as Tom. I thought about it for a few minutes that night and decided to go for it anyway. I discussed it with Annie because I was about to create a public document and I felt she needed to be consulted on this one. She wanted me to get that job at all costs. By midnight I finished my rough draft, and Annie typed it the next morning.

The next afternoon I submitted my crisp SF-171 to a pleasant woman in Civilian Personnel. I asked her if the Navy folks would be upset by my other name. She looked closely at the names of Tom and Sally, and without changing facial expression said,

"We screen the applicants' forms for qualifications and submit a list of the top three candidates to the hiring authority... current names. They will not see this page." Then her expression softened a little and she asked, "Really?" I said yes and that I could explain. She said that it did not matter to her.

Two weeks later I was called for an interview. I thought that Harry and one or two others would be there. I was ushered into a conference room with ten men seated around a table. Oh.

I had dressed in my dark blue suit, a white shirt, my magnificent inspection shoes, and a red, white, and blue regimental striped tie. I had gotten a close haircut the day before. Maybe I was twenty or thirty years older than most everyone there, but I was *just like them*. I had just finished reading a feminist book by Elizabeth Janeway wherein she made the point on the importance of being "just like them" if you want their acceptance.

There were two petty officers, two chief petty officers, two civil service men, and four commissioned officers. The first thing I felt was their curiosity; why was I not intimidated? I ignored the silent query, and just acted as though *I* had called *them* to this meeting. It was easy. I had been an actor for almost sixty years by then.

They were all gentlemen, and the questions they asked were good ones. The first thing they asked was why I thought I could help them. I told them why and how. After 45 minutes or so of questions and answers, one of the officers asked me pointedly if I thought I could get along with everyone in the squadron. I looked at the two petty officers and said, "I have worn a white hat and I know what that means." Then I looked at the two chiefs and said, "I have worn a chief's hat and I know what that means." To the officers I said, "I have worn the hat of a commissioned officer, and I know what that means." To the Civil Service men I said, "And now I am a civilian, and I know what that means." They liked that. One of the chiefs addressed me for a final question. (I guess he had just read a book too.) He said, "As fast as you can, give us two words that best describe *you*." Without a second's delay, I barked, "Navy trained!" They liked that. I was escorted from the room and advised to return home and wait for a call from the personnel office.

The drive home was a buoyant time for me. I had the feeling that the job was mine, and that I was *supposed* to have it. But why did I have the feeling that the job was the best thing for Sally? From what I could see of the squadron, it was Macho City. Even though they trained airmen to fly P-3 aircraft, a four-engine turbo prop of yesteryear, they were the next thing in glamour and heroics to the lads in *Top Gun*, a contemporary film back then. In subsequent months, I learned that the P-3 aircrews were next to nobody. Their jobs were tougher and more demanding than fighter groups. Less glamour, though.

Forty minutes later I was home. A warm sunny day and that magnificent blue Pacific Ocean across the street. I went in the house to put on my gardening clothes, alternately called my drinking clothes, depending on what I really intended to do. Annie was on the phone and said, "Just a second, Jim, here he is now." Jim was the marketing manager for Leasametrics, a competitor of USIR. We had worked together before, and he had heard that I was looking for work. He wanted to see my resume. We talked for a time, and I said I would send it to him.

Before I could get my inspection shoes off, the phone rang again. It was one of the lieutenants from the squadron at Moffett Field. He said, "Tom, I'm not supposed to be making this call, but we want you to come to the squadron." I surely did thank him and promised to wait patiently for the personnel office to call me. I was buttoning up my only-one-button-left work shirt when the phone rang again. It was Harry. "Tom, I'm not supposed to be making this call, but we all thought highly of you in that interview today. It was unanimous that we want you, so don't go anywhere else. Wait for the personnel office to call you." I thanked him for calling, and told him I would wait.

While reaching for a cold beer, Annie handed me a phone message from Sam, the headhunter. The note said I should call a certain person at Varian Associates in Palo Alto. I called, after taking a long pull on my San Miguel beer. It was another marketing job. I said I would send my resume.

I went out to the back yard to drink my suds and dig in the dirt. I needed some time to sort out these recent events. All of a sudden there were three job opportunities at the same time. The one I wanted the most was saying they wanted me. Four years earlier, I could not get anyone's attention. Now this. Is this a freak accident? Is the Cosmos trying to tell me something? Annie came out with one of her garage sale straw hats for me. "Here. Put this on. With that short hair and your sparse locks, you will get sunburn." Yes, ma'am. The next morning the civilian personnel office called me to ask if I could start work on Monday, the 11th. Yes.

I reported to Personnel at 0800. There were a few other new hires there. We were given an indoctrination lecture and some new forms to fill out. By 0900 everyone was directed to report to their new supervisors. I was not. Instead, I was given a fresh pile of new forms to fill out for the FBI, or some other Federal security agency. Oh? My job would require me to work with classified information. I had to have a security clearance or I would be disqualified. I was told to be even more careful and complete with these forms. Any errors or omissions would be considered as falsification. They wanted to know where I had lived, and where I had worked since *1937*.

Annie and I went through the same drill as before, ending with the same resolve to go for it. She wanted me to get out of the marketing business and back into education.

The lower pay was offset by the splendid working conditions and other rewards of the occupation. Those were the stated reasons. I turned in the forms the next day, promising to give Annie a super massage that night. I asked the same woman in personnel about these papers. She could only say that she hoped I was truthful, honest, complete, and not subject to blackmail. I assured her of that, and I showed her my asterisk coding system to indicate which jobs and residences were Tom's and which were Sally's. It turned out that the investigators asked *everyone* about Tom *and* Sally. Swell. A few of my references called me to ask about this Sally person. I vagued out on them and said I would explain later. (If they are reading this book, they know now.) I knew that the Feds would give me the green light because I had done nothing illegal or immoral, but I was not at all optimistic about the Navy. They have a code-of-the-hills all their own. The P-3 squadron Commanding Officer was one thing. He probably would not have nixed me, but the admiral (Commander Patrol Wings, Pacific), would take the dimmest of views. Admirals are not the jolly old sports you sometimes see in the movies. Having turned in the last set of papers, I was told to report to the Command Instructional Systems Coordinator of VP-31 in Hangar One. I asked about my security clearance. I was told that I would receive a temporary clearance. Huh? But I decided to not try to find the logic in that; I doubted there was any logic to be found. I was amazed and grateful that in a scant four weeks, I had come in off the street and secured a position in the Federal Civil Service System. I was sure the Cosmos was pushing for this.

I arrived in Harry's office and received a warm welcome. Later, I was introduced to a lot of people, and was oriented and occidized in one day. At the end of that day, I felt welcomed, wanted, needed, appreciated, challenged, and excited... all at once. Why? My guess is that Harry introduced me to everyone as a retired Chief Warrant Boatswain, a recipient of a Master's Degree in Education from Stanford University, and (in his estimation) a helluva swell guy who knows what he is doing. Any one of those accolades would have enabled me to start work with plenty of aloha.

I used that lubrication to get some reforms going right away. Because there was no resistance to my recommendations, good stuff started happening. I was able to create my own reputation based on observable results. I was thrilled to be able to please these people because they were *la creme de la creme* of Naval aviation. They had to be in order to be assigned as staff to that training squadron. Because they liked me and appreciated what I was doing, *I felt better about myself than I ever had before*. I had almost forgotten that special feeling of being a shipmate. I was regarded as such in that squadron of people who live and work in the air, the most unforgiving of environments. Everyone depends on everyone else for survival.

There was that month's interval between early April and early May when I was not working. Looking back, it was only the twinkling of an eye, but back then I was unsettled and nervous. The emotional scars of being jobless for ten months in 1983-84 were still with me. Fortunately, there were two events in April that provided pleasant distractions for me.

Mary F. had scheduled me for another speaking date that month in her classroom. She had left the librarian's desk at West Valley College to become a professor of sociology at Mission College. One of her contributions to the curriculum was to create a course dealing with the sociology of sex. Each semester, she would do her lecture/discussions every other week, and in alternate weeks she would invite a "sexpert" to speak. Some sexperts were gay men, gay women, hookers, rape victims, and so forth. And me, who appeared as Sally to talk about differences between the transsexual and the transvestite, from the viewpoint of the afflicted.

I had been doing this gig every semester since 1982, and I liked it a lot. I had a platform to use to get the message out that we were not homosexuals, but confused folk who had a problem nobody seemed to understand even then, more than 30 years after Christine Jorgensen. I shed some light and the students seemed to like my pitch on the sociological aspects, and the way I fielded their off-the-wall questions. Mary and I always met a few hours before class time to have a beer and some snacks, and to discuss how that night's presentation should be done. I, of course, enjoyed the exercise because it gave me a chance to see Mary for a few hours, and I had the opportunity to wear some of my better clothes.

The other good thing that happened that month was the Whole Earth Fair that was held in Moscone Center in San Francisco. Annie wanted to go. I was lukewarm on the idea, but went anyway. We could see what the post-hippie crowd was "into" these days. I expected to see some wild posters, hear some new-age music, and maybe eat some bean sprouts and yogurt. There must have been four acres of booths set up in that convention center. One small booth had a treasure for me. There were three nicely groomed women seated at card tables. They looked like country women, not suburban. Their sign read "Psychic Readings $20, 20 Minutes." Annie wanted to buy me a reading. Sure. One of them read palms, the second read tarot cards, and the third just sat there, smiling. I had a hunch that she read auras, and selected her. I was right, and that was how I met Rebecca.

I sat in the chair opposite her. She continued to smile, and her face turned from comely to radiantly beautiful. She asked what I wanted her to do for me. I said that she could use any avenue that she wanted to, but I just wanted to know what was going on in my life right then, and anything else that she wanted to tell me in the 20 minutes. She told me to sit up straight, uncross my legs and arms, and hold still. In less than five minutes I knew she was good. There was too much detail and too accurately told to be b.s. Everything she said about my current state was true. Other things were verifiable in a few weeks. One prediction was 18 months away and became true, on schedule.

I felt better for having just sat there, listening to her describe my aura, explaining what the colors meant, describing the major events in my life at the moment, and suggesting what I should do about those things. Her suggestions dealt with attitudes I could adopt, not specific actions like selling my nonexistent A T & T stock. She said nothing about Sally specifically, but did say at the end that there was another influence in my aura other than the usual. I took one of her business cards before I left.

The rest of spring and summer of 1985 rolled along in grand style for me. I had a job that I loved, I had a woman that I loved, and I had more opportunities for Sally. Ralph and I stayed in touch and would meet for lunch now and then. He had not been working since he left Dynatech the year before. His discipline and optimism kept him going. I was sorry that he did not have the work he wanted, but I was glad to have the opportunity to demonstrate my friendship and underscore the idea that I liked to see him whether he was my boss or not. By August, my awareness of Sally's consciousness was becoming a concern. I was feeling her presence more frequently, more intensely. Specifically, I was feeling *future*. I was leaving one plateau of the Sally consciousness, headed for a newer, higher level.

What I did about it was to telephone Rebecca for an appointment for the first Saturday she had open. I did not know what to expect from her, but the recollection of that twenty-minute session in April had stuck with me as being one of the better moments for enlightenment in recent times. I had followed her suggestions for dealing with the things that disturbed me then, and the result was tranquility and inner peace. I could not complain about such results.

On the appointment day, Tom drove to Marin to get some enlightenment and hopefully some answers. Rebecca asked that I bring a blank casette tape to record the session. Smart. I was not sure how to play the scene. Did I want to have her "discover" Sally? Should I just blurt out that I had a woman's consciousness growing within me, and what should I do about it? Or what could I do about it? Would she be good enough to help me with this? I will make no attempt to summarize the verbiage of that visit, nor any of the subsequent appointments. What I will do is to tell you what I got from those visits, and my opinion of Rebecca.

Her style was profoundly different from any psychic I had been to before, and that included at least five who read me or answered my questions from the early 70s. As I understand it, her method was to hold her crystals on her lap and begin with a short meditation. Then she would open her eyes and read my aura to see what was going on with me that moment. She would describe the colors, where they were located, and what that meant for me. Next, she would become silent to consult the *akashic* records to get some kind of meaning or rationale for what was going on. More often than not, she would ask me questions about what she had said so far, and listen for my response … also reading me as I responded to her statements. Without recognizing the point of transition, we would shift into a counselling session, like with a therapist or a very close friend. The end of the trail on any issue was invariably a short prescription for a thought process (or prayer, or proverb) that would enable me to "see the light" and deal with my own concerns, but armed with an understanding I did not have before. Now that is not fortune telling. That is what I would call psychic counselling. It worked for me. That summary of time with Rebecca does not do her justice, nor does it give an in-depth analysis of the sessions.

After that first encounter, Sally went to all the following appointments, usually once a month. At first, I felt dependent on her to keep my head together and screwed on straight. In time, I felt more confident, more learned in the ways of the earth experience, but mostly I learned how to become self sufficient in dealing with my emotions and managing my mental and spiritual resources.

One of the principal principles was to meditate daily for about twenty minutes or so. During that time I might pose questions to be answered anytime, not just at that moment, and patiently await answers that would come in minutes or days. A second principle was a reminder of the karmic laws; that I was here to grow, and so were other people. Therefore, some of my growth would be induced by others, and some of their growth would be induced by me. A third principle was that some of my discontent was brought about by my own immaturity, and other discontent was there to teach me something. Meditation would help me see the difference. That was the hard part, but I caught on eventually.

Rebecca helped me to bring a lot of ideas I had already learned into a new pattern while adding some new concepts. She knew how to twist the kaleidoscope to give me the images I needed. I am still learning, albeit more efficiently. I do not have the ability to see auras, nor do I have the key to what all the colors mean. If I were able to read Rebecca's aura, I would learn what the colors are for love, compassion, intelligence, enlightenment, patience, and womanhood in its highest manifestation.

In June I asked the squadron training officer for permission to fly on some of the training flights. He said that the Ed Specs never did that. I said that I wanted to fly so that I could see what a good aircrewman was doing when he was being a good aircrewman. I needed to know so that I could do a better job of evaluating the training materials. I knew I was rocking the boat by suggesting such a crazy idea, but what the hell.

My first hurdle was to pass a flight physical. At 59 the odds were against me, but I passed. It was then I learned my blood pressure was 116/66 and my cholesterol was 160. The next step was to get a place in the "swim school" at NAS Miramar. It was the water safety and survival program that all pilots and aircrews in the Navy must complete. Whatever it takes, I thought.

A few months later, I was flying to Fightertown, USA. The course I was given was for contractors and other civilians. All I had to do was to listen to lectures in the morning and swim in the pool in the afternoon. It sounded easy. I listened to the morning lectures as though my life depended on it. In an emergency, it would. After lunch I was told to get myself ready for the swimming pool. I had my swimming suit on with my towel draped strategically to cover my boobs, and listened to the instructor explain what the drill was going to be. Oh-oh.

So I donned a flight suit, leather flight boots with steel toes, and jumped feet-first into the pool, as directed. I swam the 75 yards, using three different strokes. (Have you ever gone swimming in your clothes, wearing boots?) Immediately after doing that, I was given an inflatable life vest and told to inflate it myself. I was then directed to swim over to the large life raft and climb aboard it. I had to figure out *how* to climb aboard it, though. From the water, one cannot reach up and grab something to pull oneself up. There is this strap below the water that can be used as a foothold, if you are observant enough to see it. I was just catching my breath when I was told to get out of the raft, out of the pool, and take my shower. I had passed the course, I was qualified to fly on training flights, and I wondered how a Pall Mall smoker my age could do all of that. There are *so many* things I don't understand.

The flights I went on seldom lasted more than four or five hours, but they were action packed. The pilot I flew with the most was my immediate supervisor. He had me belted in just behind his left seat during takeoffs and landings so that he could tell me what was happening and what the student pilots were supposed to be doing. In between, I could see what the other aircrew positions were doing. A neat plan. I was asked once if I was learning anything. I thought of Yogi Berra's line, "You can observe a lot just by watching." The most exciting thing that happened was the experience of having a brake fire while landing at 120 knots. I learned later that qualifying for that privilege to fly raised my stock even more in the squadron.

Autumn ended, the calendar said it was winter, but with little rain, again, in the Bay Area. I was feeling slightly depressed about the lack of precipitation. I asked Annie if she would like to drive up to southern Oregon (one of the places I had flown over) for a few days to see what was happening. She liked the idea and suggested that we do a Christmas-to-New Years week on the road. We would be together and not have to fiddle around with the Christmas drill without kids. They were all gone anyway, and had created their own lives in other parts of the country. We also thought it would be a nice, non-tourist time to drive it and have our choice of motels.

Another reason for the trip was to look around for a possible retirement community. We understood that cost of living was less up there, and perhaps our dollars could go farther. But was there a great place to go? Would there be any opportunities for work? We had to find out. Annie did most of the research before we went, and that saved us a lot of time once up there.

My *secret* reason, in addition to the above, was to try one more avenue to displace Sally from my future. Was there possibly a scenario for a future in Oregon that did not include Sally? I desperately wanted an answer, but oddly enough I did not especially care what the answer would be, although life could have been so much simpler if I could have found peace as Tom. I had confidence, however, that the right answer would come.

We discovered that Oregon was a beautiful state, it had a magnificent coastline, the real estate prices were less than in California, but work was not available, and the prices of everything else were the same or higher. Nice try.

My job at Moffett Field continued to be a delight. I was getting more self-actualization experiences from my tasks than ever before. I continued to get compliments from all levels of the staff for my work on a daily basis. An unexpected perk was the ease with which I could hang out once in a while with the white hats, or the chiefs, or the officers. I was welcomed in each of those select societies whenever I asked to visit. I had been one of them before, you see. The end result of my interaction in that squadron was the message, loud and clear enough to penetrate my thick head, that I was good. They told me, those first-rate airmen, that I was worth something on this planet. I had not set out to prove anything to anyone on that job, other than to show they had the best possible structure for training if they would only use it. But I ended up making a leap in my consciousness that said: "*You have crossed the finish line; you have proven that you are a good man; and you don't have to do that anymore.*"

That was a very profound message.

It took me a couple of months to let the message sink in: I did not have to be a man anymore. I had finished my male agenda. It could have been the onset of my senility, or maybe it was madness, but I don't think either one was the case. That is the way it is with us crazies.

In March of 1988, *when I was absolutely sure*, I told Annie that I had to live the rest of my life as Sally. I will spare us all the dialog as that is too personal to write about. The essence was that I asked if she could go along with me on it. She said, "No way." I said, "Too bad." The bewildering part for me was that I loved the woman, but she was a roadblock to my growth. If I had tried to reject the path of Sally to stay with her, I would have turned sour physically and mentally as I had with Helen.

From that conversation until July, we kept a peaceful coexistence going in the house. We were civil, but there was no warmth. Periodically she would ask when I was going to move out. My answer was that I would when I could figure out how. It was a matter of economics. One course of action open to me was to make the switch within the Civil Service system. Change Tom into Sally and find similar employment elsewhere. I knew that Sally would not be welcome in that squadron. It was not only my hunch, there was hard data that said I wouldn't be welcome.

Remember my security clearance? The Feds were satisfied that I was all right. They submitted my clean bill-of-health to the admiral's staff in October. The admiral seemed to be reluctant to give me the clearance, however. Can you guess why? Right. A retired male warrant officer who has successfully lived and worked as a female? I was certainly an anomaly. My successes in the squadron by that time were well known, my relationships with everyone were enormously good. I had even spent time at the monthly beer busts talking with the admiral on a congenial basis, *before* the report came in. I was an asset to the squadron on several counts, but my past was totally unacceptable for them. "People like me" could not possibly be any good. They had to deal with that cognitive dissonance, as we used to say in the ed biz.

I did not know the state of affairs until early January of 1988. A joint training conference with our sister squadron in Jacksonville was scheduled for later that month. The Jacksonville facility was such that everybody had to have the right security clearance in order to get into the place. My temporary clearance was not acceptable there. I continued to badger my boss to see what the hold up was in me getting my clearance. He was being stonewalled. *I* knew what the problem was, but I was pushing for a resolution from them. As far as I knew, only the admiral and his staff were grappling with this knot. I had never mentioned Sally or anything about her to anyone in the squadron.

A week before the conference, I was confronted with the sticky contents in the investigator's report. I will not say who laid it out for me, but I was asked for some assurance that I would not do anything to resurrect Sally around there. No problem. I got my clearance on a permanent basis, went to Jacksonville, and then wondered who else became privy to that sensitive, perfectly legal, yet unacceptable information about me. Probably no one else, because that would have been counterproductive all around.

In April, I asked the nice woman in Civilian Personnel if I could initiate the paper work to change me from Tom to Sally. Sure. By May, it was all set up, and the actual switch would take place in July. The logistics were complex, but the idea was to make the change and get out without any embarrassment to anyone. We all had too much respect for each other to want to cause a mess. I also received the papers from the Navy Reserve retirement center saying that Tom could get his new ID card that said retired on it. My modest pension would soon start.

I built a plan that included using my vacation and sick leave to get one more nose job, and have that happen after I left the squadron. In the meantime, I was looking for other GS-11 work anywhere, in or out of state. Annie was increasing the tempo of her query about me moving out.

I had the feeling that everything was moving along the way it was supposed to happen, but I did not have the whole plan worked out. Events were being set into motion, sometimes by me, sometimes by others. I was on a journey without a map. Where was my next job? How much money could I earn? I had more questions about my future than I had answers, yet I was on my way with no turning back. I think it was my first real experience at letting go and letting the Cosmos decide how everything would work out. Scary? Uh huh.

In late June, I had made the change with Social Security, had applied for a change on my driver's license. I was indeed committed to becoming Sally. Another thing that happened in late June was a telephone call from Ralph. He had gotten a position as a vice president of a local corporation. "Let's meet for lunch next week, Tom."

Chapter 20

If you ever get a lunch invitation from Ralph, accept it. You will have two lunches in one: the expected bill-of-fare from the restaurant, and plenty of food for thought from Ralph. He lived a lot, read a lot, and thought a lot. Because he began his career as a salesman, he knew his way around words and could make anything sound interesting. He read books on art, opera, economics, sociology, and could give a fine *precis* on whatever he read. As a joke once, he did an exciting twenty minutes on the information contained in one day's worth of junk mail delivered to his house.

He had been hired by The Wollongong Group six months earlier to solve some problems in distribution and in customer service. In March, he had telephoned me to ask if I would do a moonlight assignment. He needed a tape script to announce a new product. I wrote the first side of the tape by April. A budget freeze brought a halt to my freelance work, but Ralph told me to wait until next quarter. The thaw would happen in July.

His call for lunch in late June was more or less expected. He suggested that I meet him at his place of business, take a tour of his new executive suite, and drive to Palo Alto Joe's in his new company car. It was only a ten-minute drive from Moffett Field to his place. I had the tour, then we drove to the restaurant. He gave me an in-depth description of the fascinating new software products that The Wollongong Group was beginning to produce. I almost understood what he was talking about.

At the lunch table we ordered vodkas over, our menu choices, and then he started to sketch an organizational chart on his place mat to show me his new empire. In a couple of minutes I began to sense that he was telling me information that I was supposed to remember, not just be entertained. In one cluster of departments, the managerial lines all went directly to him. He said that there was to be some augmentation of staff to put a director between four of those department managers and himself. He drew in the box for the yet-to-be-hired director and the names of tech writing, training, marketing communications, and the nascent telemarketing group under it.

The drinks came, and after a short toast to the good times, his pen went back to the director's box. "I want to write your name in this space, Tom. What do you say?" It seemed like several minutes, but took no more than several seconds for me to take stock of my situation.

It was the first week of July. I had already informed my supervisors in Hanger One that I was going to resign from my job in early August, but would be on terminal leave starting the second Friday of July. It was necessary, obviously, that I was vague on my reasons for departure. I had to go *somewhere* because Annie was getting acidic about me moving out. I would certainly need a new job, and could not count on the Civil Service to provide one for me soon enough. I had a nose job scheduled for July 11 in South Lake Tahoe. My ID was in transition, and any employer would want to see it all at the time of hire. I wanted to work as Sally; I had gotten psyched up for that, had my Civil Service name change done, and was prepared for Sally to go to work. But here was Ralph, the only guy in corporate America that I trusted, offering me a job that I would have "killed for" a year ago, was certainly qualified for, and I understood why he wanted me to do it.

Ralph ended my pause by saying that he really wanted me because I had done the work of those departments, and that he needed me to manage those managers and serve as the buffer between them and himself so that he could get his own work done. I continued to look at him, wondering if I should tell him about Sally and her plans. I knew he respected me, but would he understand about Sally? I knew that he would never give the job to her. No, there was no point in muddying the waters now.

He asked what I was earning at Moffett. I told him $27,800. He said that he would pay $50,000 to start.

I must admit that some considerations are more important than others. That kind of salary would enable me to move out, thereby removing Annie's angst and mine. True, I would have to work as male, but that was only 40 hours, give or take, from the

168-hour week. The rest of the time, I could be Sally. The longevity of marketing jobs in the high tech industries was about a year or so anyway. Within a year, I should have another plan worked out to get me the rest of the way... to get launched as Sally forevermore. But I had to move fast. There could be none of that "give me a few days to think things over" routine. Ralph didn't work that way. It was one of the things I liked about him.

Significant events were unfolding because of moves I had put into motion. I had pushed off from the river bank in a small raft, and now the current was taking me into the rapids. I was not afraid of anything, I just wanted to avoid making mistakes. Was this a smart thing to do?

Yes!

"Well?"

"Okay, Ralph, you've got me again."

After I returned from lunch, I told my Navy supervisor and Harry that my new job would be a mere ten miles up the road, and that I would start work there on the 18th. I would be pleased to help get my replacement indoctrinated should they wish me to do so.

The next day Harry and I had lunch. I had to tell him about Sally because of some bureaucratic complications; he would be seeing time cards for her for the next month or so. Harry was unbelieving, but when I opened my suit jacket and threw my shoulders back, he said that he believed me. He was accepting and got straight answers to every question he cared to ask. He did not *understand* the phenomenon, but he was still my friend. A lot of my friends and associates were like that. Well, maybe 50% of those I told.

Nobody in the squadron wanted to see me go, even myself. It had been a privilege to work with those fine people, and I could have stayed there for a long time. Yet it was they who enabled me to see that the male life was over for me.

At home that night, I told Annie about my job offer from Ralph, my impending resignation from Moffett Field, and my timetable for moving out. I think she was pleased that I had a plan for leaving, but she was also facing the reality of the separation. Her countenance was stoic. All she wanted to communicate to me was her acknowledgement of my plan.

On Friday, I said my goodbyes to the guys in the squadron, turned in my several badges, and pulled chocks, as the aviators say. At home, I got my things together for my trip to South Lake Tahoe the next day. Annie went out to a meeting. I had a case of emotional overload. Too much was going on. I was leaving a job, a home, a marriage, and a way of life. Any one of those would have been enough to daunt a normal person.

But I never claimed to be normal. Yes, I was hurting, but the transsexual in me perceived this time as the moment of liberation. Or the first stage of it.

On Saturday morning, I loaded my car with everything I would need for the week in Tahoe. Annie came out, but not to kiss me. She said, in very cold, steely tones, "Good*bye*, Tom." Only wives can say it like that, and make it sting. I was really in the rapids now.

My first stop was at the nearest motel to change into Sally, then on to an apartment house in Foster City. I applied for a downstairs unit that was completely furnished, except for linens. One would be available in a few days, I was told. I wrote a check for the deposit and said I would be back in a week. By evening, I arrived in Sacramento. The motel was on the outskirts of the capital city of California, on the highway to my destination. It was hot, I was tired, and pleased that I had made reservations several days ago. I was given the key to an upstairs room. I had a lot of luggage to carry in, and I asked the reservations clerk if I could get a downstairs room instead. I let her know I was about melted, weary, and in need of a little TLC. She said she would give me the only room left on the ground level. I thanked her, and felt good about the aloha one woman will extend to another... if one does not act like a bitch.

The next morning, I drove into South Tahoe feeling refreshed by the good night's sleep and the cool morning furnished by the higher altitude. I found the Matterhorn Motel and checked in. The clerk, Ruth, was a co-owner and quite friendly. There was a pleasant relationship between the plastic surgery clinic and the motel. Most of Dr. Fosters' clients stayed there because it was close to the clinic. It was also very clean and had reasonable rates.

I was feeling happy that I was there in that cooler climate and about to get my nose done right this time. There were a lot of us transsexuals in the Bay Area who availed ourselves of his skills. He and his staff were the kindest and most efficient medical group I had ever encountered. They seemed to care about us and our quest for beautification and believability as women. Sure, they were making a ton of money, but they didn't have to be so kind and caring to do it.

I checked in on Monday morning at 9:00 and completed a few forms. The doctor came in with a Polaroid camera and took a couple of pre-operation profiles. We discussed the impending procedure, and he asked if I had any other questions. I had none. He escorted me to the operating room and administered a general anesthesia. The next day was spent in a special recovery area of his palatial home. I felt woozy and totally disoriented. There was a splint on my nose and a lot of pain underneath the splint.

I stayed there until Wednesday morning. I was back to normal, except for the pain and an outrageous hunger. I was given another pain pill, a light breakfast, and a ride back to the Matterhorn. The driver was a young man who was extremely polite. He carried all of my luggage up to my new room and made sure I was comfortable before he left. Ruth stopped by to see how I was doing. She gave me a message from Annie. I was to call her back when I could. Ruth and I talked for awhile about nothing special. She invited me to come visit her when I felt up to it. I said that I would like to do that.

When I returned Annie's call, I learned that Ralph wanted to talk with me. I got through to him by late afternoon. He wanted me to report for work on Friday instead of Monday. I told him I could not do that as I had broken my nose in a volleyball game, and the surgeon who repaired my beak wanted to see me again on Friday afternoon. He said I should have more sense than to play volleyball with such vigorous people. I slept a lot the rest of Wednesday. The pain pills did their job. A sleeping body heals faster.

On Thursday, I risked a full shower, shaved very close, and felt good about being so clean again. The splint on my nose did not add to my appearance, but it didn't detract from my attempt to look feminine. I used an ice bucket to chill the bottle of Napa Valley *fume blanc* I had brought along for a special occasion. I decided that visiting Ruth would be a special occasion.

I rang the bell on the desk. She came out, saw the bottle, smiled, invited me into her parlor, and said that she would get the glasses. I was prepared with my own corkscrew. Ruth commented on that, and I said that all of us fraternity kids learned such things. As I poured the wine, she asked what I meant by that. I said that I had been in a fraternity in college. She asked if I meant a sorority. I was suddenly aware that she believed me to be a woman. It was my understanding that she knew about me because so many of us TS people stayed at her motel. We talked about the situation, got everything straightened out as we continued to drink the wine. She said that only a fraction of their guests were transsexuals, and that some of the patients who stayed with her were pretty obvious, and I should not tell anyone else that I was a transsexual in process.

We had a fine afternoon talking about a lot of things, including her significant other, Carl. He believed I was a woman, otherwise she would not be able to spend any time talking with me. He tended to be jealous. We parted company after making a date to have dinner at one of the casinos on the Nevada side that night. Ruth said that she seldom got out at night because one of them had to be on duty all the time, and no one ever asked her to go out. I was considered safe because I was a woman, a guest, and ready for some action. Carl waved goodbye to us and wished us luck on the slot machines.

We had a delicious dinner and shared things from our pasts. Later, Ruth wanted to show me around the casino. But first, she ushered me into the ladies' room to freshen up. It was my first invitation from a woman to go to the loo. She was having as much fun as I was. Over drinks in the second floor bar, she told me that she believed me when I said I was a pre-op TS, but she still regarded me as a woman. I could have kissed her, but that would not have been appropriate there. After a few more drinks in a few more bars, she said that she wanted to invest $25 in the slots. When we left a couple of hours later, she had won $250.

Friday afternoon was checkout day at the clinic. The splint was removed by the doctor, the nose scrutinized, and photographed again. He made a set of pre and post pictures for me. There was indeed a difference even though it was still swollen. I felt I got what I wanted. He put the splint back on and told me to keep it on until Monday. After I returned to my room, Ruth telephoned to ask if I would like to come to dinner that night. Sure. It was a barbecue by the swimming pool, across from the motel's office. Ruth, Carl, and another couple were there. We all became friendly right away. Later, Ruth told me that I had been accepted by everyone as a woman. My confidence was growing.

Saturday morning, I checked out, drove back to Foster City, got the keys to my new apartment, and had a serious talk with the manager. I told her the true situation. She said there would be no problem as far as she was concerned, provided I pay my rent on time. She offered her sympathy about me having to go to work as a male.

I emptied out my car, put things away, took inventory of what I would need for the next few days, and went to Safeway for the groceries and other things a new apartment has to have. Like toilet paper and soap, to name two. After everything was put away, I opened a bottle of San Miguel and took stock of my new environment and how I (we) would operate in it. First, both Tom and Sally would have to come and go. Fortunately, the architecture of the apartment complex was such that I would be virtually invisible to my neighbors during the transit from parking lot to front door. Second, the drapes would always be closed unless I was Sally. Third, this was to be Sally's apartment, and hopefully Tom would seem to be a guest if anyone did see him.

On my first Sunday morning, I awoke and felt wonderful. I opened the drapes to see the large lagoon just outside my sliding glass door. I made the coffee, and sat on the floor staring at this new scenery. Later that day, I met my next door neighbors: Ruth and Chris, mother and daughter. We introduced ourselves and said we would be seeing each other.

I telephoned Annie, reported my presence in the Bay Area, and said that I wanted to drive over to get some of my stuff. We agreed on a time when she would be gone. She said that she hoped that Tom would make the trip. I agreed. I made two trips that Sunday evening, got a lot of my clothes, some favorite kitchen utensils I had used since my first apartment, and a few books. By midnight, everything was carried in and put away. My Tom costume was ready for the next day. I took a long hot shower and went to bed.

At 8:00 a.m. I was standing tall in the reception area of Wollongong's front office. Ralph came out, took me back to his office, and got me some coffee. We talked of this and that for awhile. I waited for him to comment on my new nose, but he never did. Instead, he asked me to sign the contract for employment. I did. He telephoned Georgina, the personnel woman, and she appeared in a minute. After introductions, she took me off to get signed up. To satisfy the federal and state regulations, she wanted to see my driver's license, and my Social Security card. I told her I knew the numbers, and I could just write them on the forms she had on her desk. No. By law, she was required to see them. Ahem. I was not totally surprised by the impasse manifesting in her office. How can I produce ID for Tom if I did not have any for him? Would this keep me from the job? Would Ralph be embarrassed in any way?

Tell the truth, dummy. You know there is no other way. By stalling or trying to avoid the inevitable, you will only screw things up.

I reached for my wallet, pulled it out, and sat there looking at her. I got up and closed the door. I said that I had some very sensitive information to transmit to her. My opener was that I was about to tell her some extremely personal information, that I would expect her complete confidence. I also acknowledged that she had responsibilities to the governmental agencies and to the company. She appreciated that. I concluded by saying that if, in her professional opinion, the information would constitute a problem for the company, then I would expect her to report it to the president. Otherwise, it would be between us only.

She agreed, and I handed her Sally's temporary driver's license and her Social Security card. She looked at them and said that she did not understand. I said that I believed that I was a transsexual, and that I was on my way to live the rest of my life as a woman when Ralph came along and offered me a job I could not refuse. I needed this job and its nice salary to get set up for the ultimate switch. She just stared at me, deadpan. To break the silence, I offered my Navy ID card with Tom's picture, Social Security number, and name on it. That tied everything together for her. She asked if Ralph knew anything about this. I said that he didn't.

She picked up all my cards, photocopied them and handed them back. She said that I did not appear to be a transsexual, and that she saw no need to trouble the president with this information as it was not illegal to want to be a woman.

I interpreted her commentary as being favorable for me. I invited her to ask me questions right then or anytime in the future. She thanked me for the invitation, said that it was a shame that I could not start work there as Sally, that this sexist society needed to loosen up, but we had better move along and find me an office to work in.

I was given a large space with new furniture, but no windows. She apologized for the dismal atmosphere saying that more space would become available soon, and that I would have a more attractive environment before long. I think she was about to ask a personal question but Ralph came in and said that there were some people I needed to meet, and then we would go to the "welcome aboard" lunch. Georgina said we would talk again, then left.

Ralph introduced me to the president and the five other vice-presidents. At Original Joe's he gave me my initial assignments. Basically, I was to give counsel to the four managers under me on the organizational chart. He was adamant with regard to me not *doing* anything within any of the departments. "This is *not* a hands-on job for you," he told me. It would be a few weeks before I felt the pain of that restriction. I could see the need for it, but I did not like to just *talk about* training, or *talk about* creating a style manual, or any of the other departments' responsibilities. I was a hands-on kind of guy.

for. I sensed that they were a little nervous, perhaps threatened in some way. It turned out they were threatened, and my first task was to convince them I really wanted to be of help. It took a few months to prove it, but I did.

During my first weekend for relaxing, I took a time-out and thought about what was happening in my life; past, present, and probable future. There had been so many events in the last four months. There was so much going on now, and I could tell that there were going to be even heavier events to come.

I had awakened at six-thirty on that Saturday morning. As I rolled over and stretched, I felt that new sensation: my developing breasts shifting with gravity. It was a special sensation, and one that would be there from now on. Thank you, makers of Estinyl. I heated some of Friday's coffee and lighted a cigarette. It was warm enough to sit in my nightgown and shag wig. It was just cool enough to see my nascent nipples signal their presence. Oh boy.

I looked out the wide window at the lagoon and saw the ducks in the early morning. The homes on the far shore blended in with the thirty-year old foliage of shrubs, trees, and vines. I knew they were no older than that because until the late 1940s, this place had been a garbage dump on the edge of San Francisco Bay. My sense of tranquility and inner peace were not dampened by the remembrance. Instead, I regarded it as an omen, or maybe an inspiration. I too was in the process of being remodelled, rebuilt into something that would be more satisfactory, more productive than before.

Another aspect of my inner peace was the sense of freedom to become me-an aging woman by now, no longer with soft, elastic skin, not oozing fertility, but nevertheless a woman of my own making.

I checked in with my two head spaces-the two viewpoints I had. Tom felt rotten about causing Annie the pain, the loss, the hurt, and the disruption. As I dwelt on it, I could feel the hurt in some way, and the hurt increased because I knew I caused it. It was a *terrible* thing I did to leave her; none of it was her fault, no deficiency on her part. All she wanted was a man to be in love with. I had been that man for as long as I could be. But she could not accept the person I *had* to be. There was no way I could get her to appreciate the fact that what made me so desirable to her was this burgeoning female consciousness that enabled me to love her in a way that no normal male can love a female. It was my chemistry and my consciousness that made it so. My consciousness was inexorably demanding full expression as a woman. I could no longer be a limited, closet woman.

The other view was that I was now Sally, and able to become me as I have needed to become for so many years. I had my own place, I was building my new identity, and a new life. I was also feeling the loss of Annie as Annie was feeling the loss of Tom.

In my journal scribbling over the recent years, I used to write about the three people in that house and marriage. Tom, Annie, and Sally. But three was a crowd, and at least one of us had to go. Well, two of us left, and Sally is now in control of Tom. It is now Sally's life and will remain so until death. Tom was made a job offer that paid well, so I let him out for the forty-hour week to bring in the money to support Annie and me. Otherwise, he is retired. All of his life experiences are within me, but I add my own feelings and experiences he could never have. He gets the benefit of my knowledge which he carefully applies to his work-especially in managing the women managers. I had to watch over Tom to make sure he didn't give himself away.

Tom and I are one as we have always been, but now I am in charge of us. Instead of him letting me out once in awhile, I let him out. I have no one else to answer to anymore. And that being the case, I feel good; I feel independent, and fulfilled. Annie, then, is in the past. I am saddened to think of her in the past. I feel frustrated that I can not do anything to keep her in the present. Is that her fault, or mine? Probably. There was an enormous price tag on my liberation.

After my third glass of coffee, I got myself put together so that I could go shopping for apartment furnishings. Most of it was done at Macy's. I needed to buy my own bed and other furniture so that I could return the rented stuff to the apartment people. I would rather pay the $90 per month to Macy's and eventually own something that would last, rather than rent the sleazy stuff. Then there was the matter of more linens, and the rest of the household things I needed to replace the rental stuff. I wanted to buy things that were immediately functional and would likely fit in wherever I ended up in the months and years ahead.

My final stop was at the super market. At the checkout stand, the cashier asked if I was Laura's mother. I said that I was not. She said that it was amazing how much I looked like her daughter's best friend. I liked her a lot, immediately. I realized that I was still appreciating validation as a woman. It was not too late for me to turn back to a male life if I learned that there was no way for me to be a believable woman. It seems silly to even think I could not pass as a woman, because I had so much experience doing it. But a lot of that success had been demonstrated some years ago. Now I was working toward a situation where I would have to be accepted as a woman all day, every day, in every kind of situation. I was in the process of betting all my chips on having a satisfactory life as a woman.

Before the end of July, I had made a number of telephone calls to inform several of my friends about my newly acquired circumstances. Some were thrilled, some were happy for me, and some were saddened that the marriage with Annie was over.

Nancy P. was a new friend who lived about a mile from me. She was on much the same journey I was. Our mutual family doctor, Susan, had introduced us a year ago. Nancy had been divorced, then went to a female status. Her employer supported the change of gender and saw to it that everyone in that international corporation who worked with Nancy would give her the same kindly reception she enjoyed as a male. Nancy had been a director of finance, and her job took her to other parts of the country from time to time, and occasionally to Europe. We both marveled at her opportunity to keep her job.

She was about sixteen years younger than me, and about six months ahead on getting things done in preparation for the sex reassignment surgery. She came over to visit me right after I made the call to her. She told me of all the things going on in her quest. I learned who the counsellors were that one had to convince in order to get the recommendation for surgery, who the surgeons were that did the operation, the different kinds of surgical procedures being done, the range of prices, and more relevant at the time, an introduction to the network of those who were like us. The Gender Clinic I had been associated with years ago had turned into something else.

Nancy was sure that she wanted the surgery. I had neither the cash, nor the conviction for taking that irreversible step. All I wanted was the ability to live as a woman and be universally accepted as such. I was more interested in what was going on between my ears than between my legs. I said as much to her. She just smiled at me. Then we began talking about plastic surgeons who do good work above the shoulders. I told her about my nose job, how much I liked Dr. Foster and his staff, and suggested she consult him rather than continue with the cutter in Los Angeles. She eventually did see Dr. Foster for such things as hair transplanting and a brow lift.

Mary F. at the college was not pleased that I had taken this step. She felt that the marriage Annie and I had was just too precious to screw up. Of course, she knew how I felt, because I spoke to her classes, and we had our own personal relationship. She could see both sides of the issue, but her own biases were preventing her from enjoying my liberation, my pursuit. At least she knew it was *her* biases that were in the way, which was more than I could say for some people. She wanted me to keep the dual existence going. I finally convinced her that the duality was no longer possible. She accepted that and said that we would need a new slant for the next lecture in the fall.

Viana was surprised to hear of my separate living arrangement. We had last seen each other at brunch in May. Her husband had called me to invite Annie and me to Viana's birthday brunch on Fisherman's Wharf. Annie was not interested in going anywhere with me. I showed up, and we were having an upbeat, friendly conversation until Viana asked why Annie wasn't there. I told them that we were on the brink of a separation. Their initial reaction was one of disbelief. Annie and I were the couple who truly loved each other and never had an ugly word to say to the other. Then they asked why the separation, so I told them I was a transsexual, and that I had to live the rest of my life as a woman.

No, this can not be true. To them, I was the sailor in Tsingtao, China, in 1946 who was not interested in men, and who seemed such a straight person. I was the product of a middle-class home where social norms did not create weirdos. I was the Naval Reservist who got to be a Chief Warrant Bosun. I was the person who unlocked the secret code of that damned computer at the Port. No, it could not be true that I was one of *those*.

All I could do was to look them straight in the eye and say that it was so; that it did not give me any pleasure to share that information with them; that I would begin living full time as a woman in the near future; and, if we were going to continue with the friendship, it would have to be on the new basis. I said those things as gently and with as much dignity as I could. They were stunned, but the message began to sink in. I invited them to ask questions.

They did ask some. Being San Franciscans, they already knew something about the phenomenon. Their questions seemed to be testing me for my conviction to invoke my plan. I told them of my earlier attempts in the 70s, and why I dropped out back then, and why the situation was different now. Their final question was why was I telling them now. I repeated my statement about wanting to remain as a friend to them, that if I did not risk this disclosure now, we might never see each other again. Furthermore, if they chose to reject me, they would at least know why we would not be friends anymore. I apologized for turning the birthday brunch conversation in such a novel direction. They appreciated the apology and my attempt at humor. Their summary statement was one of concern, and that as far as the future of our friendship-well, they would have to think about it.

When I called Viana in late July, she said that she was still undecided, but tended toward retaining the friendship. Ed, on the other hand, did not care to meet Sally, or even try to become friends with her. She asked if we could meet for dinner near the airport for one last Tom and Viana evening. She had more questions, and wanted to get answers before she met Sally. We did have that dinner, and a month or so later, she met Sally.

Our first meeting was in the lobby of the St. Francis Hotel in San Francisco. We both had appointments at nearly the same time, in the same neighborhood. We agreed to meet in the lobby of the hotel, and then find some coffee and a quiet place to talk. I got there before she did, and decided to visit the ladies' room and get that out of the way. As I was washing my hands, Viana came bursting in, looked at me without recognition. I adjourned to the outer room to brush my hair, etc. As I was finishing, Viana went breezing past and into the lobby. I gave her a minute, then walked out. She was sitting near the front doors, the better to see my impending arrival. I sat for a moment across the room to see if she would recognize me. No. I felt good about that, then got up and walked over toward her. Now she recognized me. I do not pretend to know what went on in her head. We agreed that coffee would not do it, and took a table in the little oak-paneled bar off the lobby. It was a comfortable conversation and we established our new beginning with the help of some Napa Valley chardonay.

The friendship continued, but there were some tedious moments. I knew she would have to make some radical adjustments in her thinking about me. Ours was the oldest friendship she had, and nearly my oldest. That meant quite a bit to her, but was I the same person? Yes and no. I certainly looked different, my mannerisms were a little different, and so was my consciousness. I no longer had anything to hide from her, and *I* felt more free. She, however, had the obligation to determine whether I was still enough of the old person for her to continue with. She might have to deal with that question for years to come. In the meantime, we were on friendly terms. I sensed the relationship to be better because there was tentative, provisional acknowledgement of me as a woman, and that enabled her to act on a woman-to-woman basis. Because of that, I saw a dimension in her not observable to me before. And that increased my fondness for her.

In my collection of things from the former residence I found a bundle of old letters that I intended to do something with "one of these days." One of those letters was from Anna Belle. It was a mimeographed letter-to-the-multitudes written several years ago. I was in a what the hell mood at that moment, so I called her number. It had been disconnected. Then I called Berkeley information, and sure enough, there was a new number.

A.B. was delighted to hear from me. It had been a bunch of years since we had seen each other, and there was a lot of catching up to do. The conversation focused on what was going on in her life, and what was going on in mine. She knew about me from our times together when I worked at the Port. She had met Sally once back then. While she was supportive of my desire, she felt I had a long way to go to become an acceptable woman. No matter, she liked me anyway. I thought she was a fascinating person, very bright, and as open minded as they come in Berkeley. We ended the conversation by setting a date for her to come by for dinner, a few weeks hence.

Before the dinner date, she called me to invite me to the premiere of a small San Francisco singing group called The Noe Valley Heavy Opera Company. They were going to do a bistro performance in a large bar in the south-of-market district. I suggested we meet for dinner before the show. She said that she and her gentleman friend would be delighted to meet me at the Chez Molé restaurant, a block away from the entertainment.

I worked hard at looking good that night. I got to the restaurant first. There were a number of gay men at the bar, and none of them paid any attention to me. I was thrilled as that was an indicator to me that they regarded me as a true female, a person of no social importance. I ordered a drink, then A.B. and her date came in. I was hugged by Anna Belle, and introduced to Ray, who shook my hand and exhibited courtly manners toward me. He wanted to make me feel like a lady, and he did.

During dinner, Anna Belle said that I was different-that I really seemed to be a woman now. I said that the lighting helped soften my features. She said that was not it, that there was more to it than that. I just came across as a real woman. Ray said, "Ditto, and I've never seen you before." Of course I felt good about that. After all, this was a woman who told me several years ago that I could not "make the team," and now I did. Eventually Ray went to the men's room, and A.B. and I got a few signals straight. Ray was a friend, not a romantic figure. Also, she had to sell tickets at the door, and she would have to leave our dinner early. Would I mind staying with Ray and walk up the block to the place with him? No problem. I asked if she was going to warn her friends about me. She said there was nothing to warn them about.

Ray and I had seconds on coffee, and a lively conversation. He knew a little of my past, but because he had never seen Tom, he was only able to get to know Sally. I liked that. In time, we walked to the show. There was a special feeling to that walk with Ray. He was my escort. I was really getting into the role, and I liked it more than somewhat. At the theater bar, we joined a large table of A.B.'s friends. The show was just starting, and so was one of the more memorable evenings of my life. The players had taken a lot of Kurt Weil's songs and written a simple drama to string the music together into a novel, brilliant performance. I do not know whether A.B. informed her friends of my impending arrival or not, but my presence was warmly acknowledged, and we became friendly immediately. Of course, it was a sophisticated group, and they may have been able to tell as I walked in with Ray, but no one gave any indication of anything being awry. During an intermission, I thanked Anna Belle for the loan of her gentleman. She stared at me for a moment and said that I was catching on fast.

Two weeks later, Anna Belle came for dinner. It was just the two of us. Yes, we had known each other for some years, we had spent time over a lot of lunch tables, but there had never been any romantic interest. On that evening, we began to discover what our relationship was about. We were to be the best of women friends. No more, no less. But that was quite a bit, actually. We spent hours talking, each of us sharing our recent pasts, our present circumstances, and our expected futures. We came to agreement on philosophies, on nutrition, choices of beverages, and most of all-good humor and aloha for each other. We specifically acknowledged that our relationship was karmic, that we were supposed to become close at this time in our lives.

She wanted to help me get launched as a woman, and I voted for that. She gave me all kinds of input on diverse topics such as clothing styles for me, furnishing a woman's apartment, and a lot more I don't want to talk about now. I tried to identify what she could get from me. I think that what she got was what I got: friendship, support, and love. From August, onwards, she and a gentleman friend would come to dinner. Sometimes her teen-aged daughter, Sia, would come, sometimes not. We always had a wonderful time.

Anna Belle was about a dozen years younger than I was, but it didn't seem to matter, not at our ages. She had returned from a couple of years in one of the Carolinas working for her sister. There was a family factory there, and A.B.'s job was to learn and use C, a very sophisticated and powerful computer programming language of the day. Now, she was doing clerical work for a local temporary agency.

She wanted to know what Tom was doing at Wollongong, and what did the company do? I told her, and suggested that she consider joining the team in either training or in technical publications. We needed new people, and I thought she would be an asset to either department. Ultimately Anna Belle was hired in the training department. She was smart and caught on quickly; sometimes too quickly for her manager, and thus the seeds of her termination some months away were sown.

A.B. enrolled in an evening class to learn UNIX. Due to the late hour and the distance to her house, I suggested she stay over at my place on those Monday nights. For that semester, we had our private girl talk and pajama party every week. I loved it. I think A.B. thought of me as a woman more than I did at the time. She was my support, my teacher, and my best friend. When the girl talk centered on men in her life, I could get in touch with her feelings, *and* I could identify with the man's feelings. I was in a position to help her see the male side. It was a result of those conversations that I began to identify some of the gaps between male and female motivations. Both sexes are equally smart, equally loving and caring, but the way in which a man demonstrates his love for a woman is not very often the way that the woman expects it to be demonstrated. The priorities, the agendas, the expectations, the fears, the standards are all different for men and women.

I was in touch with my brother during the initial days in the new apartment. Of course, he thought it was pretty stupid for me to do what I was doing, and very stupid for leaving Annie. Of course, I listened to him, but there was no way he could change my mind. Of course, I tried to help him understand, and of course he couldn't. But we have been brothers since I was born, and brothers we would always be. Of course.

In September, I learned of a Federal Civil Service job with the Coast Guard in Washington, D.C. The specifications described someone who had spent a few years at sea, knew something about a variety of ships, had training experience, and the ability to evaluate training programs. I met or exceeded those requirements. Because all of my Civil Service records were in my new name, Sally applied for the job. I thought a move to the other coast would do me and some others a lot of good.

The Standard Form 171 requires that everything be true and complete. What that meant here was that Tom's name had to be on that form as "other names used." The personnel evaluators don't care about that anomaly, but hiring authorities do. Very much, in this case. While the Coast Guard is an equal opportunity employer, they did not expect any women to meet those sea duty requirements of navigation and cargo handling, to name two. Evidently I was one of the top three candidates for the job, according to the Civil Service evaluators. That meant the hiring authority was obliged to interview me.

Tom got a phone call for Sally at work a few weeks later. (I sent in the application with my work phone number on it.) I suggested he call back at the residence number the next morning at 6:00 a.m. Pacific time. He did, and we had a half-hour conversation in which I learned by oblique phrasing that he knew I was a transsexual, that I was indeed qualified professionally, but no way in hell was I going to get that job. It was not until January that I got my notice that the job went to someone else. Nice try.

I stayed in touch with Harry at Moffett Field. He had found a young man to take on my old job. I renewed my offer to help bring the guy up to speed. He said it would be a month or longer before the lad would actually show up. We compared notes on how life was treating us, and vowed to stay in touch.

Life at The Wollongong Group was never comfortable for me. The task I was expected to perform was new-I was to be a counsellor for managers. They had not seen me earn my spurs in their specialties, and I was not allowed to demonstrate anything for them. Therefore, I was not credible, nor could I become credible there. The best I could do was to try to build them in some way to make them better managers. To some extent, I did it. One timid manager began to feel so good about herself that she applied for a managerial job with Apple Computers and got it. The original training manager left the company a month after I got there. One of the applicants for his job was a former Navy airman from Moffett Field. During the interview, I established that his philosophy of training was congruent with our needs. It was a pleasure to hire a Navy-trained man for the job.

In November, I got the go ahead to hire an administrative assistant. After the first day of the ad's appearance in the newspapers, the personnel assistant called to say there was a fine candidate in his office. Could he bring her over to my new corner office to interview with me? Sure. Hal came in with a woman who sent a real jolt through me. It was Nancy H., the woman who ran the web press in 1977 when Sally did the monthly newsletter for the Interpersonal Support Network. We had spent a number of hours together each month to make sure the press would do the best job. She was a little older, and so was I. There was no flicker of recognition from her. Of course, she had never met Tom, and I don't think she ever suspected there was a Tom.

It was a good interview. We got along very well because I knew her and what her philosophy was on a lot of things. Then I said that she looked familiar, and had we met before? She said we had not met before. I offered her the job, and she accepted. The relationship was very smooth and productive.

My week days started at 6:00 a.m. I would roll out of bed, do my usual morning stuff, then get dressed as Sally. I would make a modest breakfast, write in my journal, and just think about what was going on. At 7:45, I would change into Tom's clothes and drive off to work. After work, I would drive back, and within five minutes after closing the door, I would be Sally again until 7:45 the next morning.

I really was coming unglued at work. I had trouble keeping my inner self from showing to others. Right after New Years, I knew I had to do something. There were a few options open. I could quit, or I could ask to work as Sally, or I could keep on going until I got fired. A rumor started about me wearing a bra under my shirt. No way, although my breast development had become impossible for me to hide, and impossible for others to ignore. I never wore female things under Tom's clothes. I did try it once some decades before, but it was no good. Counterproductive, actually.

Every morning at 9:00 a.m., Nancy and I would have our coffee, cigarettes, and plan the day. She knew I was hurting, and asked if she could help. I asked her if she remembered printing the ISN newsletter. I gave her a couple of clues and she remembered. When I asked if she remembered Sally who brought in the mechanicals for printing, she said that she remembered, vaguely. I told her that was me, that was the way I wanted to be from now on, and that was my problem. She poured herself another cup of coffee and said that I had her permission to be Sally again. She was not being cute; she meant it. I said that I was coming to the end of my rope, and that some kind of showdown would happen soon. I suggested that she be alert for sudden changes.

On a Wednesday afternoon in the second week of January, I called the head of personnel to make an appointment. I wanted to make a clean breast of it (pardon the expression) and find out how I could gracefully leave the company-something that would be the best for all of us. I was told that I would not be able to get an appointment until Friday. Okay.

On Thursday, I had a heart-to-heart talk with the other managers. I told them that I expected to leave the company soon, perhaps in a few days, and that they were entitled to know before anyone else. We acknowledged the rumor about my chest, and I told them I was a transsexual, and that I could not maintain the charade any longer. They were polite and supportive. They did not argue with me when I said that I had been a little off-center lately. We all realized it was the end or at least the beginning of the end for me. Their opinion was that it would have been better for me if I could have worked there as Sally, but conservative organizations such as that one could not accommodate such a bizarre, but workable idea.

On Friday, I was told that I would be able to meet with the manager of personnel and Ralph at 4:00, in Ralph's office. Oh oh. I sensed that my termination was *fait accompli*. I walked into Ralph's office to find him, the personnel manager, and the vice-president for legal matters. Yep, this was it. It was a very civilized discussion. Ralph said nothing, but he didn't need to. The other V-P did the summary and laid out the company's position: I was doing a fine job and everybody liked working with me, but it was known that I was a transsexual, and that knowledge plus my physique had become unacceptable to the president. Parenthetically, I was told that had I been an employee of much lower rank, that all this could have been absorbed. Being a director, and someone with visibility to others outside the company, I constituted an embarrassment for the president. I was thereupon asked to resign "for personal reasons."

I had some trouble making my mouth work. Everything was out on the table now. My emotional resources were expended just getting through the day thus far. Sure, there was some relief knowing the game was over, but I am not accustomed to being kicked off the team. I managed to croak something. I don't remember what it was I was trying to say. The V-P interrupted me anyway, and said that the company would give me two months severance pay in lieu of notice, and that I could use the company for references under either name I chose. I think we all knew that they could not fire me for being a transsexual, but I learned a long time ago that if a person is not wanted, he will eventually go anyway. I also knew that they did not have to give me that much severance pay, and the sweetener of a reference for Sally was undreamed of. By now I could speak. I said, "Thank you for the option on the reference. After today, I will be Sally for the rest of my days."

A check for the full amount of my pay had been made out and was handed to me with the explanation for the deductions, etc. Then the V-P said that if I furnished the personnel office with the appropriate documents, they would respond favorably to inquiries about Sally.

On my way home that fine day, I realized it was Friday the 13th. I grinned when I thought of the company's newsletter being printed that day with Tom's picture on the front page along with a 2000-word article I had written. I pulled into my parking space, let Tom into the apartment, and no one has seen him since.

Chapter 21

I sat at my dining table, wearing my black skirt-and-sweater set, equipped with a glass of wine, and my thousand-yard stare. It was night, but I stared out the huge window anyway. I had turned off the electric lights and lighted five candles inside my apartment. It was raining like crazy outside. I longed for a fireplace.

I have left jobs before and I have gone through the last-day-of-finals before. In those instances, there was always a time of disorientation; a syndrome containing a mix of loss, triumph, relief, success, freedom, and feelings of disenfranchisement. On that evening of Friday-the-Thirteenth, I felt all of that end-of-an-era turmoil. Moments like that always ended up with the question, What next? In the old days, the answer would center around getting a new job, or the next classes to take. Now, I felt something I had never felt before.

The pervasive thought was that I could decide what was to be next. I mean, there were no restrictions. Until now, all decisions about the future had some built-in admonitions about my male identity, obligations to others, my geographic location, and a few other considerations to acknowledge when choosing the moves to make for my future. But now I could see that I had never had so much freedom. I had read somewhere, a very long time ago, that freedom is the optical illusion that prevents us from seeing the surrounding restrictions. Cynical perhaps, but immensely accurate. My optical system could not identify any restrictions of consequence.

I reveled in that illusion for a time, then I became aware that this new freedom carried a responsibility with it. In my philosophy, I knew there were a lot of things I had to learn in this life for my soul growth. I also acknowledged that I was, in some way, obliged to be a factor in the soul growth of other people, just as other people were involved in my growth. I dared not presume what other people needed, but it was my responsibility to be a *genuine me* when I was around them; to recognize them as fellow learners; and, that if they were to get their lessons, it was up to them, and certainly not up to me to try to tell anyone how they should live their lives, or what they were supposed to learn.

On my second glass of wine, I visualized myself all alone sitting cross-legged in a barren plane. From this unfettered, pristine condition, I could make a new start. I thought: I am as the Phoenix about to arise from the ashes of my yesterdays. I do not usually think in terms like that.

I knew that I had a lot of resources. Money was not one of them, yet I had never missed a meal in my life, nor had I ever had to sleep in the streets. I was evolving the notion that money was not my source of power as it is with so many people. Provisionally, I cited my will and my desire as my power base. Optimism, too. I had my good health-physical health certainly, and perhaps even mental health, though we may not all agree on that.

I had friends. Many of them were tried-and-true over many years, others were friends when it seemed we needed to be friends for a brief time. I had an energy and an enthusiasm for life that could not be daunted by anyone or anything. Oh, I might get annoyed from time to time, but never daunted. I had an extensive memory bank of successful experiences as a man. Most of all, I had the undeniable awareness that it was time for me to become a woman, or at least the best woman I could be. There were no more restrictions, no more namby-pamby wishing, no more doubts of any kind. The pursuit for womanhood was now a mandate.

On my third glass of wine, I thought I had better make a few phone calls. I would have to leave the life planning alone for the time being so that I could let a few people know what was going on with me as of that day. Besides, this was a moment when I felt I was relaxed enough to sound rational on the telephone.

It was still early enough to call George in Tennessee. George was the fraternity brother who introduced me to Helen in 1950. He was one of the few who I felt comfortable with in sharing my big secret back in 1976 when I did my first full year as me. He was supportive, and so was his wife, Martha. He was also supportive when Tom reappeared in late 1977, and supportive when I told him several months ago that I had left Annie. There are damned few people who can see a constancy in a person like me, and salute it. In fact, no others have stayed on my roller coaster so well and as long as George and Martha. During the conversation, I assured him that this was it for me-no more changing back. He wanted to know how I was handling this recent turn of events, and hoped that I would finally get what I wanted. He made me promise to stay in touch and let him know how I was doing. We promised to write.

Next, a local call to Nancy P. She was happy that I gained my freedom, and concerned about my emotional stability for now and the immediate future. I assured her that all was well, and that I just wanted her to know that Tom was out of the picture. We regarded that as a gain and a loss, simultaneously. We promised to get together soon.

Another local call was to Annie, to let her know that I was now unemployed, and that meant I was truly on my way to becoming Sally. Oddly enough, she was sympathetic about me losing my job. It may have been a natural reaction for her. She had ministered to me on those occasions before when I had left a job. It was a relaxed, civilized conversation. All other calls since have been civilized, but not relaxed.

The next conversation that evening was with Viana, who was still not quite comfortable with the new edition of me. She was sympathetic, but a little ill at ease. I had no specific reason for telling her about my "resignation" other than the fact that I would not be answering my telephone at work any longer. We had a brief chat, and promised to stay in touch. The last telephone call I made that night was to Tim. His answering machine promised to stay in touch, so I left a message.

I started to cook a nutritional outrage for dinner. It was to be a hamburger, with a thick slab of raw onion and lots of mustard and dill pickle slices, and pan-fried potatoes with a special seasoning salt. Before it was done, the phone rang.

It was Jim D., the technical publications manager I hired several weeks before. He wanted me to know that Ralph called a meeting of the dozen or so people who had been in my realm, and told them that I had left the company for personal reasons. Jim said that it was done in a very professional manner, layered atop the understanding everyone had from the rumor mill regarding the real reason for my exit. He said it was well handled and well received. He then gave me his personal condolences, lamenting the fact that our relationship had ended before we really had a chance to get started on a solid working basis. He went as far as saying that he wished Sally could have continued working there. The final item was that some of the crew wanted to meet with me for lunch next week. Fine with me, but I was Sally from now on. He said they wanted to meet Sally. A date was set for lunch. We promised to stay in touch.

I ate my overcooked burger. It tasted good anyway. It was a refreshing change from broiled, skinless chicken and steamed vegetables with rice. One has to eat soul food once in a while.

I also thought about my schedule for the next day, Saturday. I had made a morning appointment with Marianne, my skin lady. She was a cosmetologist and a wonderful person. She was going to do some waxing of body hair to help me get a little more believable, yet not tip my hand on what I was up to. It is incredible the number of things a male has to go through to look female. I won't even talk about body language or speech patterns now. Just to *look* like a woman is a real chore. But a labor of love.

I had an appointment with the ladies of the Wig Palace in the early afternoon to consider a new hair style. Would a new length help? A new color? I had also made a late afternoon appointment with the wonderful Dr. Foster in his San Francisco office. He was going to shoot me one more time with collagen in the upper lip. See what I mean by having a lot to do to become a woman-like person?

Instead of a fourth glass of wine, I had a generous portion of brandy in my glass of coffee. Yes, there was a lot scheduled for the next day. I had jammed as much into a Saturday as I could to accommodate my needs and the work schedule I suddenly didn't have anymore. From now on I could take my time, at least for a little while.

I really felt wonderful the next morning. There was a rainbow in my head, a song in my heart, and a smile on my lips. It was time to move off square one of my new life, and *get going*. As I was about to leave for my appointment with Marianne, the telephone rang. It was Anna Belle. She wanted to know how I was doing. We made plans for a dinner on Sunday. It was so good for me to have A.B. for a friend. We had become close during these last few months. It occurred to me that I had a sister now, the one I had always wanted.

At Marianne's I was accused of being high on some strange, exotic substance. Not true, and when I explained my termination from work, and my resolve to get on with life, they all understood. In the private room, Marianne honored my request to wax virtually *everything* from my neck down. Even a Bikini line. Talk about a labor of love! Next, she pierced my ears, and finally dyed my eyelashes black. I thought I was high when I went *into* that place.

At the Wig Palace, I had the same accusation leveled at me, and I gave them the same news. They were stunned, but happy for me. I knew that at least one of them liked Tom better than me, but what the hell. In less than twenty minutes, we all agreed that the long ash page I was wearing was the best style and color for me. I liked it when I didn't have to buy anything new. I left there early enough to stop at Caroline's for an unscheduled manicure. This time we did the acrylic nails. No more glued things that pop off at the worst moment.

By the time I got to the doctor's office in San Francisco, I was still feeling incredibly good about what was happening to me. Within the last twenty-four hours, I had burned bridges, blown up escape tunnels, and disconnected in other ways from the old life. As I sat there in the waiting room turning pages of a magazine I didn't focus on, I flashed on the custom of the groom at a Jewish wedding, when he stomps on a glass to signify that a new beginning has been made. Then it was my turn to see the doctor. Poor Barbara, his nurse, had to grip my hand during the shot. There is no way one can do a local anesthetic to deaden the pain of a collagen injection.

I got home before dark. I poured a glass of wine and was glad the pain in my upper lip was gone. That had to be the second most sensitive spot on my body. But I knew why I did it; it was optional, and it didn't happen every day. It was also my third shot, and it was likely that I would never get another one. They seem not to last. And they are expensive. I wished there was a satisfactory surgical procedure for creating more fullness in the upper lip, but alas, there wasn't. I was too happy to become unhappy about anything. It had been quite a day for getting things done, and quite a day of emotional high.

Sunday was a beautiful day inside and out. I hosted a small fizz party for my neighbors. We had become friendly a few weeks after I moved in. Ruth, Chris, Lynn, and Brian. The friendship began in late July when Brian invited me to join him and the other ladies for margaritas at Pedro's, a wonderfully yuppie Mexican restaurant next door to our apartment complex. The five of us lounged on the open deck that day, drinking and getting to know each other. A week later, I learned that each of them saw me as a male dressed as a female. They were probably the toughest crowd to convince due to their erudition, but each was tipped off by a different feature. Brian saw my posture as a giveaway; Lynn thought my hair was too ornate; Ruth and Chris thought I was overdressed in some way, but could not agree on what it was specifically. They liked me anyway.

In the months that followed that first meeting we became as close as transient apartment dwellers ever get. Now and then we had beverages or dinner at one or another's apartment. The conversations were always good; sometimes funny, sometimes serious. We became candid about me and my quest. They were supportive and promised to be ruthless about critiquing me on my dress and deportment. After a few months, they didn't say anything to me about my appearance, except to compliment me on something. Chris even asked me where I bought my rayon polka dot suit, and a few other things. I had become absorbed into their society as a woman.

We had attended the apartment's Halloween party together. I wore black fish-net pantyhose, black nylon running shorts, my sequined top from Las Vegas, golden spangled earrings that were made from ping pong balls, a truly ornate wig, and the longest rope of colored glass beads I could find. And three-inch black patent heels. I intended to go as a harlot. Their comment was that I should have worn a costume.

There was never a formal presentation of Tom, but Brian had seen him from a distance once, and Lynn had bumped into him a half dozen times in the parking lot. She had been an airline stewardess and knew how to be pleasant around strange people. So on the day of January 15, we toasted the liberation of Sally. They felt that I had improved the female presentation enormously in the six months of my residence there.

On Monday, when the rest of the world went to their jobs, I decided to get serious about my future. I called Harry at Moffett Field to let him know I was at liberty, and that I wanted to renew my offer to help the new person. He lamented that I would not be able to return to my old duties and said that the new person would be ready for my input in a few weeks. Then he asked if I would be interested in applying for a job with Lockheed in Burbank. It seemed that they needed someone who knew the P-3 aircraft and the existing Navy training program to do a project for the forthcoming update. He gave me the name and phone number of the contact person in Palmdale. I reminded Harry that I was Sally from now on. He said he knew that. Boy, what a friend!

I telephoned Mr. Paul with aircrew training in Palmdale. I identified myself as a former Ed Spec at Moffett Field. I asked if I could apply for the position that Harry had told me about. Paul was delighted to know that someone was available who had my experience. Would I like to fly down for an interview?

In a couple of days, I received the official Lockheed employment application, the airplane tickets, a room reservation, and a voucher for a rental car. I began to get the idea that they were serious about talking with me. I was expected to fill out all blank forms, and bring my Federal Civil Service stuff, i.e., (SF-171) to the initial interview. No problem, except that I knew there had to be a second set of names on those forms: mine and Tom's.

I was greeted by the head of personnel in Burbank, surrendered my paperwork, was introduced to the head of security and had a pleasant interview, and then to a support person in personnel who gave me information on housing, credit unions, the holiday schedule, and more. Now I was convinced they were serious about me.   Mr. Paul came in at that point. He introduced himself and escorted me out to the reception area where we talked for a few minutes. We left the building when the head of security sent word that my application, etc. checked out. I was given a visitor's badge to wear at all times. We drove to another facility in Burbank where I was introduced to the head of maintenance who might want to use my talents and experience at a later date.

Our last Burbank stop was at the airport, where we flew in a company plane to Palmdale to meet with the chief of the project and one of the subordinates. Paul kept a running monolog going on how good the company was, the exciting work to be done, and how lucky it was that I was available for this project. I had a running monolog going in my head that I was pleased that I was being regarded as a female by everyone so far, and pleased that I wore my new navy blue Oleg Cassini suit with white silk jacquard blouse.

In the hangar office, I was introduced to the clerical people, the young subordinate male member of the team, and then Paul and I went to the cafeteria for lunch. At the table, he stopped his commentary long enough to ask if I had any comments or questions. I had one comment and one question: "I am excited by everything I have seen and heard"; and, "When can I start?" He appreciated my enthusiasm, and said that we would be talking with the chief of the project in a half hour.

The interview was brief because the chief of the project was also the chief test pilot, and he was scheduled to fly "$32,000,000 worth of new electronics" soon. It was a relaxed conversation with no big surprises. There was one element to the job that was unfamiliar to me: MILSPEC reports. Other than that, it was an upbeat interview. Each of those three men had photocopies of all the paperwork I brought with me. No one said anything about my "other names used" declaration. On the walk back to the company plane, Paul gave me the grand tour of the Lockheed museum and a brief walk through the production lines where the new, updated P-3 aircraft were being built. That factory tour was a real privilege, I learned later.

Back in Burbank, I turned in my badge, and Paul walked me all the way to my rental car. At that point, he said that he was not authorized to make me a job offer, but unofficially speaking, he wanted me to work for him. I said I was ready.

The first thing I did when I returned home the next day was to telephone the V-P at Wollongong to alert him to the impending reference check from Burbank. He said that he had already been called and everything was all right.

The following day, Paul telephoned me to say that he would not be able to offer me the job. He cited the lack of knowledge of MILSPEC reporting to be the reason. I said that I had talked with some of my tech writer colleagues that morning about the task of learning it. I was told that it would take a tech writer, at my level, about two hours to get up to speed, but each of them asked why a training person should have to know MILSPEC. Paul said he was not too sure either.

The other thing that disturbed him was that the V-P at Wollongong did not seem to remember me, the former Director of Marketing Services in that company. Eventually, it dawned on the V-P who I was, but by then Paul must have thought something was not normal. The end of that story was that I did not get the job. The reason or reasons why not are still a mystery to me. My guess is that somebody decided to read all the paper work I submitted, and saw the other names, and drew some conclusions that were unfavorable to me. But I will probably never know for sure.

I telephoned Harry to let him know what happened. He was sympathetic and could not offer any fresh insights as to why I was not hired. He also said that my young replacement was ready to meet with me for input. Mike and I had a two-hour lunch. He was glad to get the "pass down," and said that I looked like one of his aunts. Nice.

The next big job opportunity came through Anna Belle. She had a friend employed by Civil Service in Oakland. There was an opening for an educator at the Military Sealift Command. The qualifications for that job were almost identical to the Coast Guard job I didn't get a few months earlier. I submitted the completed forms, had an interview that was very positive, and three weeks later a letter came. The job had been rescinded, therefore nobody got it. There was a clear and present need for *someone* to do that job, I had been told during the interview.

It was easy to develop a case of paranoia. I made great effort to convince myself that the universe was really behind me and my quest for employment. The perfect job was manifesting for me, and it would come when it was time. I had to believe that as fact, but it was hard to accept. It helped a little to remind myself that living in Burbank or Palmdale, or even Oakland would not be conducive to my happiness.

I telephoned the American Civil Liberties Union in San Francisco. I wanted to know what options I had on filling out those forms for employment. Was I obliged to give my former male name, or not? From that awesomely liberal temple in that awesomely liberal City of San Francisco, I was told by their spokesman that it was probably the case that job discrimination was being practiced against me, a transsexual, and there was nothing they could do for me. I was awesomely disappointed. I asked if there was any agency that could give me counsel or support. He said that the State Department of Fair Housing and Employment Practices might be able to help me.

When I called there, a very pleasant woman answered, listened to my story, then delivered the opinion that the "other names used" column was there for the sake of checking references of people who had divorced or remarried, and not a trap to catch transsexuals. Her suggestion was to just use Tom's last name in that space. Brilliant.

For next time. In late March, I was getting restless. I had been sending out resumes in response to advertised positions for over two months. No responses from anyone.

I discussed the situation with my therapist. I had started a series of appointments with Millie, a licensed psychologist and sexologist, the previous summer. According to Nancy P., Millie was one of the best for checking candidates for sex reassignment surgery, and a terrific woman to talk with. I thought that I needed to review a number of things going on in my life anyway, and *perhaps* a sex change operation would be in my future. Millie would be able to help me sort it out.

If I was to get the operation, she would be in a position to recommend me to a surgeon who does it. There are a number of reputable surgeons who will do the sex change operation, but none of them will do it without strong recommendation from a medical doctor, a psychologist, and a psychiatrist. It is a good idea to have such checks.

Millie seemed to think that I was progressing well along the road toward womanhood, but it would take at least a year for her to observe me, and for me to experience the successes one needs to be sure before the irreversible step is taken. By this date, Millie seemed to think that I was indeed a strong candidate for the operation, but "... we mustn't be hasty." I submitted the idea that perhaps I needed to consider a move to another part of the country for the sake of better employment opportunities, and a chance to create new friends. We kicked the idea around, and I continued to think about it.

In early April, Nancy P. called to ask if I was going to attend the annual conclave of transvestites and transsexuals. She said that it was in San Francisco this year, and I ought to think about attending.

My visit was on Sunday, the last day of the week-long conference. I got no farther than the lobby bar, although several floors of the hotel had meeting and seminar rooms occupied by the congress of therapists, pre- and post-ops, and transvestites. I met a number of people like me, did some fast intelligence gathering on local TV/TS support groups in different parts of the country, and had some drinks with some fascinating people. They were from all walks of life, all levels of education, a wide range of ages, and at different places on the scale of male-female consciousness and appearance. I thought that one hundred of these people would match a hundred males outside, except these people wanted to dress like women.

I introduced myself to Linda, who was also a vodka drinker and Pall Mall smoker. It turned out that Linda and I had been in the Navy about the same time, we had been on destroyers during the Korean action, and we both had a passion for words. It was her first public appearance dressed as a woman, and she was an extremely happy person. By the time I left the hotel that day, I had Linda's address, and the contact information for the Portland and Seattle gender support centers.

On Monday, I obtained fresh maps and tour guides for a trek to the great northwest. I understood that cost of living was less, but so were employment opportunities. If I had to be unemployed, I thought it would be better to do it up there somewhere. I felt there would be an advantage in finding fresh turf to establish new roots. It has been said that one place is as good as another, that you always take yourself with you wherever you go, anyway. True enough, but in this situation, I needed to be in a place where there were no reminders of my past, where new friends could be made who may or may not know there was a male in me somewhere. As long as they would never see Tom, we could establish a relationship with me as a woman.

Next, I checked with the California State Employment office about continuing my unemployment insurance claim if I moved to another state. I was assured that my claim would be valid for the period of a year, regardless of where I lived. That was comforting. As long as that biweekly check came in, I could survive until I got a job.

Finally, I made reservations for three nights in a motel north of Seattle. The choice was made with no other information than it looked good on the map. The last thing in my plan was to call Harry to see if he knew anybody in the Seattle area who might have a need for my talents. He gave me data on two men. One was at Boeing, and the other was on Whidbey Island. Harry was *surely* a good friend. Anna Belle gave me the name and address of a friend in Seattle. I wrote letters to the two people Harry told me about and to A.B.'s friend. At the end of the second week in April, I loaded my car with stuff for a few days, and headed out for greener pastures, as they say.

On my first day in Edmonds, north of Seattle, I telephoned everyone on my target list. That included the personal, professional, and gender people. Barbara, A.B.'s friend, was very pleased I called, and wanted to meet for pizza. We did, and it was the beginning of a lasting friendship.

The two men referred by Harry were unable to see me. The one from Boeing wanted me to complete an application form for personnel, and make him a copy too. He also wanted my resume, and any Civil Service documents. He said that he could use me as soon as the Navy signed the contract for his project, thereby creating a budget to pay people. He also said that he didn't want to do face-to-face interviews until it was time to hire. Harry's counterpart at Naval Air Station on Whidbey Island said that he was on his way out of town. He also said there were no openings. It was not the warmest reception I had.

The gender center had an answering machine. I left my name and my phone number where I was staying. Later that first evening, someone called me back. She welcomed me, answered my questions, and said she was looking forward to meeting me in person.

On my third day, I thought the greater Seattle area was a fine place to live. I found an apartment complex in Kent, just south of Seattle. It was kind of yuppie, but for openers, I decided it was my best bet. I signed a lease on a fireplace with an apartment wrapped around it, and drove back to California to pack. It was a better apartment and $350 per month less than renting in Foster City.

The first thing I did upon returning to Foster City, was to call Alan, who was in the moving van business. His company had provided transportation for the trade show crates I had to get moved from show to show. We had a five-year relationship for doing business, with a lot of friendly lunches in between times. I told him I was going to move to Washington, and asked if he could give me service. Sure, he said, and I would get the VIP rate because of all the business I had given him over the years. He said he would send an estimator out in a day or so. At that point, I had to tell him about my new name, etc. Alan had a problem feeling comfortable with that information. It did not screw up the moving of my furniture, but I did lose a friend. That's baseball, I guess. On May Day of 1989, I became a resident of the State of Washington.

Chapter 22

It was a week before all my stuff arrived at my new apartment, and another week before everything was unpacked. During that time, I noticed that the weather was very much like California. I thought I would be wearing woolens, but cotton was more like it. Before the end of the month, I had attended a meeting of the Ingersoll Gender Center in Seattle. The counsellors and other clients were wonderful. I was given a list of medical doctors, psychiatrists, and psychologists that would be sympathetic if I wanted to get started on an evaluation for surgery. I was also given a list of dates for transsexual meetings, for transvestite meetings, and the social calendar for both groups.

I was still not convinced that I wanted the big operation, although I thought it would be a good idea to check it out with the professionals while I checked it out with my own feelings and the amount of success I would have in establishing myself as a woman in this new land. The idea of being accepted as a woman by strangers was a challenge. So many people in California knew what I was doing, and it was all right with them. But now I was in a situation where I had to know whether I could pass as a woman, and not tell anyone, and not be asked what I was doing dressed as a woman.

So far, everything worked. I had rented my apartment, registered my car, took the written and road tests for a driver's license, transferred my auto insurance, and all the other things such as grocery shopping and negotiating the purchase of kindling wood from a local sawmill. No one looked at me strangely, or gave any indication that I was anything other than a woman. I felt good about all of that, but I was still a long way from full confidence. I was a hard case.

I took all of Tom's good suits and dress shirts, etc. to The Gentlemen's Consignment in Seattle. By now, I *knew* I would never wear those threads again. Why not convert them into cash? Sally, the owner, took my things, wrote me a receipt, and gently asked if the things belonged to a deceased husband. I thought of some cute answers, but I said no, they weren't. She continued to look at me, possibly thinking I had stolen them. Only then did I volunteer that the clothes were mine. She continued to stare. I added that I used to wear them. She asked why. I said I used to be a male. She said she didn't think so. I said a few words in my deck voice. She believed me, but her expression was another example of cognitive dissonance. She said that I should not do that again, that there was no need for me to tell people. We talked for a few minutes, and I could tell she was fascinated, but not nosey. Within a month we became close friends. And my confidence level went up another notch. Maybe two notches.

I chose a medical doctor who would monitor my health, in case I wanted to seek the operation. He did a lot of tests in a few months. He said I looked like a woman, even when I had to remove my wig so that he could evaluate my male pattern baldness. We agreed to try that prescription stuff that is supposed to regrow hair. In six months, it did not do anything except cost me a lot of money. It was worth a try.

I chose a psychologist. I needed someone to level with in my new situation. I said I was not sure that I wanted the operation, but I wanted to find out. Sandra regarded me as a woman and felt that if I wanted to live the rest of my life as a woman, I certainly could do it, operation or not. That gave me a new level of confidence. We seemed to enjoy each other's company during those biweekly appointments. It made me feel good-spending time with a therapist when I was not hurting with a problem. What used to be my problem in previous years was now my normal state: the desire to pursue womanhood. I am sure that legitimate counselling was going on, but for me it was girl talk-I was able to verify my feelings and the meanings of events unfolding around me, and getting her opinions on a lot of things.

By the end of July, she asked if I had decided yet on going for the surgery. I said I felt I was ready for more information on it. I had told her about Nancy P. going to Montreal for surgery a few weeks before, and that she was pleased by the care and the results. I was given the names and addresses of three surgeons who were deemed competent and moderately priced. They were located in Montreal, Brussels, and

Trinidad, Colorado. I had met post-op ladies who had been to them, and all were very enthusiastic about "their" surgeon. The local medical doctor said that all of my tests were normal, and that he would support my candidacy for surgery if that was what I wanted to do. At age sixty-one, I felt good about being that healthy.

I wrote letters of inquiry to the surgeons in Montreal and Brussels. I did not consider the surgeon in Trinidad because his price tag was too high for me. He had to buy malpractice insurance, whereas the foreign doctors do not. Within two weeks, I had the requirements from Montreal and from Brussels. They were similar in price, medical work ups, and therapists' recommendations. I chose to concentrate on the surgeon in Montreal. After he examined all the reports, a date would be set. In addition to the evaluations already done, I needed a recommendation from a psychiatrist. Like all surgeons, CYA is the name of the game.

My psychologist gave me some names to choose from. I picked one near Pioneer Square in Seattle. At the end of the hour session, he said he would have to see me again. I said that I understood I would only have to see him for one hour-to determine that I was not psychotic. He said that he had heard my life's story up to 1973, and needed to know more. And, no, I was not psychotic. I agreed to the second appointment and offered to lend him the first fourteen chapters of this book to read, but only if he wanted to. He readily accepted my offer. By the time of the second visit, he had read every page, and said that he knew more about me than any client he ever had. His secretary/receptionist asked if she could read the chapters too. Sure, Alice.

By September, all my tests and recommendations were sent off to Montreal, along with my request for a surgical date. On my way home from the post office that day, it struck me as odd that I had asked for a date for the surgery without a lot of conscious, decision-making anguish about it. It just seemed to be the normal thing to do. I wanted the gender reassignment surgery in order to get on with the rest of my life. In the five months that I had been in Washington, I realized that I was making it as a woman; no one questioned me about anything; I was both happy and cheerful all of the time; and, it was unthinkable to ever want to return to a male persona again.

I knew it would cost around $5,000 to make it all happen. I did not know where the money would come from, but I had childlike faith that it would be there when I needed it. After all, this was a decision made by the universe, so the universe would find the bucks. Right?

Other events had been happening in my life besides the casual quest for the change "down there." There was a divorce action in process with Annie. There was the never-ending search for a job. There was the effort to get to know more people socially in my new locale. And there was the need to find out who from my past would care to remain friends with Sally.

One of the things Millie suggested I do, as part of a demonstration of commitment, was to write a letter to one of my sons to inform him of my situation. In other words, I was to tell a son that his father wanted to become a woman-that he had always wanted to be a woman, and that he hoped to reestablish a new relationship based on the new gender choice. That was in February of 1989. I chose to write to Son #2, the one that I had the least amount of communication with over the years. I did my best to write the message in simple, compassionate terms. I also apologized for not being a better father, and attributed a lot of that lack to the distractions of Sally over the years.

He never responded, which hurt somewhat, but I cannot govern the way people react to me. All I can do is to be honest, and not tell people about me unless there is a good reason to do so. In this case I felt he should be told what happened to his father, and to use that opportunity to renew my interest in communicating with him.

In my second month in the town of Kent, I wrote a similar letter to Son #1. He was in his upper thirties, married, and had one child. I had hoped that he would be a little more mature, a little more forgiving, and perhaps a little more understanding. After all, he had a master's degree, and that implied some education as well as his experience in life.

I never did get a response from him, either. Yes, that hurt too. I had to be equally philosophical in that case as well. I wondered if his becoming a Mormon had anything to do with his reaction. I supposed that his reaction to me being a transsexual was as well-received as my reaction to him becoming a Mormon. But I don't know much about Mormons.

Son #3 continued to stay in touch. His attitude was like my brother's. They both thought I was doing a dumb thing, and neither one wanted to acknowledge me as Sally. Not in person, not in letters, not on the telephone. My brother wanted a brother, my son wanted a father. Could I not give those things to them? Sure. In fact, I was those things for them for a long, long time. But could I *continue* to do that? No. As much as I wanted their love, and as much as I wanted to be compassionate toward their feelings, I felt that they could have worked a little harder at finding out who and what I really was at that time. *Then*, if I was found unworthy, I could understand and accept their rejection. Could they do that? No. I am grateful that they chose to stay in touch, even if I have to use my old voice if I want to talk with them on the telephone. I become outraged when people say no to something when they do not know what it is that they are saying no to.

I wrote to my cousin Bill in Los Angeles. He and his wife, Pat, were the last ones on the short list of relatives to be notified of my decision for a new life. I hoped they would be a little more supportive than my primary family members. That hope was kindled by the fact that they made the effort to attend my wedding to Annie a decade earlier, whereas no other family member did. Perhaps their aloha would extend a little farther.

I received their response in a week. They were stunned, of course, because they had no idea I had been carrying this load all my life. They extended their support for what I wanted to do. They wished me well and expressed an interest in learning more about the phenomenon. I telephoned Bill that evening. We talked for a while, then I offered to send him chapters of my book to help explain myself. He said he would like that and asked if my brother was reading it. I had to tell him that he wasn't, that he knew I was writing my story, but had no interest in it at present. Bill said to give him time.

There were other old friends in California who did choose to explore the new me. Pierre and his dear friend, Joyce, wanted to meet Sally. Pierre and Tom met in high school. We were both on the swimming and water polo teams. We hung out in the same social circle back in the olden days of WW II. When I learned that Pierre was a printer, in the early 1980s, I did business with him whenever my jobs could go on his press. Before I left California, I told him about Sally. He was not put off, but was a little nervous about meeting her. The day I was scheduled to stop by the print shop to present the new version, Joyce was there too. We all talked nervously for a while, but soon became comfortable. Their opinion was that Sally was a lot happier person than Tom. Younger, too. Just before I left to move to Washington, they invited me to dinner. We had a wonderful evening out at one of the nicer restaurants on the bay. I noticed that every once in a while, Pierre would shut his eyes, trying to sense the essential difference between me and Tom. He could only say that I was the same, but different. Joyce said that I was an attractive woman, and that it was easy for her to be around me because she hardly knew Tom. Pierre has not yet made a cogent statement on his assessment of me, but we are still friends, and that is what counts.

I wrote a long letter to Ralph to see if the friendship could continue. His response was that it certainly would continue as far as he was concerned. He went on to say that we were friends before and that the friendship was based on mutual respect. Now that I was a woman, he saw nothing in that to change the relationship. We continued the correspondence, interspersed with telephone conversations.

George, my old fraternity brother, continued to write and telephone. By late summer, Martha and I began a direct correspondence. I think she sensed a need on my part to establish a communication link with the female side of the family. She was right.

My change did enable me to tune in on female topics, but more importantly I was tuning in on the female wavelength. I think she and I feel closer than George and Tom ever did. But men are like that and women are like that, aren't they?

Frances and Luke, my former neighbors in Half Moon Bay, wrote once or twice. Frances always liked Tom, but especially Sally. She expressed great joy for me in finally getting to be what I had always wanted to be. We exchanged notes and cards for a time, then we stopped. Her last card to me was so precious that I placed it in the kitchen above my microwave. Every time I heated my coffee, I read that note.

Fran was my typist in Los Altos. She did the word processing for all my resumes, cover letters, and the first seven draft chapters of this book. She wanted to stay in touch, and to read the rest of my story. Correspondence and telephone calls continued with Michal, Tim, Viana, and of course, Anna Belle.

On the spur of the moment once, I telephoned my former neighbor Chris in Foster City to see how everyone was. I learned that Lynn really did get married, that Brian had gone to Portland to seek his fortune, and that Ruth had returned to Victoria, B.C. I was given Ruth's telephone number, and then called her right away. We exchanged addresses and promised to stay in touch.

Now that I was so many miles from the Bay Area, I had to find a new word processing person. Barbara, A.B.'s friend, was in the business in Seattle. I started taking work to her. It was nice to do business with a friend, especially a woman friend. We recast my resume format and she started typing the new chapters of this book.

By the end of July, I was getting exasperated with the drill of sending out resumes and cover letters but getting no responses. After Barbara typed the latest letter/resume combination, I decided to hand carry it to the company that advertised the position. I was madder than hell, and I wasn't going to take it anymore. I entered the office of The Write Stuff, an agency for writers, approached the first person I saw, and said that I had come to claim my job. It turned out that the person was the owner of the company. She glanced at my resume, and invited me to sit while we talked. She liked the way I wrote about my work history, and seemed to like me. She said that she could place me on assignment at Boeing the next day. I *did* know Microsoft Word, didn't I? I had to say no, but I could learn. She thought that was a good attitude to have. She told me to learn it and then come back, and *do* stay in touch. Sure, Beryl.

That impromptu interview was a pivotal experience. I was heartened by having such a successful interview and about the near miss on getting a job. I began to think seriously about getting a word processor. How could I afford it? How could I afford to continue paying Barbara? How could I get a job, especially as a woman, without some recent experience with contemporary word processing? On my way back to

Kent, I stopped at a computer store to price a decent system to do my own word processing and to enable me to get up to speed for employment.

At home, I looked at my checkbook and learned that I was averaging over a hundred dollars a month getting things typed at Barbara's place. I telephoned Visa to find out what that proposed purchase would do to my monthly payment. I was told $40.00. The next day, I bought the system.

My goal was to learn Microsoft Word 5.0 and get a job. In the meantime, I could write letters, redo my resumes to suit each employment opportunity, and continue writing my book.

In early August, I saw an advertisement in the Seattle paper asking for a business partner in a bed and breakfast place located on Lopez Island, in the San Juan group. My fantasies went wild! I studied the maps and the ferry schedules, and realized that I could drive to Port Angeles, ride the ferry to Victoria, visit with my former neighbor, Ruth, then take the other ferry system to Lopez Island and interview with the B & B people. I spent two days with Ruth and it was wonderful to be with her again. I got to see a lot of the sights and ate too much of the delicious foods in the local restaurants.

I spent one night with the beautiful people on Lopez Island. We got along fine, and their home was magnificent. I had a real problem with the pace of life on Lopez. It was not only too quiet, too rural, but too slow. Slower than lawyers. I had to decline their offer for inclusion in the enterprise. I knew that I would kick myself someday for rejecting that opportunity, but I simply was not ready for it. Of course, I was pleased that they accepted me as a woman.

In late August, I drove to Whidbey Island to see the head of air crew training about a job. I felt that a personal appearance would get me farther than a letter. I did get to see the man, we talked for almost an hour, and I got a lead for a job in Bremerton at the Navy base.

On my way home from that interview, I listened to a radio talk show. The topic for the two-hour segment was transsexualism, of all things. The guests in the Seattle studio consisted of my therapist, a sister (male-to-female), and a brother (female-to-male). They were there to explain to the listeners what the phenomenon was about. I knew all of them from the group meetings. I thought they did a great job of explaining what it is and how it works, and what it is like after the sex reassignment surgery. The host of the show was sympathetic and gave them every chance to speak on the topic. The odd thing was that the listeners did not seem to care. There were several callers who gave support to the idea, but nobody called up to say it was wrong or dumb to do that. There were a few questions, but no complaints. Never before and never since has there been a topic to meet with such indifference from the listeners of that talk show. Strange. My guess was that not enough people knew enough about transsexualism to talk about it, or argue about it.

At home that day, I telephoned the contact in Bremerton about applying for a job. I was told to send my SF 171 for consideration. The next day I was contacted and asked if I could come for an interview for a non-Civil Service teaching position. And that was how I met Tami, a youthful, friendly person who was glad to see me. One of her teachers was going to resign the next day. Could I take over that math class? Sure, Tami.

It was early September, just over four months since I started looking for work. I was thrilled to have the opportunity to do something. I was estatic that I was hired without having to explain my past to Tami or anyone else. Before I left California, I had changed all of my transcripts and credentials to my new name. I had even taken the CBEST Test, a proficiency test of basic skills that was new for teachers in California and Oregon. I had my record of passing grades for that test, too. The documents were all asked for and were given, just as though it happened every day. I had passed for being a woman by a hiring authority. Oh *yes*, I really felt good about that.

Now that I had a job, I wanted to tell my friends. In a state of high humor, I wrote a whimsical newspaper-style article, did it on my word processor using 10-point type, in two columns with a 14-point head. One of the people I sent a copy to was Beryl, owner of The Write Stuff. I wanted her to know that I could handle such a format on my new machine, and perhaps deliver a small tweak for not hiring me herself. Three weeks later she called me to say that everyone thought my copy was very funny, and that it was posted on their bulletin board. Then she asked if I would do a funny piece for their company newsletter that would go to 500 customers. Sure, Beryl, how many words, and what do you want me to write about?

I wrote it in less than two days, sent it off, and it was printed in the newsletter with absolutely no copy changes. That made my ego soar. I got a byline and a lunch. More importantly, I became friends with Beryl.

I was only a little nervous about the job in Bremerton. The task was to teach basic skills to sailors who wanted to get ready for college courses. It was something I had done for sixteen years in the public school system and several years of night classes. The part that caused me concern was the ability to sustain my female image to the same group of sailors for the five weeks left in that class. I had stood in front of enlisted men as a Warrant Officer, but now I was something else. I entered that classroom knowing that I knew my subject, I knew the Navy, and I knew that I was now a woman. From that moment on, it was easy.

The hard part was the commute from Kent to Bremerton, 53 miles each way. I was motivated to move to the western side of Puget Sound, even though I travelled only two days per week. In late September, I found a two-bedroom duplex for $130 less than the apartment in Kent. It was the least expensive, yet the best place I had lived in since Half Moon Bay.

During a break time one day, I mentioned to some of my students that I was getting ready to move to Port Orchard. One of them volunteered to round up some buddies and move my stuff if I rented the truck. They did move my stuff, all right, and in the process I got to meet two wives and several kids. A few weeks later, I served them a grand dinner. One of my first tasks in October, upon taking the new residence, was to apply for a library card. While chatting with the librarian, I asked if there was a local chapter of American Association of University Women. The librarian said she would call one of her friends who was a member, and she would call me. I did get a call, an invitation to attend the next meeting, and the offer of a ride with Kay who turned out to be a good friend.

Anna Belle and I continued to exchange notes, but mostly we had extended telephone calls over the months. She was my support now, more than ever. In late October, she asked if she could come visit. Of course, A.B. Then I asked her how she, as poor as a church mouse as I was, could take off from work and buy an airplane ticket to Seattle. She said that her aunt passed away, and left everything to her. We made plans for her to come in November. Oh boy!

The visit was wonderful. We talked all the time and about everything. She wanted to know how I was doing with regard to surgery. I told her that I had not heard from the surgeon yet, and that I did not have the money anyway because the divorce had not become final and no settlement had been made. "Let me lend you the money," she said. I thought it over for a picosecond or two, and said I would accept her generous offer. First, however, I would need the green light from the surgeon in Montreal. She said that she would need a week or two in order to produce the bucks, and be sure to let her know.

The next business day after Anna Belle left, I telephoned the surgeon's office to see what the hold up was in getting notification. I was told that the report from the psychiatrist had not arrived. I knew it had been sent in early September, because I had a copy. I called Alice, a friend by now, and asked if she could Fed Ex a copy to the cutter. Sure.

In mid-November, I actually got to speak with Dr. Yvon Ménard, the surgeon in Montreal. He said that I had sent him *reports* of the several tests, but he needed the actual test results for his files. Right, CYA. Also, I would need another blood test: this time for AIDS.

Those demands were met in early December. By now I was no longer in the casual mode for that surgery. I wanted a firm date. Besides, if I were to travel to Montreal, I had to make a reservation soon to get the cheapest airplane seat I could. I made another call to Montreal, and miraculously spoke with the surgeon again. The conversation ended when he gave me a firm appointment for an office visit on Friday, January 19, and a *tentative* surgical date of Monday, January 22. I made travel plans to leave on January 17, and return on Groundhog Day.

I knew that Dr. Ménard wanted to make sure for his own sake that I was an acceptable candidate for the operation. Of course, he had a folder full of documents from the qualified professionals in Seattle. Still, I would be on his hands for a week or so, and he wanted to make sure I would not cause trouble in any way during that time. I had been told by Nancy P. that he had been known to deny the operation to a lot of those who caused him concern during the office interview. Also, the majority of candidates never even got as far as the office visit. Was this man a prima donna? Maybe, but he was good, and I saw no reason not to play his game. I learned later that he had a lot of heat put on him by the Canadian government with regard to this particular operation. His surgical records were inspected regularly.

When I boarded that Air Canada flight to Montreal, I knew I had an office visit, and maybe an operation in my future. Sure it was dicey, but I've played long shots before.

During the flight, I had a chance to catch my breath and think about a lot of things. The hours before the flight were harrowing. I was to catch a bus to SeaTac Airport from my neighborhood. Anna Belle was having the funds for the surgery wired from an out-of-state bank to my bank in Bremerton. An hour before my bus was to leave, the funds were not there. Come on, universe, where are the bucks? A half hour later, the money came in. I got my cashier's check in Canadian funds, and had five minutes to spare to catch the bus. I knew it would work out because it was supposed to, but I did not appreciate the cliff hanger on that day.

I had an aisle seat, my favorite, with no one next to me. Good. I wanted some quiet time to think about what was ahead for me in Montreal. As usual, I thought about what I expected, and then considered back-up plans if anything went wrong. I am an optimist, but it never hurts to have a Plan B.

I thought about the person I wrote to regarding my arrival. She was a friend of Nancy's who had been through all of this years before. Would she be friendly? Would she even talk to me? Would she consider me to be a sister and be helpful? In my letters, I said what my timetable was and that I would call when I arrived.

I thought about the schedule in the event that I did get the operation. I knew I would be in a recovery mode for five days, but I would have to leave the clinic on a Friday, spend the weekend *somewhere*, and return to the clinic on the following week for examination. Where would I go for that time? I suspected I would need some TLC, but who in a strange city would provide it for me?

I thought about what I was doing. Did I really want the surgery? Of course I did. On that date, it was a year and a couple of days since Tom's last appearance. During that time I became more sure that this was what I wanted above all else. I had grown more confident of my ability to be perceived as a woman, and I was continuously happy with my new place in society. Mostly, I was pleased by a new state of mind. Sandra, my therapist had said that I could be considered a woman whether I had the operation or not. That was comforting, coming from someone who serves as a gatekeeper for those wanting entrance into the surgical corral.

So I could live the life of a woman without the surgery, except for one thing; an important part of being a woman is to be able to function as one for a man. During my year, I had a number of men make advances, or flirt, or display interest in me. Or so it seemed. I had developed a way of letting them know I was flattered, but not interested in a relationship beyond being a pleasant person.

If I was to have a total life as a woman, I had to have the operation. What I fantasized about was meeting a man and being in love with him. I believed that I needed to be in love with someone. I was totally unacceptable to Annie, that was for sure. I also thought that I could be one hell of a good woman for a man. I had the experience, you see, of knowing what a man wants-really wants—- from a woman. I was prepared to give that to the right man. I believed that when I was ready for such a relationship, I would indeed meet Mr. Right. A childish notion, perhaps, but I didn't think so.

The real question I had consisted of thoughts about sexuality. Specifically, if I was not able to feel sexually-oriented toward males now, how would I ever expect to become sexually-oriented toward males later? I could envision myself as a loving sister for a man, but not a bed partner for a man. Would the operation change that? Not in itself, I guessed, but perhaps in the months or years afterward it would. Because anticipated sexual activity was not my motivation for surgery, I decided to let the question linger unanswered, and was comfortable with no answer. I had been guided by instinct thus far, why not continue with that kind of counsel?

During that first year in my new life, I considered my male organs to be an anomaly. They were something to be hidden at all costs. Towards the end of that year, I began to think of them as a birth defect that had to be surgically corrected.

I also thought about the document my lawyer sent to me just before I left. The divorce became final in December. I still cared about Annie. I may never know a love like that again.

The flight was without incident, but the customs people north of the border were curious about why I was entering their country. I prefer to tell the truth, so I told them I was coming in to get an operation. That set off some bells in their heads because of their socialized medical program. They thought I might be trying to get some of their medical attention for free. I assured them I was paying for it, and showed them the cashier's check made out to the doctor for the operation, although I did not specify the kind of operation. That put them at rest and they went on with more bureaucratic questions about the nature of my visit. I was asked if I was bringing anything into the country that I would be leaving there. I almost collapsed at that question, but told them they would have to ask my surgeon. I was passed through customs.

I called Lynn, the sister I wrote to, and we agreed to meet at her apartment that evening. I thought it would be smart to rent a car from Hertz and save on taxicabs. It was not a good idea, but I had no way of knowing that when I did it. I never would have guessed how easy it was to get lost in that city. I checked into the motel where I had made a reservation weeks before. After I got settled, I went to see Lynn.

She was a wonderful person. Extremely friendly and sensitive to my novel situation. I relaxed right away in her apartment. She telephoned for pizza, saying that it was not a night to be outdoors. The Celsius temperatures were in the negative numbers. We spent the evening getting to know each other, but I felt I had known her all my life.

On Friday morning, I was at the surgeon's office fifteen minutes early. Because of the snowfall during the night, he was a half hour late. I was glad that I had waiting room delays many times before in my life, or I would have been a nervous wreck. I mean, this was it. Would I get the operation or not?

The doctor came into the waiting room and beckoned me. We talked in his office for almost an hour. It was pleasant and relaxed. English was a second language for him, but he was fluent.

I knew I had passed the critical phase when he asked if I had a place to stay during the week end after surgery. I had no special plan, and said so. He said he would have someone call me in a few days to work out some arrangements. He then showed me color photos of the operation. They showed a pre-op shot, the post-op immediately after, and additional photos taken at monthly intervals for the next six months. I looked at them and said, "Yes, that is what I want."

I was instructed to check into the clinic on Sunday, and he gave me a list of things to get and things to do before I checked in. He also gave me a prescription for a hundred tablets of powerful painkillers. He said there would be some discomfort after surgery. I had heard that before, and had no reason to doubt it. One of his questions during the interview was why I waited so long to seek the surgery. I told him that I just wanted to be sure.

I returned to my motel after getting all the things from the pharmacy. I telephoned Lynn to give her the results of my morning's activities, and we made a plan for getting together that night. She asked if I would like to meet Jennifer, and perhaps drive her to the airport. Jennifer was going to fly to San Francisco, and spend a week with Nancy P.

I called Jennifer, got directions to her place, picked her up, and proceeded to the airport. I turned in the rental car, and we walked into the terminal with her luggage. After getting her checked in, we sat at a table to drink espresso and talk. I wondered why it was so easy to feel comfortable with her (and Lynn) immediately. It could have been something subliminal.

We *really were* sisters of a sort. Natural siblings have an unspoken language and the ability to communicate a lot without words. Perhaps this kind of sisterhood was a phenomenon based on having the same yearnings and same stresses over the years, and that we, in one sense, *were* the same. Or at least made of the same stuff. There was no need to explain ourselves.

Jennifer asked about my office visit with the surgeon. I told her. She asked if I got a good look at the pictures, and I said that I certainly did. She said that it was her. Golly, I was having coffee with a celebrity. When the plane carried her off to see Nancy, I took the world's longest bus route back to Lynn's place. We had dinner, more conversation, and then I went back to my motel. Sleep came easy. I was temporarily without anything to worry about. Everything was working as expected, and better.

I spent Saturday alone. It was an adventure being by myself in a strange city in a foreign country. How many years had it been since I had done that? Maybe forty, in the Orient. I walked to a shopping center, then to a restaurant for lunch.

In the evening, I wanted to take another nice long walk around the neighborhood, but the snowfall suggested I not do that. When my appetite alarm went off later, I donned my five-pound wool coat and walked a few hundred yards to a takeout pizza place. While waiting for my order, I had a cup of decent coffee. A man, about thirty-five, came in and placed his order, speaking rapidly in French. He evidently asked for coffee too. All of a sudden he was at a table next to mine. He smiled and said something in French. I could only shrug and smile. He grinned and asked, in flawless

English if I was a tourist. I said I was. I thought he was a nice person, totally without malice. You can sense those things. You can also sense when the person is about to make a friendly offer of companionship for the evening. His name was Andre. The conversation was of no importance in itself, but it did tell me that I wanted that surgery more than ever. Maybe I could go to bed with a man. Maybe I was just pleased that I was validated as a woman by this nice man. I picked up my pizza order and went back to my warm room, alone.

On Sunday, I packed my stuff after doing some personal things to myself so that the nurses would not have to do it. O. K. with me. I'd rather shave myself down there, anyway. I mean, even though I knew what was going to happen, I still wanted no unnecessary roughness. I paid my motel bill, called a taxi, rode to the clinic for plastic and reconstructive surgery, and checked in.

The duty nurse was almost fluent enough in English to communicate with me. Only a minimal amount of pantomime was needed to get me into a two-bed room, get undressed, and slip into the regimen of the place. I was shown which buttons to push on my telephone. Lynn called and asked if I was settled in and did I want visitors in a few days. We talked awhile about nothing special.

Nancy called to see if I was settled in and promised to call back in a few days.

I went to sleep after taking a pill to keep me constipated for a few days.

The nurses were friendly, and wondered why I had waited so long to get the operation. I said that I wanted to make sure it was what I wanted. I wondered if I looked that old to prompt such questions, and concluded that I did.

Monday morning. I had breakfast and wondered when I would go off to... I complimented myself again for bringing my own coffee making equipment. I made a fresh pot and hoped I would not be in the room long enough to drink it all. I looked out the window and saw the snow piling up in the parking lot. I wondered if the surgeon would be able to drive in. But I reminded myself that the universe was supportive of this, so there was no need to fret.

The anesthesiologist came in to welcome me, and to ask a lot of questions about allergies and so forth. He said surgery would happen soon. I was supposed to relax, but I made a second pot of coffee.

The nurses were attentive. I noticed they came around just to make small talk. Before I knew it, the lunch trays were being distributed. I had expected to be in the operating room by 10:00. I was assured that all was well. Evidently Dr. Ménard was a little late, then the patient before me needed more time on the table than they expected. Did I still want the surgery? What a question! But I was polite, and merely said that I did.

At 1:00 I was asked to follow a nurse down the hall to a pre-op room. I was told to rest on a table with wheels on it, and asked one more time if I was ready for the operation. I said yes I was, and then I was given a pill that set me free. I had a hazy recollection of being wheeled away, but no recollection of arriving anywhere.

The next thing I knew it was Tuesday morning. It could have been Wednesday or the next week, for all I knew. I wondered what was going on. I mean, I was fuzzy headed, but I did not have any pain anywhere. The disturbing notion crossed my mind that I did not get the operation. A nurse was fussing with something in the room. I asked what time it was. She said it was almost breakfast time, and did I want one of my pain pills. I said that I did not hurt, and asked if I got the operation. She looked at me strangely and assured me that I certainly did. By now I was up on my elbows and could see some tubes and stuff emanating from the place where they should have been emanating from. *All right.*

I managed to eat the light breakfast. During that repast, the surgeon came in to see how I was doing. The nurse excitedly told him I had no pain. He was stunned. He said that everyone had pain after that surgery. I did not.

In my wooziness, I did something no human being is ever supposed to do: I tried to explain a medical phenomenon to a surgeon. I simply said that I had no pain because I was so old, and that such surgery was less of an assault on my body than it would be for a younger, vibrant male. He grimaced a bit, then reluctantly said maybe I was correct. He would have to think about that. He also said that I was the oldest patient he had for that operation.

By the time lunch arrived, I had my own coffee made. I was ambulatory, but my constant companion was a two-liter bag to collect that stuff that flowed from the catheter. That catheter would stay in there for a week.

I decided to take a walk after lunch. My bag needed emptying anyway. The loo was just outside my door near the central corridor. I was the only patient in my room, and the only one in for sex reassignment surgery that week. There were a lot of women patients in the other rooms. All of us had received surgery on Monday, and all of us would be out of the clinic Friday evening. The facility was closed over the week end.

The central corridor of the clinic became a promenade from Tuesday on. Bathrobe-clad figures with heads wrapped to look like Claude Rains in *The Invisible Man*. They walked in pairs or singly. I thought I was on the set for *Twilight Zone*. I was sure they wondered about me. I just grinned like a happy idiot, and they nodded their heads in response to me, or mumbled something. It was difficult to tell whether the mumbles were in French or in English.

Nancy sent flowers and a card. Lynn came by to visit with some friends that evening. They could not believe I had no pain. Some telephone calls came in. I was prepared to do the whole experience all by myself, but the support group out there would not have it. I felt good about that.

On Wednesday morning, the nurse came in with the same allotment of pills and asked if I was ready to receive visitors. It seemed that the other patients had noticed I had a surgical procedure different from theirs, and asked the nurses what I had done. They were told that I was a sex change, and now they wanted to meet me. Sure.

For the next few days I had visitors. I served coffee and shared my ashtray with the affluent, maturing ladies from Ottawa, Winnipeg, and New Brunswick. They welcomed me to the superior sex and asked a lot of the predictable questions. Some of us exchanged addresses because they wanted to know how I would fare in the future.

The future. What was there for me?

The surgeon told me that full recovery would take six months. After that, I could have normal relations with a man if that was what I wanted to do. I could not, at that moment, believe I would. I would have to reserve judgment until I could determine what changes would manifest in the months to come. There were no more male hormones being generated and the estrogen was now having full sway. What mental changes could I expect? What other physical changes could I expect?

You can believe I would be on the lookout for a certain someone who would think my liver spots were sexy, and consider the varicose veins on my legs to be a highway map to adventure. But would I want to respond?

There was a whole new world waiting for me out there. Sure, I was getting close to my 62nd birthday, but I still felt more like 35. I had energy and experience to share. I had a new enthusiasm for life-a life without the old frustration. I knew that if I tried to guide my actions toward giving to others, and sharing whatever gifts I had, I would find fulfillment.

I was fixed for life.

Chapter 23

January 1993

Here is an account of the immediate effects after surgery.

Three years have passed since the surgical magic was performed in Montreal. It seems like a million years ago and possibly something that really happened to someone else. In another sense, it was as though I emerged from the anesthesia just this morning. I recall raising up on my elbows, looking down at my loins, and knew I no longer had the organs of a male. I do not dwell on that instant much these days, but the moment can be recalled quite easily, I assure you.

I looked at the heavy bandaging and the catheter tube coming out from all that packing material and thought, I really did it! It it is hard to spin brilliant phrases or wax poetic with regard to that instant of achieving one's heart's desire. There was relief. And satisfaction. A moment of intense pleasure. If it hasn't happened to you, no one else can explain it. I had known for weeks that it was going to happen. The biggest thrill was getting the approval for the surgery. It was like getting a major tax refund from the IRS. I knew it was really going to happen. Getting the surgery was like getting the refund check in the mail: unquestionably important, but expected.

I laughed and said out loud, *"You silly bastard, you really did it!"* Then the small, niggling thought of Did I do the right thing? And quickly the answer, Hell yes! Triumph. There had been a battle, all my life, between the forces that wanted to keep me male and my will to become female. I had just won. Forever. I sighed, laid back on my pillow and reveled for a time in the reality of it all. Then up on my elbows again, checking, just to make sure.

No matter what would happen in the months and years ahead, I had achieved what I wanted. Oh yes. There was a feeling of delight in knowing I could never go back. No one could take away that which was taken away.

You may recall that I had, in desperation, taken steps years before to sample life as a woman. The great summer vacation in 1973, that wild year in 1976, and all those countless, stolen weekends. Every one of those times striving for feminine expression came to an unhappy conclusion when I had to return to the responsibilities of Tom. Tom, the stalwart male person I had created because family and society expected it. Anyone able to share my painful feelings of temporarily being a butterfly that had to revert to caterpillar status each of those times, would certainly be able to share my relief when I knew I would never have to go through that unnatural act again.

I might have a new set of painful experiences waiting for me, but certainly not those of prior decades. Being a Gemini, I would welcome any change, any new experience. I did not consider notions that my life would go down hill, or that I might fail in becoming whatever I wanted. While I was not prepared to say what my future held, exactly, I knew that I would be all right, that I would win at whatever I set out to do. It had been my style to be successful. Why should that pattern change just because I was now surgically corrected? I had no fear. Instead, I had a new strength because I was no longer living in a house divided.

One of the nurses said the technical details of my operation would be described for me, and the care I was required to observe to achieve recovery would be explained before I left the clinic. The surgeon was busy doing noses and face lifts elsewhere and would see me on Friday.

The several days until Friday were days filled with an emotional high that I cannot describe with any clarity. Similes and metaphors fail. I wondered if it was like being on drugs. Because I was not in pain, the clinic was not giving me anything. I was still drinking my own coffee and smoking my own American cigarettes. The food was hospital bland. So where was the high coming from? I didn't know. The nurses didn't know, either. They said all the others who had the operation had been in pain during the time I was being ecstatic. They wanted to know why I wasn't in pain. I had a fleeting thought that my guardian angels were celebrating my victory and were, in some way, sharing their happiness with me. For those who don't believe in fairy tales, maybe I was just generating gallons of endorphins.

Dr. Ménard stopped by late Friday morning to give me detailed instructions for my care and feeding for the weekend. I was to return for a visit on Monday to see if there was anything to be mended, or whether I could go home. I asked him to describe for me what he actually did, and tell me if there were any complications I should know about. And this is what he told me.

First, he did the castration, but saved the scrotum to fashion the labia major. (Remember, this was a plastic surgeon who was concerned for cosmetic effect as well as functionality.) Next, an incision was made a few inches in front of the anus to create an opening, later to be called a vagina. The new canal was made to parallel the lower colon, and in front of it, as you might guess. The penis was removed, then subjected to some topological wizardry. It was slit on the long axis, and the tissue inside was removed. (Think of a hot dog being slit, having the meat removed, retaining the casing, and throwing everything else away.) The skin of the penis was then sewn back together, but inside out. The tip was sewn together, and that little sleeve was then inserted into the newly-created cavity and stapled in place at the far end, about five and a half inches up there. The bottom edge of the tube was sewn around the entrance of the new opening, forming the labia minor. A *faux* penis was inserted into the new vagina. It was a rubberized plastic dildo sheathed in a condom and well greased. Its purpose was twofold: First, it would press the internal tissue of my old penis to the walls of the new opening so that the blood vessels and nerve endings would grow to their new home. Second, the new cavity had to be kept open, otherwise it would grow shut, a consequence not wished for.

To recap, then, the old exterior of my former penis was now the lining of my new vagina; the old inside of my penis was now growing to new tissue. The formerly exterior skin of my former penis would begin to change to mucous membrane like a standard vaginal wall, or like the inside of one's mouth. Finally, the urethra was re-routed from where the penis had been based to a new location more appropriate for a female.

The icing on the cake was the creation of something that functioned like a clitoris, or at least the surgeon told me he had hopes for it continuing to survive. I asked that French-Canadian miracle man how he managed to provide a clit, but alas, his command of English failed to explain the medical terminology so that my American mind could understand. Who knows, maybe it was really a trade secret he did not want to share. Not every sex change gets that. I am pleased to report that mine subsequently flourished.

Some surgeons discard the penis entirely, and use a section of one's colon as the vaginal wall. There is no standard procedure used by all surgeons. In fact, they seem to continually modify their techniques based on experience or new technology.

I was released that Friday evening, well-packed with industrial-size sanitary napkins, and with a short-stemmed catheter still hanging out. It had a stopper in the end so that I could control the discharge of urine in a socially-acceptable manner, in a socially-acceptable place. I spent the weekend in the nearby home of a former patient of Dr. Ménard where I was well treated and made most comfortable. The emotional high continued. Fifi and her natural sister owned a home in a suburb of Montreal. Fifi was queen of the castle; Florence held a job outside the home.

They had a collection of video tapes of foreign films about transsexuals and one dealing with transvestite entertainers. They were filmed in France, Spain, and Italy, but with English subtitles. I was fascinated by the artistic achievements of those foreign film makers. They captured all the emotions and subtlety that we experience as we go through the living of the duality, then go for the big change. The story of Christine Jorgensen was also shown. By contrast, it was a disappointment. It was clumsy, like an amateur documentary by comparison, not an exploration of the emotional part. American film makers have not even come close to the artistry of the Europeans when portraying this segment of humanity. Our domestic films have brought amazing new heights to violence, death, and destruction, but seem incapable of delivering the poignancies experienced by transsexuals. I thought "The Crying Game" was all right.

The second day, Saturday, Fifi telephoned some of her friends to tell them to come by and meet the new girl—me. The designation titillated me. Yes, I was on a high, all right. Marie was the first to come. She was small-boned and skinny. As a male she could have been a jockey. She had lived with a foster mother since infancy. Her foster mother wanted Marie to dress as a girl and consider prostitution as a career. After completing high school, she was able to get the sex change through Canada's medical system, then decided to become a nurse. She had a warmth and a sense of humor that would serve her well in her chosen occupation. She insisted on looking at the site of my operation, but did not touch the bandages. She smiled and said to Fifi, "Let's sprinkle some holy water on this."

On Sunday, Christine came by with her boyfriend, Herve. They were certainly in love with life and each other. During the work week, Christopher was the financial executive for a very conservative, old Montreal manufacturer whose products were sold in the world market. Herve was the sales manager for a Canadian trucking company. Still in their thirties, they'had known each other for a decade and were saving up for the day Chris could leave the job, have the surgery, and they could get married. I had been moved by their playfulness in the snow as I stood at the big window and watched them come from their car to Fifi's house, throwing snowballs at each other. Chris was a lot better with English than Herve. We talked about the frustrations of living the dual life, and I learned once again that the phenomenon is international. I have thought about those two in subsequent years because the energy was so high and their loving glances to each other were so pleasant to see. Later, I realized they reminded me of the old film, *Love Story*. I hope their lives will turn out better.

Lynn, who had visited me in the clinic several days before, came for dinner Sunday evening. I had spent maybe five hours total in her presence, yet she seemed like a relative. So warm, so friendly, so funny.

On Monday I returned to the clinic. The surgeon removed all the bandages and wrappings, and looked at his handiwork. He pronounced it good and removed a few stitches, which tickled. Then he removed the catheter, which did not tickle. Lordy, no. He said that the remaining stitches were the dissolving kind, and I was not to worry about them. He handed me a sheet of instructions to follow for the next six months, things like douching, betadine sitz baths, the care and use of the dildo, and so forth. He told me to see a gynecologist in about three months. His final remark was that my surgery was easy for him because my old penis still had a foreskin, thereby giving him more material to work with. (Thanks, Mom and Dad.)

The return flight lasted about eight hours due to fierce head winds and stops at Ottawa and Winnipeg. There was still no sharp pain, but there was a lot of discomfort, the beginning of a general soreness of the target area. I was pleased I had the foresight to bring that little inflatable rubber cushion. When the flight attendant for my section saw me standing, blowing into the tube, she expressed concern for my comfort. I explained that I recently had some surgery "down there," and that the sore places were beginning to introduce themselves. She checked on me continually. I wondered if it was because I, a *passenger*, had surgery, or I, *a woman*, had surgery. It was probably the first time I remember of taking such a question seriously. I began to wonder what else I would be wondering about in the months and years to come.

Stopping in Ottawa and Winnipeg gave us a chance to get off the plane for a while. We smokers raced off to find the small areas catering to the addicted. I, with the longest stride, got there first, both times. I was joined immediately, both times, by two other women who lit up and started talking with me right away, about this and that. As a male, I would have stood alone; no one would have joined me.

After the plane arrived in Vancouver, B.C., I caught the connecting flight to Seattle. At 1:30 a.m., Groundhog Day, I had retrieved my suitcase on wheels, and began looking for the airporter to drive me to Port Orchard. I was stiff from sitting, sore from you-know-what, and very sleepy. Seeing the small van, I asked the driver for help getting my case loaded. She took a look at me and swung the case aboard saying, "You look pooped, sweetie." I nodded and found a seat.

The scheduled stopping point for me was the Safeway parking lot, a half mile from my home. We got there around 2:45 a.m. The driver asked if someone was coming to get me. I said there was no one coming for me. She said, "What the hell. Give me directions to your house." Snow began to fall as she parked in my driveway, carried my suitcase to the front door, and whispered, "We have to stick together, you know." I gave her an extra five dollars and said, "Believe it." I let myself in, locked the door, got out of my Oleg Cassini navy suit with pleated skirt, and fell into my bed. Face down.

For the next three months, I cared for myself as directed by the printed instructions from the surgeon. It was an awful lot of trouble. Sitz baths three times a day in a betadine solution for the first three weeks, then once per day thereafter. Removing the dildo every time I had to use the toilet, cleaning or replacing the condom encasing it, greasing it with K-Y jelly, and reinserting it. And constantly wearing a panty girdle with a sanitary napkin inside to keep everything in place. I mean 24 hours a day. Gravity and muscular forces were at work trying to shoot that thing out.

A few visitors came. A half dozen people called. The most welcomed visitor was my supervisor, Tami, who knew my secret. She brought me baked things, a lot of conversation, and the offer for a new teaching assignment, when I was ready for it. After three weeks of cabin fever I was ready.

The teaching assignment was another trial, a test of my mettle. The class to be taught was for some sailors on a ship in drydock in West Seattle, about 55 miles away from home. The commute would have been a bother for anyone, but for me the logistics presented special considerations. Fortunately, I had to do it only three days per week. It meant driving an hour to the parking lot of the shipyard, walking a quarter mile carrying the student workbooks to the mess hall on the pier, and setting up a classroom while other sailors were cleaning up after the noon mess. There was no wall-mounted chalkboard for the math class. The mess hall had no ladies' room, yet I had a craving to use one, at least once before I set out for home. I had to ask one of the sailors to clear the facility for me and stand guard whilst I did my complex business. They thought the idea of a woman using their facility was special, but I don't think they suspected how special it really was.

That class ended five weeks later. By that time I was much stronger, and each day's three-hour class seemed easier to do. I am glad I had the experience because it was one of those times that I had to meld the attitude of John Wayne, my diminished physical condition, the need to become ladylike, and be a decent math teacher. Quite a mix. Each day on my commute I would tell myself that if I could do this, I could do *anything*.

In late April I was ready to have an appointment with a gynecologist. I knew I was mending because I felt like I was. I needed a professional opinion, however, and to connect with a doctor I could turn to if the need should arise. One of my friends from the Ingersoll Gender Center recommended a doctor in Federal Way, a suburb of Seattle. I made my appointment by phone. I was asked what the nature of my problem was. I stated my problem in the simplest terms I could. No problem.

I checked in and took a seat in the waiting room. Other women there did not stare at me, as I thought maybe they would, but I had a sense that I was being looked at. It occurred to me later that I was overdressed. They were in sweat suits, or blue jeans. I was in my business duds, like the attire suitable for any corporate board room. I was disappointed that feminine clothing was not in style for daytime wear. I believed I needed feminine clothing to look like a woman. Now I was beginning to understand that relaxed, comfortable clothing would be more convincing. Maybe I could compromise by wearing cotton skirts, and such.

I was shown to an examination room and told to get undressed, put on the paper gown, and wait. As I sat on the table, I flashed back to a time forty years earlier when I was in college and did week end work as a cleaning man in an OB/GYN office. I used to look at those tables with the stirrups and feel a bit envious of those who received medical attention on such a device. Now I was there. Evidence of my doctor being a woman was the sheepskin covering on each cold, metal stirrup. Nice touch, and one that made me feel better about connecting with a female gynecologist. She had been there.

My doctor was an attractive, young, competent physician. Businesslike, but friendly. I put my heels in the hallowed position and was invaded. I no longer have such romantic thoughts about that kind of place. She spent several minutes poking and looking; looking and poking. Eventually, she looked up and said everything was fine, excellent surgical technique, and could see no problems manifesting in my future. I was told to get dressed and come to her office.

Seated across from her, she gave me the obligatory five-minute lecture on cigarette smoking and that I should definitely quit. Then she asked if I had any questions. "Yes," I said, "How much of a woman am I?" She blinked and asked what I meant. I said I understood that women are subject to a lot of physical problems, such as osteoporosis, breast cancer, and such. Would I be susceptible to any of those or other maladies?

Her response was thoughtful, as though no one had ever asked her such a question before but considered it a good question. She began by pointing out the obvious. My skeleton would not change to female proportions, and the composition of bone was so established by now that osteoporosis was not a possibility. My chromosomes would remain XY—not become the XX of females, regardless of how many estrogen pills I took. She said my breasts, surprisingly bountiful as a result of chemicals previously ingested, would not be subject to the causes of breast cancer in women. She started to ruminate, to herself mostly, on milk glands which were only nascent in me, then trailed off into silence for a moment. Then the flat statement that I would not be a candidate for breast cancer unless there was a history of such on the male side of my family. She concluded by saying that my muscles would show the greatest change, as well as my general skin tone. That would be due to the loss of testosterone-producing equipment and the estrogen pills she would be prescribing for me. Beyond that, most of the changes I could expect would be in my head. Good enough, I thought.

The doctor gave me two prescriptions. The first was for Premarin, 1.25 mg. I had been using Estinyl, but she said Premarin would be better now. The second was for Premarin vaginal cream. I was to load the applicator with one gram, insert it all the way up inside, then shoot the stuff and remove the applicator. I was to do that three times per week. Both prescriptions were for a year's supply. We made an appointment for next year. She stood to shake my hand as a farewell gesture and asked if there was anything else I wanted to know. I said there was nothing else I could think of, but could I legitimately consider myself as an Xy? She smiled and said, "Of course."

My drive home that day was occupied by more questions that seem to live in perpetuity inside my pumpkin head. "How much of a woman am I?" "How much of a woman can I be?" "What does it mean to me to be a woman?" "How am I different?" I continue to get partial answers, even as I write today. I will do my best to share my answers, provisional though they may be. But first, other events were commanding my attention.

About that time (early spring, 1990) I was treated to something called *mood swings*. I had heard the term before, but never thought it would have anything to do with me. Wrong. I don't know exactly when or how I became aware of the swings. A week or so after I had returned from Montreal I noticed that I was feeling very up, or very down. Very little in between, or so-called normal. Being a little confused about it all, it was not easy to formulate a plan to deal with this new emotional roller coaster. I was two months into it before I realized that was what it was. Did it cause confusion? Yes.

At least I knew *something* was not going well. In private, I was a mess. In public, I did a lot better because I was, after all, an ~~actor~~ actress. I had learned a trick many years earlier. It was to *pretend* that I was feeling good even though I wasn't. A simple thing to do, really. I would acknowledge that it was a crappy day, everything was turning sour, and I felt like hell. And then I would say to myself, How would you be acting if everything was wonderful? Act it out. Put a big smile on your face, say something funny or show enthusiasm about something. Act it out. Pretty soon those false feelings of being upbeat magically turned to genuine feelings of being upbeat. Perhaps it is a variant form of self-hypnosis, though I'm not sure. I think of it as priming the pump. It works, and that is what is important.

Making an effort to be upbeat in public worked just fine, the real problem was feeling good when alone. I love living alone. I am never lonely, but I am obliged to live inside my head. Therefore, I felt a need to get a better understanding about this mood swing thing, and do it fast.

I listened to a few women friends tell me about their experiences with it. When Sandra, my former therapist, called to ask about me, I asked her about the swings. I was given essentially the same answer from all parties; namely, that they seem to be triggered by a hormone imbalance, and there is no cure, but there are ways to deal with it. Some steps include proper diet and reasonable care for the body. The other part is to be aware that the swings keep on swinging, but good mental health practices will moderate the magnitude of the swings.

I was also told about depression. It is supposed to affect women much more than men. The best definition I could get was that depression is a feeling of powerlessness. While I could understand the words, I rejected the concept of powerlessness. I knew very well that I sometimes lost a fight for something, but that is not the same as being powerless. If I lost all of the time, I might be powerless. I concluded that for me powerlessness is a lot of crap. I still think so. Oh, it can be easy to feel oneself not in control, but it is not a necessary condition. Anyone can be in control of their life if they are willing to fight for it. The secret to avoiding depression is *to never, ever quit fighting* for what you want. At least, that has been my experience.

Spring of 1990 was a confusing time, all right. It was obvious to me that a sea change had taken place. What were the elements of that change? For one thing, I was being constantly reminded that I was no longer a male. Every time I went to the bathroom I got that message. Not male, but only rudimentarily female. I was delighted by what had been done, and it seemed silly to expect more. I had not heard of anyone getting ovary transplants, or fallopian tubes installed, nor the rest of the female system. I did, in my warped mind, wonder if this six months of care-down-there would count as an equivalent for all the menstrual periods I never had. Maybe, but probably not. I certainly had all the concern for "security" down there that a menstruating woman has, and I sat on those damned pads for a solid six months.

Further realization of my change came with the preponderance of documentary evidence I had acquired. Driver's license, Social Security card, checking account, transcripts and diplomas, and much, much more were all in my new name and new sexual designation. I would have one hell of a time trying to go back to being male again. The thought delighted me.

And my social identity was being established. Very few people in my new state knew of my past, and none of those ever knew Tom. New people I had met by then, as well as those in my future, would not be told there had been a Tom. Maybe they wondered, or maybe they were sure in their own minds that I was a change, but I would never tell them. It would have been counterproductive for me to tell. Let them guess if they wanted to. The most wonderful thing is that no one has ever asked me. I concluded that I am woman enough by their standards, and it might be too embarrassing for either of us to risk the question. I'd like to keep it that way.

Another aspect of the change was the issue of what kind of a woman was I, and what kind of a woman could I hope to become? My gynecologist answered the physiological portion of the questions; the countless bureaucracies I am known to had done their best to make me a woman; but what about the rest of the identity? What about my inner feelings, and what about my social future? The quick answer, more than three years later, is that I am doing just fine, but I am still in process. I expect the process to continue indefinity. I think the direction is clear but I wonder how far it will go. I can hardly wait to find out.

But sometimes I wonder about "my sisters" who have become unhappy after surgery. Some have given up on the pursuit for womanhood and reclaimed as much of their manhood as possible. Or, they have committed suicide. I have no statistics on the post-operatives group and I don't think anyone else does either. We tend to seek anonymity, you see.

Of course, most who have the surgery manage to achieve the future they wanted. We don't always live out the exact scenario we dreamed of before surgery, but we do get something that is plenty all right, but with aspects not considered before. Eleanor, for example, fell in love with a male friend of hers, got married, then got the surgery. It happens.

Tomika, a third generation Japanese-American, had been Senjo's lover. He went through an enormous amount of trauma because loving the not-yet-surgically-corrected Tomika was so outrageously contrary to Japanese culture; something very much in force for both of them. Despite the affront to their cultural heritage, they were very much in love. They will, in all likelihood, get married after Tomika's surgery. Senjo never knew Tomika as a male. I have not met Senjo, but I know Tomika well enough to bet the rent money on her success to achieve whatever goal she aims for.

Wilma has been a friend since my early days of the change. She had her surgery before I did. As soon as it was possible, she dated then had sex with some man she had met at her church. She reveled in being able to be laid. The novelty wore off when she realized her life was being shaped by that male partner who sometimes did what he said he would do, sometimes not. After a few months, she closed him out and went shopping for a new partner. After all, Wilma had been a corporate executive who was fortunate enough (and valuable enough) to keep her job after the change. She wasn't going to be shat upon by anyone. The new partner turned out to be a lesbian. They have been lovers and very happy for the past three years and show signs of settling in as an old married couple, complete with their own house and a legal contract as binding as a marriage contract. Who would have thought?

Joan had been a sugar beet farmer in San Joaquin Valley. When she "answered the call" to change, she moved to another state, got a civil service job with that state, and made her change. We stay in touch by phone, and a few times each year we get together for dinner. She is very much as I am—nothing but contentment, not sure what will come down the pike next month, but we are both happy and pleased with our new front-end realignments and the way society treats us.

I can make only tentative, provisional generalizations about who gets to be happy after surgery, and who ends up a mess. Using unscientific and semiprofessional language, it goes like this: If I were asked to sort all potential sex changes into two piles—those who will be happy and those who will be unhappy—I would have to determine whether the candidates were *inner directed* or *other directed*. Some people, you see, are satisfied that they are okay. Not perfect, but good enough. There are the others who cannot feel good about themselves unless others tell them they are okay. This latter group, the other directed, will almost surely fail after surgery because nothing has really changed for them, and no one is going to tell them how wonderful they are because they had a sex-change operation. Life will be as frightful for them as before. The inner directed people will always have faith in themselves, know who and what they are, and continue to triumph over whatever obstacles life tosses their way. I know this smacks of Carl Rogers' psychology, but he offers accurate, descriptive vocabulary. It is certainly not limited to transsexuals, but appropriate for everyone on the journey through life.

Eventually, all transsexuals have to arrive at an understanding of what manhood is and womanhood is *for them*. I have recounted enough of my life so that you will know that I achieved a level of manhood that could pass muster anywhere. Something deep within me kept saying that it was not enough.

For me the issue is not manhood or womanhood, but personhood. It is a wimpy word, I'll admit, but accurate. It is my opinion that the stereotypical male and female are merely opposite ends of the same stick called personhood. Our traditional culture urges us to be one or the other. I say I want the whole stick, the whole pie, the whole enchilada. I want to be a balanced blend of the two. Why not? Maybe it is the yin and yang thing famous in oriental philosophy. I intend to be composed of the best parts of each sexual stereotype. Yes, I have created the exterior of a female, and I have embraced several elements of the female persuasion such as sensitivity to others, a caring countenance, a willingness to help others. But I still hold on to those aspects of manhood that let everyone know I am not a doormat, I am an emotionally strong person, I do not crumble under anyone's negativism, nor do I depend on others to help me. I am presently still feeling my way along this path toward total integration, or what I think would be total integration. I am not able to state any final remarks about this effort, but what does occur to me is the feeling that I am getting close to my inner core, inner self. I don't know whether it is a soul search, or essence of humanity, or what. Traditional labels are useless for me.

The *inner* identity issue began to take shape soon after coming back from Montreal. The first step was to take an inventory of what I had in my conscious mind. I had been a man who had been moderately successful as such. I had done a lot of things that required guts, some brains, some luck, a lot of energy, a lot of patience, and an incredible amount of optimism. I knew I had those basic resources to work with.

I knew there was *something* out there that supported what I was doing. I did not know what, but I had so much evidence that it was there, that I never doubted I would evolve into a future that was "supposed to be." Oh, I was impatient a lot, but never in doubt. Whatever cosmic force was at work had taken me from a boy who wanted to dress up in women's clothes, to a man who wanted to appear in public as a woman, then to a man who wanted to be accepted as a woman in social and employment contexts, and finally to the sea change status provided by surgery. In attempting to achieve each stage, I felt that it was *the* destination. If I could achieve *that* much, I would be happy. Yet, the achievement of each stage required me to go to a newer stage. I never once, as a young person, ever thought the surgery was possible, or that it would be possible to live the life I am living now. Looking back, it seems I was *baited* all those years.

So what is the next step in that progression? I suppose intimate relations with a man seems logical. Somehow I am not excited by the idea. One would think that I would be eager to try out my new capacity. I, too, am surprised I am not. I have thought about it. Specifically:

1. As a male, I had no desire to have sexual contact with other men.

2. Moving towards femininity was not a means to an end, it *was* the end.

3. Now that I have lived some years as a woman, no latent, nascent desire for men has emerged.

4. Why not? I am not sure. Some early thoughts include

    a) I am officially a senior citizen. While that does not mean the end of sexual appetites, it does not signal the onset of raging sexual desires either.

    b) No man has made a move on me. Flirted, yes, but no real passes. I am friendly with several males not too much younger than myself, but only in the work place. We have enjoyable collegial friendships, period.

    c) I do not feel comfortable initiating flirtatious behavior.

    d) I spend a lot of my time focusing my attention on women, because I learn from them. I study the diversity of women, and the range of their behavior and feelings. Can I say I am just as much a social woman as any of them? I think I am closing in on yes for an answer.

5. I have a confusion or dichotomy of thought; I am both a new woman and an old woman. The new might want to be frisky and explore new limits, but the old is more interested in exploring the deeper questions of life. I spend my free time, and there is a lot of it, reading books that offer me a better understanding of life. I want to live the rest of my life as emotionally efficient as possible. I wonder why there is an earth, why there are living things on it, what are people for, what are we supposed to do. I am getting some new answers that do make sense. That pleases me, but I still do not know why I am not looking for a mate. It is just barely possible that one should not look for a mate; but instead, be ready to accept a loving relationship when it comes one's way. I'm still thinking about that notion.

6. I have to acknowledge the fact that I may not be an attractive, sensual package. Men may find me easy to work with, and we may be able to key in on the same wavelength in conversation, that does not trigger sexual overture. I may be perceived as exactly what I am: a former male. Even *I* can get in touch with the reluctance to make a move on me. Does that mean I fail as a woman?

7. So where do I fit? Who and what am I really? How much of the female attributes are mine? And another question, seldom discussed in contemporary

society. What are the relevant and useful attributes for an old lady who lives alone? And do I have them? And if I don't, how do I get them? And, finally, do I have any attributes that are counterproductive? One major lesson I learned was never to tell anyone I was a change. While some may suspect I am, they really don't want to have to deal with the confirmation of it.

8. A parallel issue, while dealing with the desire for the external trappings of womanhood as a youngster, was the development of an ego. I felt that I wanted to be among the females, knew I could not, and knew I had to develop a male image. The attributes were selected by me as though I were choosing clothing in a store. Being aware of the fashions, I chose things from the racks of my father, my brother, the movie heroes, my friends at school, until I had a wardrobe of attributes to be well dressed in any circumstance. I copied the attitudes and behaviors of those who were considered good males. Because I was successful at it, I could be comfortable projecting such a persona, but I always felt it was an act. A sham. Not me. For me a male ego was a burdensome, constricting thing to wear.

9. Now I am without a male ego. It was the first thing I dropped back in 1989. Sometimes I think it was dissolving for a decade or so before then. My focus now is choosing attributes from the female racks, and I am choosing the behaviors and attributes that truly fit. I cannot say how many male attributes remain. I am amazed and pleased by the diversity of women, in both the physical and attitudinal aspects. It makes life a lot easier for me. I can even be a curmudgeon if I want to, and get away with it.

I can only speak from experience about the male to female transsexual. I think I made the point earlier, albeit clumsily, that we don't really make the full, complete, 100% change to a female body. The expectation we have is to get *close enough* in appearance so that we can achieve womanhood. Each of us must decide for "hermself" what close enough means. A short answer is that we must do the very best we can to become what we want to be, and do it in a way so there will be no question about acceptance from those we encounter as we function in our new roles. The goal is to achieve a complete change of gender, and that is 100% achievable.

There is not much understanding about transsexualism among the general public. Despite the occasional television shows and interviews, most citizens still don't understand. Part of the reason is we don't or can't articulate the phenomenon very well. I am of two minds about this lack of publicity.

One part of me thinks it is very helpful because the greater society we live in is not thinking about us very much. They are not sensitized to us. That helps us pass as normal taxpaying citizens like everyone else. That is what we want. It would be silly to go around asking for acceptance for being who we are. No, it would be tragic to do that, and it would defeat the whole point of what we are doing.

The other part of me thinks there needs to more information available for those who are considering (or making) the change, the families and friends of those making the change, the sundry types of counsellors for those making the change, and employers. That is the segment of the population who needs all the information possible. It would also be helpful for the general society to have a better understanding of us so they will realize we are not bad people, but I am at a loss for ideas on how to do that.

Homosexuals have had a rough time ever since they got that bad press in *Leviticus* four thousand years ago. But the Bible does not mention males who want to become women. Therefore, there is no *institutionalized* opinion about us sex changes. Many people think that a transsexual must be a homosexual. The facts do not support such a conclusion. The only passage I could find in the Bible that is even *close* to a sex change is in St. Matthew, Ch 19: 11, 12. And even Jesus said that not everyone would understand.

I needed a belief system. I think we all do. We need something that will help us interpret events in our lives, something that will script our imaginations so that no matter what comes our way, we can make some sense of it. What I needed was a concept or set of them that would provide me with a rudder and a keel that would keep this little craft upright and headed in the right direction during my final years. Events in my life have to make sense. I do not require scientific proof, nor do I employ Aristotelian logic. I can and do accept ideas on faith if they make sense.

I was no stranger to books on religions, philosophies, psychology, and New Age thought. I reread several of them, then went on a search for more, a *lot* more. I read, mulled, and reflected. I reexamined a lot of my experiences (distant past and recent) in light of what I read. I projected those thoughts onto what I felt would be my future.

One notion really intrigues me. In the Abrahamic religions—Judaism, Christianity, and Moslem—mankind is made up of humans seeking spiritual experiences and transcendence. Suppose instead that we are spiritual beings seeking human experiences. The notion that one's core self must be allowed to manifest has been espoused by a number of philosophers. "To thine own self be true," comes to mind.

In the meantime I will continue on with my punky little job. I mean the part-time job is enormously important, but the demands on my time and energy are minimal.

But that's okay. I can use the rest for while. I've worked for many decades and I've earned this time for coasting and for getting caught up with my new place-in-space. As I said before, I am a new woman, but I am an old woman. It will take time for those two states of mind to even out.

Chapter 24

September 1999

And this is the wrap up—after nearly ten years.

My punky little job turned into something else in 1995. I was settling into the very comfortable routine of teaching English grammar and basic math to sailors at the submarine base. There is no end to the number of high school graduates who are without acceptable proficiency in the three Rs. By the time they leave boot camp, they suddenly realize that their future depends upon their literacy. The problem has been so widespread that the Navy entered into a contract with my college some decades ago to teach those classes wherever and whenever they were needed. The sailors welcomed the opportunity to "do it right this time."

I was grooving on the feelings generated by knowing I was a successful school marm. It was a new head space and one I wasn't sure I would be able to attain until it really happened. I found that I was evolving into a new consciousness—a day in, day out life of just being an old lady who was teaching the basics to a splendid group of sailors who really wanted to learn. One can imagine the gem-like moments for me when a sailor would say that I reminded him of Mrs. Schultz back home, or I was just like Ms. Gates. They would sometimes ask how come their high school teachers didn't explain certain concepts as well as I did. And I would reply that their teachers probably had, but they probably weren't paying attention in class. We all would chuckle, then get on with the lesson. And that was all that was going on from 1989 until July of 1995. Bliss. I had found it; I knew it; and I was luxuriating in it. But The Universe seemed to have something else in mind for me.

My boss was located at the Naval Air Station in Alameda, CA. He phoned me in the early summer of 1995 to say that the Pentagon's base closure program had given him notice to vacate the office space. He said that his work load was going to be transferred to Puget Sound, and that his boss in San Diego would be calling me very soon. He also said I should brace myself. Before that day was over, the Associate Dean—whose office was in San Diego—called. He said that he was going to fly up to see me next week, and that my former boss, Doug, was going to retire. The Dean's mission was to travel to all the bases in Puget Sound to determine how big a job it would be for the new area coordinator to deal with.

He arrived and checked into a motel right on schedule, and we spent the next four days in my car as we drove from one naval base to another. For those who have never explored Puget Sound, it must be explained that one does not travel very far west of Seattle without boarding a ferry boat. Mostly, it is a fun thing to do—possibly romantic, but if one is in a hurry it can be an aggravation. From the Bremerton area, it was a full day's travel to go to Whidbey Island where the Naval Air Station is located, even though one logs only 102 miles round trip. Another day for Everett. By the end of the grand tour, my boss's boss declared himself to be my boss. Specifically, he wanted me to be the area coordinator for all of Puget Sound. Oh.

The job description was a lengthy list of tasks. Simply, it would be my duty to abandon teaching, and be the local authority figure for the college. There were two contracts, actually. The one I had been doing would continue, but I would have to hire and assign others to do that part. The other contract was to set up college-level classes on board ships home ported in this area. The details are too lengthy and possibly too boring to relate here. The essence of the job was to go aboard each ship to meet with the captain, describe our service, explain how we could serve his crew, and get a commitment form him to go ahead. Next, I was to work closely with each ship's Educational Services Officer to set up schedules so that I could meet with the crew—possibly a dozen sessions for 20 to 50 sailors at a time—to survey their interests and then test to determine their readiness for college courses. And a lot of other details. The end result was to establish six months worth of classes, order the textbooks, hire the professors, and deal with their travel. There were three aircraft carriers, two large cruisers, three replenishment vessels, four destroyers, and two fast frigates. Let us not forget the air squadrons that go aboard the carriers. Each ship and squadron was to have the service. To help me, the woman who had the assistant's job in Alameda would be moving to this area to continue doing what she had been doing. As the dean was leaving for his return flight to San Diego, he said he would send me some printed information and a lot of blank forms. I don't remember him asking me if I wanted to do this new job. He did say a few things about my qualifications and prior experience, and that this would be good for all of us.

I was very pleased to have a full time job, and empowered to provide such a wonderful program for shipboard sailors. I was not pleased about leaving the school marm role, however. It would have been pointless to complain. Besides, I would be working closely with Vicki. We had done our business by telephone for several years. Now she would be in the same office space with me on an all day, every day basis. I had no intention of sharing my big secret with her, but I had some concern that she might figure me out in time. It was not my first risk, was it?

Before the end of July, I had been aboard one of the aircraft carriers and one of the cruisers. They both wanted the program, and I set about to make it happen. Vicki arrived in late November. We had been telephone pals, now we were office mates. The working relationship was even more comfortable than before. If she had confronted me with her suspicions, I would have simply confessed and asked for her cooperation. She never did. If she did subsequently figure it out, or ever wondered, she never let on. Nobody ever questioned me, never said anything to indicate the possibility existed that I was a change. I mean no one. And I was dealing with one of the toughest crowds imaginable. There is nothing shy about sailors. If the idea crossed any of their minds, nothing was said or hinted at in any way. I think a lot of my success in that regard was due to the context. Presenting myself aboard a ship, being introduced to the sailors by one of their officers was a way of legitimizing my presence. If any of them ever saw me walk into a tavern at night by myself, I think there would have been a different reaction. I am grateful for that experience. I would never, ever have doubts about myself again. Oh I know there are some citizens around who must wonder. I let them.

In January of 1996 the college sent out new security clearance forms, an event that occurred every couple of years. Because I had to spend so much time aboard ships, and possibly encounter classified information, I had to have a confidential security clearance. It was not as high as the secret clearance I had to have at Moffett Field, but it was another blank form I had to complete. In the past, there was the other-names-used-box where I was able to simply write in Tom's last name. It was truthful, but now there was a different form. This one specifically asked for other first and middle and last names ever used. Cripes! I felt cornered and intimidated more than somewhat by this new form. One thing one must keep in mind with these security forms is that one must always tell the truth. That is what the agencies are looking for—Does this person tell the truth? A lie will get you fired. The truth may not be pleasant, but that's okay. Do not ever lie. I had no qualms about telling the whole truth to the FBI (they knew about me already), but in this case, the forms were to be filled out and routed to my boss in San Diego who would forward them to the college who would forward them to the FBI. I was concerned about the number of college employees handling the forms who would learn that Sally used to be Tom. I telephoned the dean in San Diego and said I was concerned about some sensitive information I had to reveal about me, and concerned about the number of people who would be looking at my forms before they got to the FBI. I was told to send the completed forms to him marked personal and confidential. He would then endorse the packet and send it to the college security person who would send it to the feds. No problem. Of course, I had to write a letter of explanation to the dean. A few days later he called to say that he was amazed. He never would have guessed, especially after all that time we spent together. He did not think anyone at the main campus would object, or be concerned if he was not concerned. Vicki was curious about my secrecy, but not really nosey. I took a chance and offered to let her see my forms. But she hesitated, then declined. Good. It was important for me to let her know I would trust her with sensitive information.

Another thing was happening about the same time. It occurred to me that it was Tom who was doing this job. Without being aware at the beginning, I had to rely on Tom's experiences. When one deals with shipboard personnel, especially captains, one must be sharp, sure, and decisive. They also expect one to operate on their wavelength, e.g., use their vocabulary, understand their routines, their lines of authority, and more. Tom knew that stuff. He had gone on the Navy's retired list before any of these present day senior officers and older enlisted men had joined the Navy. They were like recruits as far as Tom was concerned. Is there no end to the irony?

It was a strange head space for me whenever I went aboard a ship—which was almost every day. I would walk up the brow (gangplank) of a ship, cross the side, salute—as a civilian salutes—and request permission to come aboard. It is the Navy way. I was Sally, yet it was Tom's comfort level that enabled me to do my job. I knew that the quarterdeck people were amused that an old lady could come aboard ship in the same precise manner as the crew. I was amused by their amusement.

In talking and working with the various crews, something would eventually be said that caused them to ask how come I knew such and such. I would simply say that I had retired out of this canoe club in 1972, after 26-plus years of service. They would be very interested, and wanted to know what I had done. I would then tell my only lie.

I would say that I had been a journalist, then as a Warrant Officer was a Ship's Clerk. I could not tell them I had been a quartermaster and later a Warrant Boatswain. Women could not have that career path back then.

It helped me enormously to let them know that I had been where they were now. It was like the group at Moffett Field—*I was one of them*, or close enough. Communications improved greatly and mutual respect was easily established. The main thing was to get the job done. We did that, all right.

There would be an occasional *deja vu* kind of moment. On my way one day to a ship tied up at Pier A, I walked past a huge bollard (big steel stump use to tie a ship to the pier) near the head of the pier. It was my first time to go to that location in this new job. The last time I had been on that spot was in February of 1949 when Tom's ship had been in a nearby drydock. It was a snowy day, and Tom had to lead a small detail of sailors in the duty section to this location to receive the mooring lines from the inbound *USS Columbus*, a heavy cruiser. It was an eerie feeling as I walked past that bollard, having the flashback, in my cotton skirt and blouse.

I had to admit that my new assignment was really good. One benefit was the secret game of Tom & Sally jointly doing the job. The larger benefit was in knowing I was doing something good for the "white hats," the enlisted sailors. Another not-at-all-small benefit was the close relationship I had with Vicki. It was the best woman-to-woman friendship I ever had.

The job came to an end for me in June of 1997. Due to new security rules, I was no longer permitted to drive my car on the piers to park near the ships. I found that walking a half mile from a parking lot, carrying 20 pounds of printed materials, was no longer possible. My legs gave out. I'd just had my 69th birthday and thought that perhaps I should consider a new occupation. I resist the concept of retirement. I would rather wear out than rust out.

And sure enough, the Universe agreed I was not ready to vegetate. I was asked, in the spring of 1998, if I would become a member of a small start-up company in Bremerton. I am not earning any money, but I am having a ball being of some use to these "young Turks" who have a splendid new product. I am a corporate officer and do some sales and marketing tasks, but mostly I just hang out a few hours per week. They seem to appreciate the opinions emanating from an old gray head. I think it a fair to call it a symbiotic relationship.

In between times one of the things I do is to reflect on my life. With the exception of the pain I caused for two wives and three sons, I like to think my life has been worth the effort. I cannot dwell on my sins and transgressions because I cannot change the past. I do try to learn from the past, and my purpose in writing this account of my life is to help others. I would like others like me to have a more efficient transition, and to do it with the least amount of hurt for their loved ones. I wonder what else I could do.

One thing I did five years ago was to join PFLAG (Parents and Friends of Lesbians and Gays). It is an organization for non-gay people to try to gain some insights into what is going on with their gay friends or children or parents. Sometimes gays attend. I thought I would *be there* for the parents of a young person who declared his or her transsexuality. I have tried to make the point earlier that transsexuals are not the same as homosexuals. The only similarity is the rejection we all get from society. It seems there is a natural affinity the two groups have for each other. Not one transgendered parent has appeared in our local group. No transsexual persons, either.

So what could I do for the transsexual? I do not think any self-respecting post-op transsexual would want me to do anything for her. Any crusade I muse upon would be directed toward easing the transition for the pre-op transsexual. Pre-op and potentially pre-op transsexuals need information about a number of things. They need to meet in a professional setting and talk with others like themselves. They need to get the clearest vision possible of what their lives would be like for them and for others if they pursue the course. They need to find the vendors of feminine artifice who will be sympathetic for their quest. They need to find the proper medical and psychological providers who will help them get ready for the surgery, or help them realize it might not be a good idea. There are many groups that offer such services these days. The situation was primitive when I was getting started a generation ago. I am sure there are Internet sources readily available if one looks. In Seattle, for example, the Ingersoll Gender Center is a first-rate place. It is listed in the white pages of the telephone directory. There are national organizations, such as AEGIS, in Portland, Oregon. No aspiring transsexual should try to go through the process alone.

During this past year I learned of a new wing created within the PFLAG organization. It is called T-SON, the Transgendered Special Outreach Network. PFLAG, the parent organization, has active chapters in over 400 cities in the US and foreign countries. At last count, 170 of those chapters have T-SON coordinators. For a list of their chapters, write the PFLAG national office in Washington, DC. Where were you guys when I needed you? No matter. You are there now.

Another needed effort is to enlighten the greater society about the irrevocability of the desire to become the other sex. Anyone who is aware of being a transsexual can get help and succor from psychologists, psychiatrists, and even some ministers. Those aids are like aspirin, and can help the poor devil cope somewhat. There is no "cure" for transsexualism any more than there is a cure for homosexuality or a cure for heterosexuality. Whichever way a person is born is simply that—the way a person is born. Period. I know there is a lot of controversy about that. But I think I have just spent a lot of time and ink trying to illustrate that one does not have the power to change their basic nature. The bigots can't do it, neither can the transgendered. Everyone *does* have the power *to deny* acting on their inner nature. But I think we know what that leads to. So, the only issue for discussion is what one will do about it. Those who govern themselves according to their nature and a loving attitude will find a blissful life.

That leads to my final statement: If you are a transsexual, don't screw up anyone else's life by trying to prove you are not a transsexual. You may love women very much, but they cannot cure you of transsexualism. All they can do is suffer when you turn honest and realize you cannot change, no matter how much you love them.

END

Printed in the United States
739400002B